OSBORNE CP/M® USER GUIDE

BY THOM HOGAN

OSBORNE
CP/M®
USER GUIDE

OSBORNE
CP/M®
USER GUIDE

By Thom Hogan

OSBORNE/McGraw-Hill
Berkeley, California

Published by
OSBORNE/McGraw-Hill
630 Bancroft Way
Berkeley, California 94710
U.S.A.

For information on translations and book distributors
outside of the U.S.A., please write OSBORNE/McGraw-Hill
at the above address.

OSBORNE CP/M® USER GUIDE

4567890   DODO   898765432

This book was reviewed for technical content by William Fairman of Faircom.
Technical editor was Curtis A. Ingraham. Compositional editor was Denise
E. M. Penrose.

Photos by Harvey Schwartz. Cover design by Timothy Sullivan.

Hogan, Thom, 1952-
    OSBORNE CP/M user guide.

    Bibliography: p. 267
    Includes index.
    1. CP/M (Computer program)   2. Operating systems
(Computers)   I. Title.   II. Title: CP/M user guide.
QA76.6.H62   001.64'2   81-3948
ISBN 0-931988-44-6   AACR2

This book is dedicated to Lore Harp, Carole Ely, Steve Jobs, Steven Wozniak, Gary Kildall, and Seymour Rubenstein, who gave me the tools to write it.

Contents

Introduction

Your computer is not a single unit, but an interrelated system of devices and programs. You must direct these components to carry out any program you wish to run. CP/M is an operating system which does this job for you. CP/M directs the activities of your computer's components, and manages files which contain computer instructions or data.

Although CP/M is a complex computer program, you can learn to use it without any prior computer experience. This book introduces the novice to the microcomputer system and examines CP/M's function within that system.

Chapter 1 provides the basic, practical information you need to get started. Chapters 2 and 3 detail the CP/M commands. This is information you will use every day. We recommend that you study the examples carefully, and review the applicable appendices where each command is capsulized for quick reference. These three chapters provide a solid foundation for understanding CP/M.

Chapter 5 supplements your understanding of CP/M by describing the support programs compatible with CP/M. Application packages, high level languages, and solution programs combine with CP/M to answer a user's computer needs. This section discusses how the support programs work with and supplement CP/M.

Chapter 6 explains the functions of MP/M and CP/NET and examines the commands unique to these operating systems. The differences between Cromemco CDOS and Digital Research CP/M are highlighted to enable Cromemco operators to use this book.

Chapters 4 and 7 are written for assembly language programmers who wish to modify CP/M or use CP/M for program development. This information is not essential to CP/M users. We present it to provide a more complete discussion of CP/M, and to stimulate the reader to make full use of CP/M utilities.

A final section, Chapter 8, distills the author's experience with CP/M and offers a number of helpful hints.

An annotated bibliography provides directions for additional reading, and several appendices offer practical consumer information about CP/M-compatible programs, languages, and products.

If you have a working computer system, read this book while seated in front of your computer. Try the commands and examples presented here; do not just read about them. You will be comfortable with CP/M much sooner than you expected.

CP/M® is a registed trademark of Digital Research. MP/M[tm], MAC[tm] SID[tm], and DESPOOL[tm] are trademarks of Digital Research.

This book is the work of the author and the publisher; it was not reviewed, authorized, or endorsed by Digital Research.

Books, like computer programs, are never completely error-free. The publisher invites your comments and corrections.

1

An Introduction to CP/M and Operating Systems

CP/M is a disk operating system for microcomputers, produced by a company named Digital Research. It was designed for use on 8080 and Z80-based microcomputer systems. CP/M stands for "Control Program/ Monitor." Versions of CP/M are available for a wide variety of microcomputers using 8-inch and 5¼-inch floppy disk drives.

HISTORY OF CP/M

CP/M was developed in 1973 by Gary Kildall, then a software consultant for Intel. The earliest version was written for Kildall's own experimental system, which included one of the first 8-inch diskette drives built by Shugart Associates; it was a shopworn drive that had been used for equipment life tests before it was passed on to Kildall.

By 1975 a number of companies were marketing microcomputers. Most of these companies preferred to develop their own disk operating systems. Had these pioneers (Altair, Polymorphic, and Processor Technology, for example) been able to get their products to consumers quickly, CP/M might not have become the quasi-standard operating system it is today.

Instead, several small microcomputer manufacturers eliminated this costly research and development stage, and adopted Kildall's CP/M operating system for their products. Most notable among these smaller companies were Tarbell Electronics and Digital Microsystems; they were among the first to ship working disk systems. Because these firms manufactured "add-on" components, owners of compatible equipment were at last able to install disk drives, sidestepping the primary manufacturer of their equipment which had not shipped drives yet. In addition, IMSAI, another microcomputer pioneer, had been shipping disk systems and promised to ship an operating system shortly. This operating system turned out to be IMDOS, which was really a disguised version of CP/M.

Another important element in CP/M history is the enthusiasm of its first users. These true hobbyists tackled normally insurmountable problems in their pursuit of new knowledge and experience. Theoretically, CP/M could link any 8080 or Z80-based microcomputer with any disk system, and a group of hobbyists with "mix and match" systems emerged to test Kildall's product. These hobbyists developed a number of refinements and, more importantly, a strong and visible users' group.

The support of a strong users' group cannot be underestimated. During the infant years of the microcomputer industry, accurate product information was not readily available. Manufacturers often released products with incomplete documentation, computer stores were still relatively unknown, and in some cases users' groups were more stable than the companies who developed the product at the focus of the users' group.

After manufacturers delivered reliable disk drives, software developers launched the next vital phase of CP/M's evolution. The key to making software development financially feasible is to write programs that run on many different microcomputers. CP/M made this possible, since it was one of the few operating systems that could run on just about any 8080 or Z80-based microcomputer, using any disk drive. The first programs available were *development tools*, or programs that generate other programs. Among these development tool programs were CBASIC, Microsoft BASIC, and other languages used to write application programs such as general ledger and word processing.

The popularity of the CP/M operating system thus became part of an escalating pattern: CP/M spawned programming languages and development tools, which in turn gave birth to application programs. These CP/M-dependent application programs increased CP/M sales, and the sales spiral continued.

CP/M MANUALS

Now you come into the picture. You probably purchased this book because you need CP/M to run an application program. The program may be a simple accounting system or a sophisticated word processing package, but both require an understanding of CP/M. Digital Research manuals were not written for you. They were written for professional programmers. This book attempts to bridge the gap between Digital Research manuals and your knowledge of computers. The CP/M manuals you have will depend on your version of CP/M and where you got it.

Digital Research is constantly upgrading CP/M, so like any good software product, new versions are released from time to time. The most recently released CP/M is version 2.2; before version 2.2, version 1.4 was commonly distributed.

If the CP/M you bought is version 2.0 or newer, you should have the following manuals:

An Introduction to CP/M Features and Facilities

CP/M 2.0 User's Guide

ED: A Context Editor for the CP/M Disk System

CP/M Assembler (ASM)

CP/M Dynamic Debugging Tool (DDT)

CP/M System Alteration Guide (1.4)

CP/M 2.0 Alteration Guide

CP/M Interface Guide (1.4)

CP/M 2.0 Interface Guide

Users of CP/M version 1.4 or earlier will be missing the *CP/M 2.0 User's Guide, CP/M 2.0 Alteration Guide*, and *CP/M 2.0 Interface Guide*.

For most users only the first two manuals are helpful. This book covers the material in the first five manuals, and summarizes the four remaining manuals. You may have additional manuals if you bought CP/M from someone other than Digital Research.

THE FUNCTION OF CP/M WITHIN A MICROCOMPUTER SYSTEM

It is important to understand the functions served by CP/M within a microcomputer system. If you know what is going on you are less likely to make mistakes. We will describe the function of CP/M (or any operating system) within a computer system. This description assumes an elementary understanding of microcomputers and how they function.*

A microcomputer system is illustrated in Figure 1-1. The system illustrated is typical of configurations that you may encounter. It includes the microcomputer itself, a terminal which combines a keyboard and display, a pair of diskette drives, and a printer.

You could make numerous changes to this system. Instead of the terminal you could have a separate display and keyboard. The keyboard could be part of the microcomputer while the display is separate, or the keyboard, display and microcomputer may be packaged together.

Small systems may use cassette tape and cassette tape drives instead of floppy disks and floppy disk drives. In the early days microcomputer systems used paper tape to store information and read it back, requiring a paper tape reader and a paper tape punch. The use of cassettes and paper tape with CP/M is uncommon because disks are faster and more reliable.

Microcomputers spend a lot of time transferring information between the microcomputer and various other components of the system. Microcomputers must also control operations at these other components. Microcomputers perform these operations by executing programs which are referred to collectively as an *operating system*. CP/M is such an operating system. By using appropriate CP/M commands you can transfer data from a disk to the microcomputer, print data at a printer, or perform any operation which the microcomputer system is physically capable of handling.

In order to perform these microcomputer system functions for a wide variety of different configurations, CP/M (and all other operating systems) ignores the *physical units* that comprise the microcomputer system, dealing instead with *logical units*. In other words, rather than addressing a printer, the operating system assumes a *listing device* is present. Likewise, rather than reading from a paper tape reader, the operating system assumes the input comes from a *reader device*.

The manufacturer of your microcomputer system will ensure that the system's actual physical units connect properly to the logical units CP/M uses. These program modifications are invisible if made correctly, but if the proper changes are not made, CP/M may not work accurately.

As an operator you may occasionally be concerned with physical and logical units. For example, you may have the option of sending output to a printer or a display. Likewise you may have the option of typing input at a keyboard or receiving input over a telephone line. You can make such physical unit choices easily using the appropriate CP/M command we

---

* If you need more information about microcomputer systems, see *An Introduction to Microcomputers, Volume 0, The Beginner's Book* by Adam Osborne, Osborne/McGraw-Hill, Berkeley, Calif., 1978.

describe later in the book. For the moment, you need only understand the general function of CP/M, or any operating system. You do not need to understand the operating system's specific activities in order to use CP/M.

An operating system such as CP/M is itself a computer program which must be executed by a microcomputer. Being a program, CP/M must be written in a programming language. The programming language which a microcomputer understands is determined by the *microprocessor* that the microcomputer contains.

A microprocessor is a very small and unassuming device; Figure 1-2 illustrates a microprocessor. The microprocessor is a microcomputer's most important component; it actually translates a program and causes the action. Some microprocessors execute CP/M, but others do not.

CP/M was initially written for the 8080A microprocessor. Since the 8085 and the Z80 also execute 8080A programs, CP/M will run on microcomputers containing these two microprocessors. A version of CP/M will soon be available for a new, more powerful microprocessor, the 8086.

SOME USEFUL TERMS

Consider the following information on microprocessors when you purchase a microcomputer system to run CP/M and other compatible software. You will learn some computer jargon, too.

Byte. The storage capacity of a microcomputer's memory, or its disks, is always described as some number of *bytes*. A byte is a memory unit capable of storing a single character. For example, the letter A or the digit 1 could be stored in one byte of memory. Numbers without decimal

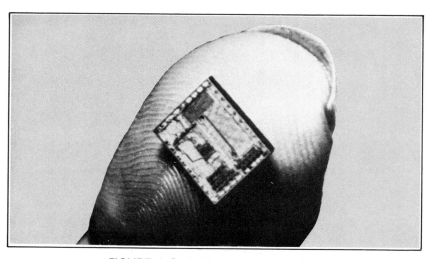

FIGURE 1-2. A Microprocessor Chip

points are usually stored in two bytes of memory, while numbers with decimal points may require five or more bytes of memory per number. Memory size is usually expressed, not as thousands of bytes, but as some number of K bytes. 1K equals 1024. All computers are binary machines that count in twos. You will get the number 1024 if you double 2 to give 4, then double 4 to give 8, and keep on doubling in this fashion ten times.

Sectors and Tracks. When information is stored on a cassette tape, it is stored as a single track of data down the length of the tape. When information is stored on a diskette, the surface of the diskette is divided into a number of concentric tracks. Each track is divided into a number of *sectors*, so that CP/M can access any point on the diskette surface, given a sector and track number. Figure 1-3 illustrates the sectors and tracks.

TYPES OF CP/M

CP/M may be a quasi-standard operating system in the microcomputing field at present, but all CP/Ms are not equal. CP/M varies with the input and output programs (I/O) peculiar to each machine.

In addition, computer technology is not standing still. New ways of doing things are invented every day. The machine you now own does far more, far faster than the vacuum tube computers of the fifties. The recent introduction of hard disk units may become one of the most significant developments. These new disk units can store far more

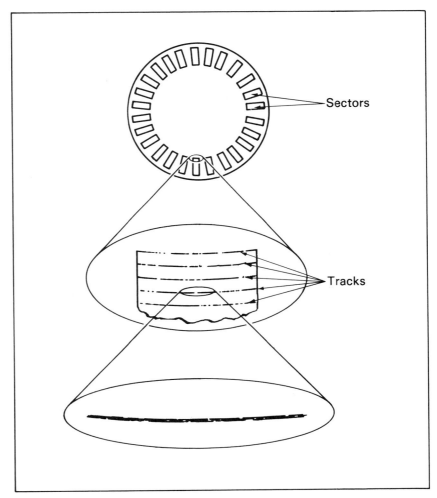

FIGURE 1-3. A Diskette's Recorded Surface

information than the current diskette technology. While diskette units may store up to 2 megabytes (2,000,000 characters of information), hard disks may store up to 300 megabytes. Since CP/M was designed for floppy diskette systems, it required changes to use hard disk units. This is the primary difference between versions 1.4 and 2.0 (see Appendix C).

The different types of CP/M also reflect the large number of manufacturers using CP/M. Each may add utility programs or refinements to CP/M to improve performance on a particular machine.

CP/M Compatibility

Unfortunately, not all CP/Ms are compatible, and even the degree of compatibility can vary. The primary ways CP/M varies are:

1. Version number (1.3, 1.4, 2.0, etc.).
2. Location of CP/M within memory.
3. Type of diskettes used.
4. Logical layout on the diskette (the way the information is stored on the diskette).
5. Vendor (usually this results in a combination of variations 1 through 4).

To list every different type of CP/M would be futile. First of all, the list would be out of date by the time you read this book; but despite the possibilities for variation, CP/M still remains more machine-independent than most operating systems. By linking computers using two disparate versions of CP/M, programs or data transfers can usually be accomplished.

CP/M Version Numbers

As stated earlier, there are several versions of CP/M. In general, this book is applicable to CP/M versions 1.4 and 2.0. CP/M versions are identified by one number to the left of a decimal point, which refers to the overall version number, and one number to the right of the decimal point, which refers to a revision within a version.

A second number to the right of the decimal point, as in 1.42, identifies subtle or machine-dependent modifications. If your version of CP/M is not 1.4x, 2.0x, 2.1x, or 2.2x (where x represents any release number), ask your supplier for a newer release. Versions of CP/M include:

1.3   The original release version of CP/M.
1.4   A more error-free version of CP/M release 1.
2.0   The original release version of CP/M release 2.
2.1   A field update of version 2.0.
2.2   The current revision of CP/M version 2.

Version numbers can vary from vendor to vendor. Some CP/M vendors released several different CP/M revisions as version 1.4, while others indicated their own updates by numbers 1.41 and 1.42. In general, only the first two numbers in a version number indicate changes to CP/M by Digital Research.

Digital Research CP/M Products

Since Digital Research wrote CP/M and supports it, we will compare other products with theirs. Currently, Digital Research supports the following CP/M products:

Single Density 8-inch uses a predefined (IBM 3740) format for storing information on the diskette. CP/M was originally designed for this format. Versions 1.4 and 2.2 are available, differing primarily in the number of disk drives and capacities they can address.

Double Density 8-inch stores more information on a diskette than single density 8-inch. Caution: there are a few double density implementations of CP/M that are not directly compatible; a diskette created on one manufacturer's drive may not always be inserted and directly read by another manufacturer's drives. As with single density drives, the industry standard is based on existing IBM specifications.

MP/M is a multi-user form of CP/M. Instead of supporting just one terminal, MP/M supports several. See Chapter 6 for more information about MP/M.

CP/NET is a multi-computer form of CP/M which allows one computer to use the resources of another (printers, disks, etc.). In order to use CP/NET, at least one of the computers must be equipped with MP/M, and all others must use CP/M. Again, see Chapter 6 for more details on this operating system.

Please note: Digital Research provides a ready-to-run CP/M for the Intel MDS Development System only. For other microcomputer systems Digital Research provides no terminal, modem, printer, or special disk drive. Only a skilled assembly language programmer should buy CP/M from Digital Research.

Lifeboat Associates CP/M Products

In addition to selling Digital Research CP/M products, Lifeboat Associates has altered the part of CP/M which contains instructions to the disk drives and other devices (the BIOS section, described in Chapter 7). Lifeboat Associates CP/M products are available for the Radio Shack TRS-80, Micropolis, North Star, Polymorphic, Altair, Heathkit, and a number of other systems. While programs written using Lifeboat Associates CP/M products are almost universally compatible with other

CP/Ms, the physical program storage media are not. Thus the end result may disappoint you. Since the physical media, the diskettes, may differ from one machine to the next, copying programs or data from one microcomputer to another may be difficult. On the other hand, if both systems have modems, you could send programs via phone lines to a different system.

Because Lifeboat Associates is only a distributor of CP/M, their products are released after Digital Research updates. For instance, Lifeboat Associates released products for disk drives other than standard 8-inch floppies one year after Digital Research introduced CP/M 2.0.

Furthermore, all diskette systems do not universally use all CP/M utility programs. For example, formatting a diskette, the process of putting "dummy" information on a previously unused diskette so that the operating system recognizes where data lies, is not provided for under Lifeboat's North Star Single-Density CP/M.

Caution: TRS-80 Model I and early Heath versions from Lifeboat, load at a different spot in memory than standard CP/M.

Manufacturers' CP/M Products

Many microcomputer manufacturers provide CP/M as a standard operating system on the computers they sell. Manufacturers include Micromation, Dynabyte, Vector Graphic, Onyx, Altos, Industrial Micro Systems, Digital Microsystems, and Exidy.

Manufacturers' CP/M products differ slightly from Lifeboat Associates CP/M products; manufacturers all reconfigure portions of CP/M for their own equipment. Some manufacturers add subtle traps for the unwary, however. These traps are often labeled "features." For example, Vector Graphic CP/M 2.2 includes some complicated checking for the computer model in use. They also added a routine to check for the depression of certain keys. In the Vector Graphic product, these additional routines make some otherwise standard CP/M-compatible programs incompatible with their implementation of CP/M.

CP/M Lookalikes

Another category of CP/M products is non-CP/M operating systems which look like CP/M. Some of these systems claim to be "CP/M-compatible." Of these, the most popular are TP/M from Computer Design Labs, SDOS from SD Systems, and IO/S, the disk operating system offered by TSA Software. In addition, CDOS, the Cromemco Disk Operating System, claims compatibility with CP/M version 1.3.

For the most part, these lookalikes will run standard CP/M software. For those of you who might have purchased a CP/M substitute, Chapter 6 is devoted to these lookalikes.

DISKETTES

The backbone of any disk operating system is, of course, the disk itself. It may be difficult to comprehend that 150 single-spaced typed pages (the equivalent of 30 hours typing) can be stored on one flimsy magnetic disk in a thin cardboard coat. Unfortunately, we can easily forget to take the proper steps to protect the information stored on the diskette. Before discussing more detailed information about CP/M, we will pause for a quick course on diskette care and usage.

Comparing Diskettes

Walk into a computer store, ask for a diskette, and the salesperson will ask you what kind you need. For an idea of the possibilities, here are some features to consider:

- 8-inch and 5¼-inch diskettes
- Single-sided and double-sided diskettes
- Single-density and double-density diskettes
- Soft-sectored and hard-sectored diskettes
- 10-sector and 16-sector hard-sectored diskettes
- Write-protect notch and no notch

A confusing array, and there are as many brands as there are types. We could not possibly list all of the combinations. In fact, diskette manufacturers publish long lists of compatible diskettes, computers, and disk drives. Check with any reputable computer store to learn which diskettes to use with various brands of microcomputers; or better yet, check with your computer vendor.

A brief summary of the more popular types of diskettes and microcomputers is provided in Appendix E.

Describing Diskettes

Diskettes are flimsy. That is why they are sometimes called *floppies*. If you have an extra diskette around, go get it right now, as we are about to take a "diskette tour."

First you will notice the diskette is accompanied by a thin cardboard envelope. This envelope protects about two-thirds of the diskette from such data killers as dirt, food, liquids, and thumbprints. Since it is very thin cardboard, it provides limited protection, so be careful. Many diskette manufacturers print handling tips on the back of this envelope. Read any information printed on your diskette; someday it may mean the difference between retyping for five hours and spending a relaxing evening at home.

Carefully pull the diskette out of the envelope (Note: it slides right out. If it looks like you must cut something open to get inside, you are mistaking the diskette sleeve for the envelope.) The diskette has a square cardboard sleeve which protects a thin circular *disk*. The sleeve has a circular hole in the center (as does the disk surface inside) and there is an oblong cutout at one edge of the sleeve (see Figure 1-4). Also, there is a smaller hole just to one side of the central hole. Identify these parts:

> *Centering Hole.* The disk drive mechanism locks onto this hole to spin the diskette.
>
> *Indexing Hole.* The disk drive looks here to find the starting *sector* (and in some cases, each individual sector) for each track on the diskette. Imagine a line drawn across the disk surface at this point; the drive waits for the starting line, then counts characters of information from there.
>
> *Access Hole.* The head of the disk drive comes in contact with the magnetic surface through this cutout. The head moves back and forth in this opening, from *track to track*.
>
> *Notch.* This is a write-protect notch. Writing on the diskette means adding information to the diskette. A point of confusion: on 8-inch diskettes, if the notch is covered up, you can write on the diskette, and if the notch is left uncovered, you cannot write on the diskette. On 5¼-inch diskettes the opposite is true. If the notch is uncovered you can write on the disk; if the notch is covered, the disk is protected against write. (You might circle the appropriate section of this paragraph for future reference.) To compound the problem further, the 8-inch diskette write-protect notch is located near the access hole, while 5¼-inch diskettes have the write-protect notch on another side (see Figure 1-4). Learn where your write-protect notch is and how to enable the protect mechanism.

Handling Diskettes

Now that you are familiar with parts of the diskette, it's time to learn how to handle it.

First, the *don'ts*.

Never touch the diskette surface. You may handle the cardboard sleeve when necessary, but do not touch the actual magnetic surface of the diskette. No matter how clean your hands are, even a slight residue might prohibit your computer from reading some data.

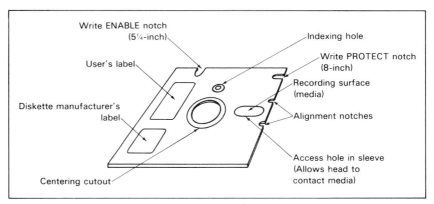

FIGURE 1-4. Typical Diskette

Keep diskettes away from magnets. Silly instruction, you say? You think you don't have magnets where you work? Think again. If your computer has a video terminal (one with a television-like display tube), you have a magnet. Strong electrical fields can also act as magnets. The speakers in any sound system almost certainly contain magnets. Actually, the magnetic field most appliances generate is not enough to erase the information on your diskettes except through direct contact. Even so, it is a good idea to keep your diskettes at least a foot away from anything magnetic. Also, contrary to popular belief, it is best to store magnetic media in a *metal* box, not a plastic one. Plastic does not intercept stray magnetic fields; metal does.

Do not bend your diskettes. The information on a diskette is packed into a very small area. Think about it for a moment: 2,000,000 characters (on some diskettes) in an area of two surfaces, eight inches in diameter. Any crease in the diskette can make the read head of the disk drive lose contact with the disk surface, and a lot of information could be lost in that crease.

Do not keep diskettes in a dirty environment. If you allow computer users to eat, drink, or smoke while they use the computer, you are asking for trouble. Filmmakers routinely use cola to erase extraneous noises from magnetic sound tracks; it works better than some commercial alternatives!

Never leave a diskette in the computer when you power down. Remove the diskettes before you turn off the computer and/or the diskette drives. Likewise, turn the power on before inserting the diskettes. Most of the time, if you do not follow this advice, nothing will happen. However, a "spike" of power could reach the magnetic head of the diskette drive and write spurious information. This can prove disastrous.

Do not let your diskettes get too full. Many programs use a diskette to temporarily store data or to generate data. If this temporary or new data does not fit, you could lose it.

Two factors limit diskette capacity: the number of files and the number of characters. Standard CP/M allows no more than 64 files, no matter how small they might be, although some manufacturers have expanded the directory space to allow as many as 1024. The number of characters on a diskette is determined by the drive and ranges between about 100,000 and one million characters. Hard disks can generally store several million characters.

Now for some *do's.*

Always insert diskettes slowly and carefully. Many of the mini-disk (5¼-inch) drives have a very small tolerance for alignment between the diskette and the magnetic head which reads and writes information. In particular, Micropolis drives can mis-center a hastily entered diskette since the drives actually move the diskette before it is positioned for reading. Diskettes are fragile; they should be handled slowly and deliberately. Saving one second by rushing to get the diskette into the drive may waste hours when you must reenter the lost information.

Label all your diskettes. Nothing is more frustrating than having fifty identical diskettes and not knowing their contents. Diskettes, especially if you follow the backup recommendations given later in this chapter, have a tendency to multiply like rabbits. Consider this book. The text barely fits onto one diskette. However, copies of the last three revisions, plus backups, are stored. In addition, the text editor program occupies most of another diskette. Add the programming diskettes, another set of diskettes to keep important records and data, plus a few for games and recreational purposes, and you can imagine the stack of cardboard envelopes.

So take heed: label your diskettes. Develop procedures to distinguish older versions or copies of your data from the current (or "use") one. The label should contain your name and the date, the name and version number of the operating system, and some description of the diskette's contents.

Keep backup and rarely used diskettes away from the computer. Limit those diskettes you keep at the computer to those you constantly use. Since you will generate a number of diskettes, why complicate locating you might accumulate.

Make sure your diskettes are stored correctly. Just like phonograph records, diskettes will be damaged if stored for long periods of time in other than a horizontal or perfectly vertical manner. If diskettes are allowed to slant diagonally, gravity will in time subtly bend the diskette. While diskettes do not warp like records, when that bend gets to a certain point it will crease the diskette.

Maintain your equipment. Disk drives are not as persnickety as cars; they do not require oil changes every 10,000 reads. Actually, diskette equipment can be *over* maintained. Constant adjustment of the mechanism may erode the tolerances built into the drives. Constant cleaning of the magnetic heads may be more abusive to the heads than normal wear. Use a *cleaning diskette* (available from diskette suppliers) once every three months or whenever you suspect diskette read errors. The latest diskette drives need maintenance only once a year (and in the case of the newer Winchester Technology hard disk drives, there is nothing to adjust; the unit is a sealed mechanism).

Buy quality diskettes. Mail-order bargains for minidiskettes (5¼-inch) are priced below what most dealers pay. At that price the diskettes have not been *verified,* or checked for their ability to store and retrieve data. You can hear the difference in quality between diskettes; a poor quality diskette will make more rubbing noises. You don't keep your personal and business records on napkins and paper towels; do not entrust your valuable information to their computer equivalents.

Inserting and Removing Diskettes

Consult the microcomputer manual to learn how the diskette goes into the drive. For horizontally-mounted drives, hold the diskette (remember not to touch the surface of the diskette) so it is also in a horizontal plane. The label side must be up. Insert the end with the head access hole (the oblong one) into the drive first (see Figure 1-5). The writing on the label usually faces away from you as you insert the diskette.

Once the diskette is entirely in the drive, you close a door or hinge; this step varies among disk drives. Usually drives have a small door that must be moved *over* the diskette slot after it has been inserted. Micropolis drives have a small latch which must be pushed down after the diskette has been inserted.

Vertically-mounted drives are a bit more difficult to describe, as they may be mounted with the label either on the left-hand or right-hand side as you insert the diskette. If you insert a diskette upside down in these drives, you run the risk of creating errors. For loading instructions see your microcomputer manual.

Almost all diskette drives tell the user when the drive is accessing a diskette. Usually a small red light, the *disk activity light,* comes on each time a diskette is accessed. *Never put in or take out a diskette when the disk activity light is on.* To do so is disastrous because it may cause data to be written randomly across the diskette surface.

Rational handling of diskettes is applied common sense. Though diskettes are new to the computer novice there is no excuse for ignoring

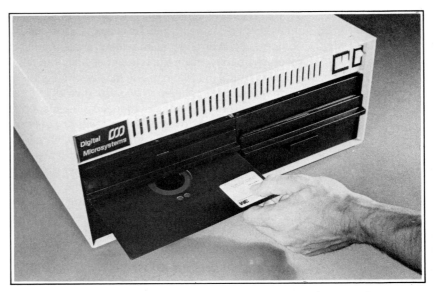

FIGURE 1-5. Inserting Diskette in Horizontally-Mounted Drive

the implications of misuse. CP/M can only be as good as the environment you create for it. Properly maintain the equipment and carefully handle your data on the diskettes.

STARTING UP CP/M

When CP/M is loaded into your computer, several things happen. First, a *cold start loader* moves into your computer memory from the diskette. This loader varies from machine to machine and may differ between CP/M versions, but its function is always to load CP/M. The cold start loader is a distinct program stored with CP/M on the diskette.

Why load something into your computer in order to load something else? The reasons are complex (and are discussed in Chapter 7), but primarily it facilitates *machine independence*, which means that completely different computers can use the same disk drives and the same copy of CP/M.

After the cold start loader brings in CP/M, a number of things happen. In order, they are: 1) CP/M is loaded into your computer's memory. 2) Program execution is passed to CP/M, which 3) performs various initialization operations, and 4) places a "sign-on" message on your screen, followed by 5) the prompt A >. 6) Finally, CP/M waits for you to type a command. At this point, your display looks something like this:

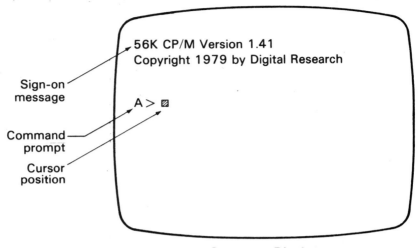

Computer Display

As you can see, CP/M does nothing particularly mysterious when you start up your computer. The whirring and clacking you hear from the computer's disk drives indicates everything is working properly.

Next consider the physical process *you* undertake to initialize CP/M. Since every computer system is different, we will talk in general terms. If you are not sure of the correct procedure, read the manuals that accompanied your computer.

Some peripheral devices must be turned on first. If you have a hard disk drive, turn it on first, preferably several minutes before the system is to be used, as it needs to get up to speed (imagine how long it takes to get a 20-pound, 14-inch metal platter spinning at 3000 revolutions per minute).

If you have floppy disk drives, do not insert any diskette yet (unless your computer manuals tell you to do so). If you insert the diskettes and *then* turn the computer on or off, a small transient voltage may be applied to the diskette drive head, and accidentally erase or add information to the diskette.

Turn the computer on. In some cases, the computer immediately attempts to load programs from the diskette when you turn the power on. Do not insert a diskette into a drive while the drive is accessing a diskette unless your manual tells you it is okay to do so. If you do, information may be erased or added to the diskette.

Most manufacturers use a cold start loader (discussed earlier in this chapter) to get things started. When you "power on" such machines, they display a message on the screen and wait for your instruction. Some wait for you to press the Carriage Return key several times (to determine the speed the keyboard sends characters). Usually the instruction is a single letter (like B, which stands for "boot"). On these systems, you turn on the power, place your diskette in the first drive, and press the B key or the instruction your system requires.

Here is a summary of startup steps:

1. Switch on peripherals' power.
2. Insert diskette (some systems).
3. Power on computer.
4. Insert diskette (remaining systems).
5. Press Carriage Return (some systems).
6. Type boot instruction (usually B).
7. Wait for CP/M to "sign on."

See your computer manual for specific startup procedures.

DAY-TO-DAY ROUTINES

There are other day-to-day operating routines you need to know.

Reset the Computer: Pressing the Panic Button

There are a number of other fatal errors that can endanger the data on your diskette. Fatal errors are guaranteed if you turn off the power or press the RESET button while writing information on the diskette. Unfortunately, there is no steadfast rule on this one. You may resort to pressing the RESET button to stop an endless loop of continuously executed instructions. Thoroughly tested programs rarely get stuck in such a loop but newly developed programs can.

If one of these endless loops includes an instruction to write information onto the diskette, the diskette activity light could come on and stay on. After a few minutes of waiting for something to happen, panic may set in. Be certain the computer is in an endless loop before proceeding. Good computer programs will give periodic messages like:

I'M WORKING. . .

or

THIS MAY TAKE A WHILE. . .

While these messages are not exactly foolproof (how long is "a while"?), they are somewhat reassuring when the diskette activity light comes on and stays on.

If you are entirely convinced that your computer is in an endless loop, press the RESET button on the computer. Almost all computers have one, but some of them are hidden on the back. Pressing the RESET button on most computers has the same effect as turning the power off and back on. However, the power is not interrupted to any component, and any program or data that was stored in the computer's memory will remain.

If your manuals are not clear about what to do after pressing RESET, *call your computer store before doing anything else.* If important data still remains in the computer and you want to preserve it, reloading CP/M or another program may destroy it!

Backup the Diskettes

Almost every implementation of CP/M has a *copy program* (see Chapter 5). Before ending a session at the computer, make copies of any diskettes you have changed or updated. This process is called *backup*.

Consider the following information on backing up diskettes:

1. *Label all diskettes.* Distinguish the original diskette from the copy. One way is the *father-son method.* The original diskette is labeled "father," and the copy is labeled "son." If you maintain an extra copy of the diskette for archive purposes, this is the "grandfather" (original), and the "father" and "son" diskettes are subsequent copies. This may not be the best way to maintain copies, as it is far too easy to slip into the habit of making infrequent backups.

   A far better method is the *rotating backup procedure.* You have one data diskette for each day you use the computer (e.g., Monday-Friday). At the end of Monday's processing, you copy the Monday diskette onto the Tuesday diskette. At the end of Tuesday's processing you copy the information onto Wednesday's diskette. Using this method (assuming that you labeled each diskette carefully), you know immediately if you are using the right diskette, and there is a natural backup sequence.

2. *Diskettes are not permanent.* No diskette will last forever. The reason for this fact is simple: there is a great deal of physical contact between the diskette surface and the inside of its sleeve. Also, a poorly aligned drive will create excessive head wear.

   Estimates of the life of a diskette have an extraordinary range. One manufacturer claims their diskettes will endure a year of continuous use. In any case, do not expect diskettes to last forever. If you use the rotating backup procedure, retire diskettes after six months of use. This is a conservative practice, since each diskette has been used only 27 days. But considering the price of a diskette versus the cost of reentering lost data, it seems a wise practice.

3. *Never use programs on their original diskettes.* When you receive a new program (or CP/M update) on diskette, make a copy of it, label the original "master," and safely store the master diskette. Using an original diskette is foolhardy. Someday your computer may sit idle while you wait for a replacement diskette. Some software vendors provide an update only on return of the original diskette.

Shutting Off the System

Earlier you learned how to turn on your computer system. The procedure for shutting off the computer system is *not* the reverse of the power-on procedure.

First, use a normal exit from any program you might be running.

Second, remove any diskettes from their drives. Then turn the power off on the disk drives, terminal(s), printer(s), and any other peripheral. Turn power off at the microcomputer last. If you have hard disk drives on your system (with non-removable media) turn off the power to those drives before turning off the microcomputer's power. Failure to do so may result in loss of information on the disk. If your manual tells you to do the opposite, follow its instructions, or consult your computer retailer or manufacturer to verify the manual's procedures.

2

CP/M Built-In
Commands

We described how to start up CP/M in Chapter 1. Now it is time to make
CP/M work for you. We convey that work by typing commands.

COMMANDS ARE INSTRUCTIONS

Commands are your instructions to CP/M. When CP/M is ready to receive
a command, it displays its prompt (usually A >). To express a command,
type the command and then press the Carriage Return key.

CP/M has two types of commands: built-in commands and transient
commands.

The distinction is a subtle one. The short programs which carry out
built-in commands are always present in memory with CP/M. The
programs which carry out transient commands are not automatically
loaded into memory when CP/M is started up. A transient command
causes CP/M to get a program from the disk, load it into computer
memory, and execute the program. The program, called a transient
program, would not otherwise be present in memory.

To make things a little clearer, we will distinguish between
built-in commands and transient commands in this way:

A *built-in command* is immediately executed by CP/M without
consulting further instructions on disk.

A *transient command* requires a set of instructions stored on
disk to be brought into memory before each use. It is

important to note that CP/M executes all commands. Both built-in and transient command programs are invoked by typing a command such as LOAD or DIR in response to the CP/M prompt.

Commands Operate on Disk Files

CP/M commands access and manipulate information stored on disks in files. A *file* is any information stored as a single entity, with a unique name. The length of a file may vary from no characters to the maximum capacity of the disk. Here are some examples of files:

- A single program
- All of the data used by a program
- An entire mailing list
- A single letter
- A large group of standard form letters
- A chapter of this book
- The entire contents of this book

No rule determines the information you may store in a file. You define a file's contents when you create the file.

All files consist of *fields:* single words, numbers, or any other convenient, small unit of information. You can also divide files into *records*, to represent another division of information larger than fields.

How files are divided into records and fields again depends on how you create the file. To illustrate records and fields, consider a mailing list file. All the names and addresses may constitute a single file, but each name and address could be designated a single record, while the name and each line of the address might each become a single field.

Built-In Commands Summary

Only *six built-in commands are recognized by CP/M 1.4*, and *seven are recognized by CP/M 2.0*. The six commands are DIR, TYPE, ERA, REN, SAVE, and x:, and the seventh is USER. The format and operation of the commands are summarized below. Detailed descriptions are given later in this chapter.

DIR x:filename.typ
Displays a directory of the file names on a disk.

TYPE x:filename.typ
Displays the contents of a disk file on your console screen.

ERA x:filename.typ
Erases a file from a disk.

REN x:newname.typ=s:oldname.typ
Renames a file on a disk.

SAVE nn x:filename.typ
Saves the contents of the computer memory as a file on a disk.

x:
Changes the currently logged disk.

USER nn
Changes the currently logged user number (CP/M version 2.0 and newer).

LINE EDITING COMMANDS

In addition to the basic built-in commands there are several immediately interpreted line editing commands. They are summarized below:

Control-C
Restarts CP/M if it is the first character typed in a command line. Called a *warm start*.

Control-E
Moves to beginning of next line. Used for typing long commands.

Control-H or Backspace
Deletes one character and erases it from the screen (CP/M version 2.0 and newer).

Control-J or Line Feed
Same as carriage return (CP/M version 2.0 and newer).

Control-M
Same as carriage return (<cr>).

Control-P
Turns on the *list device* (usually your printer). Type it again to turn off the list device.

Control-R
Repeats current command line (useful with version 1.4); it verifies the line is corrected after deleting several characters. Control-R does not work with CP/M version 1.3.

Control-S
> Temporarily stops display of data on the console. Press any key to continue.

Control-U or Control-X
> Cancels current command line. Control-X does not work with CP/M version 1.3.

Rubout (RUB) or Delete (DEL)
> Deletes one character and echoes (repeats) it.

These line editing commands are described in detail later in this chapter.

Entering the Commands

We use these conventions to denote commands and keystrokes:

> *Press* means to press a single key.
>
> *Type* means to press a sequence of keys.
>
> <cr> means to press Carriage Return.
>
> ^x means to enter control character x.
>
> <u>Underline</u> distinguishes user input from computer output (when necessary); user input is underlined.

The Carriage Return key will be represented by the symbol <cr>. A typical example is:

DIR <cr>

This means type the letters D, I, and R, and then press the Carriage Return key. The Carriage Return key can be labeled RETURN, CARR RET, CR, ENTER, or other abbreviations.

Control characters are subject to special interpretation by a computer. Just as you hold down the Shift key to type a capital letter on a typewriter, you hold down the Control key to type a control letter (or control character in computer jargon). This is illustrated in Figure 2-1. Therefore, ^C means press and hold down the Control key, type a letter C, then release the Control key.

The Control key is often abbreviated as "CTRL" or "CTL" or sometimes "ALT"; it is almost always found in the lower left-hand corner of the keyboard near the left-hand Shift key.

Your console displays both what you type and the computer response. This book uses the following convention to differentiate between output from the computer and data typed at the keyboard: operator input is underlined, while all computer-generated characters are not underlined.

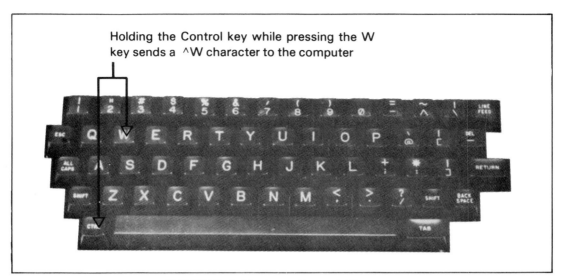

Holding the Control key while pressing the W
key sends a ^W character to the computer

FIGURE 2-1. Typing a Control Character

Here is an example:

```
A>DIR<cr>
A:STAT.COM
A:MBASIC.COM
A:BACKUP.COM
A>MBASIC<cr>
Microsoft BASIC version 5.1
copyright 1977,1978,1979,1980
by Microsoft, Inc.
14,568 bytes free
OK
```

In this example, the computer places a prompt A> on the screen (or
printer). You type DIR<cr>. The computer replies with STAT.COM,
MBASIC.COM, BACKUP.COM, and another prompt A>. Then you type
MBASIC<cr> and a five-line message indicates Microsoft BASIC has
been loaded and is ready to use.

The space character, which is typed by pressing the Space Bar, is
frequently required in commands. Even though it appears to be "nothing"
or "blank space" when typed on a typewriter, within a computer system
it is just as important as any other character. In fact, your computer and
CP/M are quite finicky about spaces. Generally, where the examples in
this book show a space you must press the Space Bar, and where no
space is shown you must not press the Space Bar.

Upper- and lower-case letters are used in command line and other user
input examples to differentiate the fixed and variable portions of the

input. You must type the upper-case portion exactly as it appears; this unvarying part of your input is usually the command name. In place of the lower-case portions you must substitute information of your choosing; this is the variable part of your input. For example, one form of the directory command is:

> DIR *.typ < cr >

You must choose an extension (file type) to replace "typ" when you type this directory command. Here are some specific examples which fit the form above:

> DIR *.ASM < cr >
> DIR *.BAK < cr >
> DIR *.DOC < cr >

CP/M File Conventions

Each CP/M file is identified by a *name* and an *extension*. These identifiers are discussed in detail below.

FILE NAMES

Each CP/M file has a unique name. CP/M file names may have from one to eight characters. A word of caution: it *is* possible for a file to have no name. In addition, a file name can include lower-case characters. Both possibilities cause problems; CP/M automatically converts characters you type in a command line (following the A >) from lower-case to upper-case, and will not accept a blank file name in a command line. How could the lower-case letters get there? If you save the file with BASIC or some other program which does not convert file name characters from lower-case to upper-case (Microsoft BASIC and CBASIC are two examples), you could end up with a file name with lower-case letters in it. You may find such files inaccessible since you cannot name them in a CP/M command. As a matter of course, *always use upper-case characters when referencing a CP/M file*.

To veteran computer and CP/M users, this admonition may seem a bit strong, but if you are a newcomer to computers, or you generally use packaged software, it is a good rule to follow.

Several characters may not be used in a file name. These characters are:

> < > . , ; : = ? * []

Since CP/M uses these characters in special ways, they are invalid as file name characters.

Nor may you use control characters (or other characters that do not appear on your screen) in a file name.

Here are some samples of valid and invalid CP/M file names:

Valid	Reason	Invalid	Reason
FILENAME	Uses valid letters*	ISFILENAME	Too many characters
filename	Uses valid letters*	IS.FILE	Contains .
FiLeNaMe	Uses valid letters*	<FILE>	Contains < and >
IS-FILE	- is valid character	WORD*	Contains *
IS/FILE	/ is valid character	MYN=YORS	Contains =
OH!	! is valid character	OH?	Contains ?
A)FILE	) is valid character	A:FILE	Contains :
87654321	Numbers okay	500,000	Contains ,
A+B+C/D	+ is valid character	A+B=C	Contains =
		^C	^C is sub-command

* These three files are the same since CP/M converts all lower-case letters to upper-case. These names will not be the same if saved by a CBASIC or Microsoft BASIC program. These BASICs bypass the CP/M automatic lower-to-upper case conversion process for file names and commands; thus "FiLeNaMe" would exist exactly as typed.

FILE EXTENSIONS

It is a good idea to identify files in a manner that lets you know what a file is going to be used for, since different types of information are handled in different ways. For example, certain program file operations could destroy the contents of a data file, were it accessed by mistake.

To keep such disasters from happening, CP/M relies upon a file extension to express the file function. The file extension follows the file name and consists of three characters chosen from the list of valid file name characters. The extension is separated from the file name by a period; that is why a period cannot be imbedded within a file name.

Several quasi-standard file extensions are used:

.ASM   ASseMbly language source file

.BAK   BAcKup file

.BAS   BASIC program source file

.COB   COBOL source file

.COM   Directly executable transient program (COMmand file)

.DAT   DATa file

.DOC	Text (DOCument) file
.FOR	Microsoft FORTRAN source file
.HEX	Intel HEX format object code file
.INT	BASIC program compiled in INTermediate code
.LIB	Extension for a LIBrary file
.MAC	MACro file (usually a subroutine used in assembly language programs)
.OBJ	Machine code (OBJect code)
.PAS	PAScal source file
.PCO	Sorcim Pascal run-time module
.PRL	Page ReLocatable MP/M file
.PRN	Assembly language listing file (PRiNt file)
.REL	RELocatable machine code program
.SRC	SouRCe file for CP/M Users' Group
.SUB	Command file for a SUBmit run
.TXT	TeXT file
.$$$	Temporary file or an improperly saved, unusable file

While there are other extension names in use, this list represents about 95% of those you will encounter. As you can see, these extensions help to identify particular programs. In addition, they aid in selecting files to use or to print.

You can also make up your own file extensions. For example, try using the version number of a program during the development stage. If you were working on a program called THEBEST, your list of files on a disk might look like this:

THEBEST.001
THEBEST.002
THEBEST.003
THEBEST.004
THEBEST.BAS

THEBEST.BAS represents the finished product, and each of the other file extensions represents the program at a different stage of development.

File extensions can be one, two, or three characters long, or nonexistent. That is, the file extension may be omitted when you name a file.

While CP/M itself ignores the file extension, many programs that use CP/M demand specific file extensions. For example, the CBASIC compiler requires source program files to have the extension "BAS," while a CBASIC compiled program file needs the extension "INT." But these extensions are meaningful to the CBASIC compiler only; CP/M knows nothing about the CBASIC compiler needs, nor does it take such needs into account in any way.

Combining File Name and File Extension

Sometimes in a command you can specify a file by typing just the file name (the eight-character label). Other times you must type the file name and file extension. Some valid examples of the combined file name and extension are:

WATNOWMY.LUV
ROBOT.AGE
MICRO.COM
THX1138.PIC
KINGAND.I

Notice eight characters are not required in the file name, nor are three characters required in the extension. A file name must have at least one character, and it does not need an extension. In other words, you may have file names of one to eight characters in length, and file extensions of zero to three characters.

Now for a caveat: computer language is not standardized enough for universal definitions. For some programmers "file name" represents the *entire* combination of file name, period, and file extension. Terms like "file reference," "file type," "primary name," and "secondary name" refer to the various parts and combinations of the file identification. In this book, *file name* describes the label (one to eight characters long) used to refer to the file (Digital Research *primary name*), and *file type* or *extension* refers to the type (zero to three characters long; Digital Research *secondary name*).

Disk Drive Identifiers

CP/M addresses its available disk drives with the letters A, B, C, D, etc. The first, or *primary drive* of your system is the A drive. Other drives follow in alphabetical order (i.e., the second drive is B, etc.). The only exception occurs when hard disk and floppy disk drives are mixed on a computer system. Some manufacturers use the letters M, N, O, and P to refer to the hard disk drive surfaces. Check your manuals if your system uses mixed drives.

Since file names and commands consist of letters, CP/M must determine when the letter A refers to a drive and when it is part of a command or file name. To denote a disk drive enter a colon (:) after the drive letter; for example, A:. In this book and in all CP/M manuals, A:, B:, C:, etc., always pertain to disk drive devices.

If you have used other disk operating systems you may have trouble with the drive identifiers; many operating systems use numbers instead of letters to identify drives. Since most manufacturers do not label the disk drives it makes sense for you to label each drive with its identifier A, B, C, etc.

When you start CP/M you will use the A drive. Unless you specify another drive, the A drive will be the *default* or currently logged drive for all commands and programs you invoke. This means that to use the A (default) drive, you need not type its identifier.

Ambiguous and Unambiguous File References

Another set of keystrokes comprises the *ambiguous file references*:

* The asterisk represents either an ambiguous file name or file type. It replaces an *entire* file name or file extension.

? The question mark represents a single ambiguous character *within* a file name or extension.

These ambiguous file reference characters may be used in the specifications of the file name or extension. In the Digital Research manuals, ambiguous file references are abbreviated afn (for ambiguous file name) while complete file name/extension combinations are abbreviated ufn (for unambiguous file name).

Many CP/M commands require you to enter unambiguous file references in the command line. This means you must precisely specify the complete file name and file type to invoke the command properly.

The asterisk (*) can represent the *entire* set of characters on either side of the period in a complete file name. For instance, all of the following are valid, ambiguous file specifications in CP/M:

*.BAS
THEBEST.*

.

Now wait a minute, you ask, what good is that? Consider the directory command. To learn the names of all of the BASIC programs on drive A, type the following command line:

DIR *.BAS <cr>

The computer displays all files with the extension BAS. To erase all BASIC source program files on your disk A, type:

ERA *.BAS <cr>

Unfortunately, CP/M does not print out file names as they are erased; we see nothing else until the prompt A > returns after CP/M finishes its job; this is a weakness in the CP/M system. Think twice before using the ERA command with ambiguous file references. Always enter the DIR command to test file specification before invoking ERA.

You may have already guessed that we can use the question mark like the asterisk. For instance, if PROGRAM1.ASM is the only file with extension ASM, the following three commands will be treated identically in CP/M:

    ERA *.ASM < cr >
    ERA PROGRAM1.ASM < cr >
    ERA ????????.ASM < cr >

Notice how all eight file name characters must be identified, using question marks, while only one, the asterisk, appears in the first example. (Try typing DIR ???.* < cr > to see what happens.)

Remember that the question mark always represents a single ambiguous character. To display all your BASIC programs (extension BAS) *and* backup files (extension BAK) type:

    DIR * .BA? < cr >

Both file types are listed since the file extensions BAS and BAK differ only in the final character, which is ambiguous (?).

Most CP/M systems have two or more drives. Remember that CP/M identifies a disk drive with a letter and a colon. The command:

    DIR B:*.* < cr >

displays ALL file names on drive B:. The prompt A > indicates A: is the *current* default drive. If we do not type B: in front of the file reference, all files on drive A: will be displayed by default.

Built-In Commands — Detailed

Built-in commands were introduced earlier in this chapter. In the following section each built-in command is described in detail.

DIR — DISPLAY THE FILE DIRECTORY

The DIR command displays a directory of files on a diskette.

    DIR x: < cr >
        Displays directory of all files present on drive x. x: is optional;
        if omitted, the currently logged drive is used.

DIR x:filename.typ < cr >
Displays directory of all files present on drive x whose names
match the unambiguous or ambiguous "filename.typ." x: is
optional; if omitted, the currently logged drive is used.

DIR x: < cr >

Display directory of all files present on drive x.

```
A > DIR B: < cr >
B: DOCUMENT MAR
B: DOCUMENT APR
B: DOCUMENT JUN
A >
```

A >   CP/M prompt; CP/M waiting for your
                                       command

DIR B: Display a directory of files on
                                       disk drive B

B: DOCUMENT MAR   List of files from disk drive
B: DOCUMENT APR   B is displayed
B: DOCUMENT JUN

A >   CP/M prompt returns

Display directory of all files on the currently logged disk drive.

```
A > DIR < cr >
A: EENIE       BAS
A: MEENIE      BAS
A: MINEY       BAS
A: MO          BAS
A >
```

A >   CP/M prompt; CP/M waiting for your
                                       command; currently logged drive is A

DIR < cr >   Display directory of all files on
                                       the currently logged disk drive

A: EENIE   BAS   All file names are displayed
A: MEENIE   BAS
A: MINEY   BAS
A: MO   BAS
A >   CP/M prompt returns

DIR x:filename.typ < cr >

Display directory of files which match ambiguous or unambiguous file
names and/or file extensions.

```
A > DIR B:*.BAS < cr >
B: FRESHWTR    BAS
A >
```

A>   CP/M prompt; CP/M waiting for your
                                       command

DIR *.BAS <cr>   Display the directory of the
                                       file with the name FRESHWTR and
                                       extension "BAS" on drive B

B: FRESHWTR BAS   .   Display the file name

A>   CP/M prompt returns

```
A >DIR B:*.BAS <cr>
B: FRESHWTR BAS
B: SALTWTR  BAS
A>
```

Displays the directory of all files on drive B with extension BAS.

```
A >DIR FISH. <cr>
A: FISH   TRT
A: FISH   CRP
A: FISH   ING
A>
```

Display the directory of all files on the currently logged drive with the file name FISH.

```
A >DIR *.* <cr>
```

Same as DIR <cr>. Displays the directory of all files on the currently logged drive.

Error Messages

NO FILE or NOT FOUND

The disk does not contain the files you specified (if you type DIR *.BAS, "NO FILE" means no files with the file extension of BAS are on the disk).

BDOS ERR ON x:

(where x is a drive identifier). CP/M could not find a disk in the selected drive: there is no disk in that drive, the disk is not properly formatted, the power to the drives is off, or the drive door has not been closed. An old disk can deteriorate to the point where CP/M thinks there is no disk in the drive.

DIT?

You mistyped the command DIR by striking the T key instead of the R. An unrecognized command is repeated with a ? after it. Check carefully for typing errors when you see such a message.

Notes on DIR *.*

All file names can be displayed, or directories may be searched, using the * and ? characters to select a group of similarly-named files. Employ the ambiguous file references (* and ?) to search for a particular file when you do not know the exact file name. For example, to look for a BASIC program if you know only that the file name starts with an A, you might type: DIR A???????.BAS.

CP/M versions 1.4 and 2.0 display the file directory in different ways. CP/M version 1.4 displays one filename per line. CP/M versions 2.0 through 2.2 display four file names on each line; each file reference is separated by a vertical line, another graphic indication. Each directory line starts with the disk drive identifier.

ERA — ERASE A FILE

ERA stands for erase. Type the file name after the command to erase the file.

ERA x:filename.typ < cr >
Erase the file, filename.typ, on the disk in drive x. filename and/ or typ can be ambiguous. x: is optional; if omitted, the currently logged drive is used.

ERA x:*.* <cr >
Erase all files on the diskette in the default drive.

ERA x:filename.typ < cr >

Erase the file "filename.typ" on the disk in drive x.

```
A >DIR C: <cr >
C: QUALITY  CTL
C: MIND     CTL
C: WEIGHT   CTL
A >ERA C:QUALITY.CTL < cr >
A >DIR C: <cr >
C: MIND     CTL
C: WEIGHT   CTL
A >
```

A>	CP/M prompt
DIR C:	Display directory of all files on the disk in drive C
C: QUALITY CTL. . .	Displays the file names
A>	CP/M prompt returns
ERA C:QUALITY.CTL	Erase file, QUALITY.CTL from the disk on drive C
A>	CP/M prompt returns
DIR C:	Display a directory of files on the disks in drive C, to verify proper erasure
C: MIND CTL	Verify file erased
C: WEIGHT CTL	

A>   CP/M prompt returns

```
A>DIR B:*.BAS<cr>
B: NOW     BAS
B: THEN    BAS
B: ALWAYS BAS
A>ERA B:*.BAS<cr>
A>DIR B:*.BAS<cr>
NOT FOUND
A>
```

Erase all files on drive B with the extension BAS, and check the results.

```
A>DIR SNJAQUIN.*<cr>
A: SNJAQUIN VLY
A: SNJAQUIN RVR
A: SNJAQUIN BDG
A>ERA SNJAQUIN.*<cr>
A>DIR SNJAQUIN.*<cr>
NO FILES
A>
```

Erase the files with the name SNJAQUIN from the currently logged disk drive.

```
B>DIR<cr>
B: SOHO       NY
B: CHELSEA    NY
B: UPREST     NY
B: UPRWST     NY
B>ERA *.*<cr>
ALL FILES (Y/N)?Y<cr>
B>DIR<cr>
B: NOT FOUND
B>
```

Erase all files from the currently logged disk drive.

ALL FILES (Y/N)?   CP/M verifies your intent

Y<cr>   Affirmative

Error Messages

NO FILE or NOT FOUND
   The file you specified cannot be found. If you type ERA
   KNOW<cr> instead of ERA NOW<cr>, this message might
   appear. But if you have a file named KNOW, it would have
   been erased! Do not count on this error message to catch your
   typing mistakes.

BDOS ERROR ON x:
   CP/M could not find a valid diskette in drive x. Either the door
   is open, no disk has been inserted, the disk is improperly

formatted, the power is not turned on for the drives, or the
disk is write-protected.

Notes on ERA *.*

Since it is extremely rare to remove *all* files from the disk, CP/M makes
one last check before erasing all your valuable information. CP/M version
1.3 does not display the cautionary (Y/N)? message.

Notes on ERA

Checking the directory before invoking ERA is a good habit to develop.
You verify the file exists on the disk in the form you have entered. And
the *only* way to verify CP/M correctly erased the selected file(s) is to
enter the DIR command after executing the erasure.

REN — RENAME A FILE

There is only one form of the REN command.

REN newname.typ=oldname.typ < cr >

Finds the file oldname.typ and renames it newname.typ; the new name
for the file is always to the left of the equal sign.

```
A > DIR < cr >
A: HOLDEN  ONE
A: PHOEBE  TWO
A > REN NOVEL.BST=HOLDEN.ONE < cr >
A > DIR < cr >
A: NOVEL  BST
A: PHOEBE  TWO
A >
```

A >	CP/M prompt
DIR < cr >	Display all file names on drive A
A: HOLDEN ONE. . .	Display file names
A >	CP/M prompt returns
REN NOVEL.BST=HOLDEN.ONE	Rename the file HOLDEN.ONE as NOVEL.BST
A >	CP/M prompt returns
DIR < cr >	Display directory, to verify name change
A: NOVEL BST. . .	Displays all file names on drive A. Verifies HOLDEN.ONE changed to NOVEL.BST
A >	CP/M prompt returns

Error Messages

FILENAME?
You incorrectly used an ambiguous file reference in the REN

command line. For instance, if you type REN
TAL.CAR=SHORT???.CAR the error message
SHORT???.CAR? appears.

NO FILE

The file you wish to rename does not exist. Check the
specified drive and file name for typing errors.

FILE EXISTS

The new name specified is the name of a file which already
exists. You cannot rename a file with the name of an existing
file. If you wish to replace an existing file with a newer version
of the same file, either rename or erase the existing file or use
the PIP utility, described in Chapter 3.

Notes on REN

Almost universally, whenever the computer deciphers an *equivalence*
statement, the *new* formation or result is to the left of the equal sign, and
the *old* formation or result appears on the right.

Contrary to the conventions of the DIR and ERA commands, you may
not use the ambiguous file references (* and ?) when using the REN
command. Typing REN NEWTHOM.BAS=THOM'S.BA? <cr> results in
an error message.

In our example we first asked for a directory of files; again this is a
good habit to develop because CP/M does not display the results of your
renaming.

A disk drive specifier may be included with either or both file names. If
included with one name, it applies to both. If included with both file
names, the same drive specifier must be used with both. If omitted, the
currently logged disk is used.

TYPE — DISPLAY FILE CONTAINING
ASCII-CODED INFORMATION

There is only one form of the TYPE command.

TYPE x:filename.typ <cr>

Displays the contents of file filename.typ from drive x: on the console.

A>TYPE O.POS <cr>
Had Henry Ecpuck been present, and had he been able
to see inside the NASCOM Cray-1 computer, he would
have seen a long string of bits spelling out his name
computer style. But the National Security Computer
Center was 1500 miles away; in fact, Henry
was not aware of its existence. The

```
A>                          CP/M prompt
TYPE O.POS                  Display the contents of the file O.POS
Had Henry. . .              File contents (text) displayed
```

Input other than Command Line

Press any key to abort display of file contents.

^S — temporary pause in display; then press any key to restart listing; or press ^C to abort listing.

Error Messages

FILENAME?

The file you named does not exist; you used ambiguous file references * or ?; you misspelled TYPE.

Notes on TYPE

The file must consist of *printable* characters to be seen on the display. Do not TYPE files containing non-printable characters, such as files with extensions COM, OBJ, etc., as gibberish appears on the screen.

TYPE *does* work for files with extensions BAS, ASM, BAK, DAT, HEX, DOC, and any other file which contains ASCII text or data. *ASCII* is a character recognition and storage scheme for computers; each letter and character has a unique representation that can be saved or used by the computer in ASCII code.

You can use a text editor or word processing program to see a file, but not everyone using CP/M has a word processing program available. If you only want to take a peek at your program or data, why run a text editor? The TYPE command is built into CP/M and is always available.

SAVE — SAVE MEMORY CONTENTS IN A DISK FILE

Saves the contents of the Transient Program Area in a diskette file. There is only one form of the SAVE command.

SAVE nnn x:filename.typ <cr>

Save a portion of memory in a file, filename.typ, on drive x where nnn is a decimal number representing the number of pages of memory.

```
A>DDT CURSEAND.HEX <cr>
DDT VERS 2.2
NEXT PC
1100 0100
-^C
A>SAVE 16 CURSEAND.COM <cr>
A>
```

A>	CP/M prompt
DDT CURSEAND.HEX	Load the file CURSEAND.HEX into memory
DDT VERS. 2.2	DDT identifies itself
NEXT 1100	Display the first available hexadecimal address (1100) following the program
PC 0100	The program counter is set at 0100
—	DDT prompt
^C	We have the information we need from DDT; now we pass control back
A>	to CP/M
SAVE 16 CURSEAND.COM	Save 16 pages of memory in the new file CURSEAND.COM
A>	CP/M prompt returns

Notes on SAVE

The disk drive specifier x: is optional; if omitted, the file will be placed on the currently logged drive.

Select the file name carefully. SAVE will erase any existing file of the same name before creating the new one.

You will rarely use the SAVE command if you only use CP/M to run off-the-shelf or *canned* business application programs. On the other hand, assembly language programmers will use this command frequently. For continuity's sake, the SAVE command is presented at this point in the book; if you are not familiar with assembly language, or want more background before tackling the particulars of SAVE, you should read Chapter 3 before proceeding with the rest of this description.

Since DDT, the debugger utility program, is normally used in conjunction with the SAVE command, we have used DDT in our example. DDT is examined in Chapter 4, Assembly Language Utilities.

In order to perform a SAVE, you must know the number of "pages" in memory to be saved. A *page of memory* is a block consisting of 256 bytes. The first page saved usually begins at memory location 0100 hexadecimal. The number of pages to be saved must be expressed as a decimal number.

Beginners often encounter problems with the "page of memory" concept; 256 decimal is equivalent to 100 hexadecimal. The number conversion involved is not an easy one, especially if you have "math anxiety." If you are susceptible to math anxiety and do not plan to learn assembly language programming, skip this command.

The *hexadecimal system* (abbreviated hex by almost everyone) is equivalent to base 16. In other words, the one's place can have 16 digits, as opposed to the ten digits in base 10. In base 10 we count:

0 1 2 3 4 5 6 7 8 9

In hex math we count:

0 1 2 3 4 5 6 7 8 9 A B C D E F

The letter A represents our normal number 10, B represents our usual number 11, etc. In everyday math we would interpret 111 to mean:

One in the one's place   =   1
One in the ten's place   =   10
One in the hundred's place = 100

In hex math 111 means:

One in the one's place   =   1
One in the sixteen's place =   16
One in the 256's place   = 256
                       Result = 273 (in base 10)

Okay, so it's different; what good is it? A complete answer would fill a book. Suffice it to say, we must talk to the computer using the hexadecimal system.

Remember 0100 hex equals one page of memory. Does 0200 hex equal two pages of memory? Yes. The math conversion is easy when you can drop the last two digits.

To save the portion of memory from 0100 hex to 2785 hex:

1. Round the upper memory location to the next *higher* page (that is 2800 hex in our example).

2. Drop the last two hexadecimal digits from each location (we now have 01 and 28 in our example).

3. Convert the two numbers to decimal and subtract the lower from the upper. Thus 28 minus 01 is not 27 but 39 decimal. We get this by first converting 28 to decimal:

   8 in the 1's place   =   8
   2 in the 16's place = 32
               Result = 40

   then subtracting 1; the first page of memory is not used in the SAVE command.

4. You now have the number of pages of memory to use in your SAVE command: 39.

There is an easier way to calculate the number of pages to save. To save memory from 0100 hex to 2785 hex:

1. First forget 0100; the SAVE command always starts at this address.

2. Drop the last two hex digits from the higher address. In this case 2785 becomes 27.

3. Convert the remaining number to decimal. For our example:

7 in the 1's place   =   7
2 in the 16's place = 32
Result = 39

4. Step 3 gives the correct result except for one special case. If the last two digits dropped in Step 2 were 00, you must subtract 1 from the result in Step 3. For example, if the higher address were 2700 instead of 2785, the correct result would have been 38.

The SAVE command is used with DDT, the debugging program that accompanies CP/M. DDT is discussed in Chapter 4.

Error Messages

FILENAME?

You failed to specify how many pages of memory to save or the file reference you specified makes no sense; you typed an ambiguous file reference.

NO SPACE

Too many files are already on the disk, or no room is left on the disk to save the information.

USER — CHANGE THE CURRENTLY LOGGED USER NUMBER

There is only one form of the USER command.

USER n < cr >

Set the user number to n, where n is an integer decimal number from 0 to 15, inclusive.

Error Messages

n?

You specified a number greater than 15 for a user area number (i.e., you will see 16? on the screen when you type USER 16 < cr >).

FILENAME or NO FILE

These messages appear in response to other commands which reference a file outside the current user area.

Notes on USER

CP/M versions 2.0 and newer include USER. CP/M versions 1.3 and 1.4 do not.

When you cold start in CP/M, user number zero is assumed. Your disk operations will reference files in user area zero only. In other words, if you save a new file called JUNK.AGN after a cold start, it will always appear in directories assigned to user area zero. Type USER 2 <cr> before you save the file, and it will appear only in the user area 2 directory.

The user areas are imaginary. Every file on a diskette has a user number associated with it, stored on the disk as an additional piece of information about that file. Thus it is not necessary to set aside room on the disk for each user area.

The USER command is of minimal value in running canned programs. However, when several users share disk drives, one user can save files in user area 1 and another in user area 2, and both can share files in user area 0.

The ERA command functions differently when you have files in different user areas. For example, ERA *.* <cr> only erases all files with the currently logged user number. There is no way to erase all files on the disk unless they are all in the same user area, or USER commands are alternated with ERA commands.

x: <cr> — LOG IN ANOTHER DISK DRIVE

On a CP/M system with two or more disk drives, change the currently logged drive by typing the letter representing the drive being logged into, followed by a colon and a carriage return:

> B: <cr>
> C: <cr>
> D: <cr>

To revert to drive A, type:

> A: <cr>

When you change the currently logged drive, CP/M changes its prompt letter. Following B: <cr>, CP/M returns with a prompt B >. You can always tell which drive you are logged into by the CP/M prompt. When selecting a file on the currently logged drive you do not have to type the drive letter; but in any reference to files on other drives you must specify the desired drive.

The currently logged drive functions as the default drive when no drive is explicitly specified; for this reason it is often called the *default drive*.

Line Editing Commands — Detailed

The line editing commands let you correct typing errors while entering command lines and give you some control over the console display

TABLE 2-1. Line Editing Commands Grouped by Function

Function	Commands
Terminate command line	Carriage Return Line Feed Control-J Control-M
Cancel command line	Control-U Control-X
Cancel one character of command line	Backspace Delete Rubout Control-H
Display control	Control-E Control-R Control-S
Printer control	Control-P
Warm start	Control-C

(output). They are grouped by function in Table 2-1.

The Control-P and Control-S commands are useful at any time. The other line editing commands must be typed within a command line, that is, after the CP/M prompt appears and before you press the carriage return.

The line editing commands can often be used when typing input requested by transient programs. Their usefulness is this case will depend on the program.

CONTROL-C — PERFORM A WARM START

A *warm start* restores CP/M's internal information to a predefined state without destroying programs or data stored in memory. A *cold start* starts a system from scratch, destroying programs which were in memory before the cold start.

A cold start is often called a *cold boot*, and a warm start is often called a *warm boot*.

In CP/M the warm start command has two primary uses:

1. To "log in" a diskette when you insert a different diskette into one or more drives.
2. To interrupt the current transient program and return to the CP/M command mode.

You can create problems if you do not close files at the proper time. You can avoid such problems by always allowing a program to end normally.

If you change diskettes without telling CP/M, strange things happen. Always press Control-C after you insert a different diskette in a drive. There are some exceptions to this rule.

Error Messages

BDOS ERROR ON x: R/O
   Read-only error on disk x. (BDOS stands for Basic Disk
   Operating System, which is part of CP/M.)

CP/M can sometimes detect a switched disk. When it does, it will set the read-only attribute for that disk. If a program subsequently tries to write on the disk, this error message appears. *The only way to recover from this error and not destroy information on your disk is to type Control-C for a warm start.*

If a program does not tell you to change disks, assume that you must perform a warm start after changing any disk.

For the experienced or brave: you will notice that the error message you receive when CP/M detects the switch in diskettes mentions the diskette is "read-only." This error message appears when you try to write new information onto the diskette. This implies you can switch diskettes at any time *as long as you only read from the diskette.* If you use your system like most users, however, it is rare for a diskette to be read, but not written to.

CONTROL-E — CONTINUE TYPING ON NEXT LINE

To continue typing a long command line on the next line of the display, type Control-E. This will move the cursor to the beginning of the next line. When you ultimately press the Carriage Return, the entire command line will be considered, even though it may appear as several lines on the screen.

The Control-E line editing command can also be used when typing input requested by a transient program, depending on the program.

CONTROL-H OR BACKSPACE — DELETE
LAST CHARACTER AND ERASE IT

Use Control-H or Backspace to correct simple typing errors before pressing the Carriage Return.

If your keyboard has a key labeled "Backspace" or "BS" you can use it; in any case you can type Control-H. The two are just different names for the same function.

Control-H is similar to Rubout or Delete; it differs in that it erases the unwanted character from the screen, while Rubout or Delete leaves the unwanted character on the screen and repeats it.

Control-H or Backspace is intended for video displays rather than printers. But CP/M will still respond correctly to Control-H even if you are using a printer and the printer responds strangely.

Control-H operates in CP/M version 2.0 and newer.

CONTROL-J — LINE FEED

If you are using CP/M version 2.0 or newer, you can substitute Control-J or the Line Feed key (if your keyboard has one) for the Carriage Return key. If your keyboard has a Line Feed key, it might be marked "LF."

CONTROL-M — CARRIAGE RETURN

Typing Control-M is exactly the same as pressing the Carriage Return key.

CONTROL-P — ASSIGN OUTPUT TO THE PRINTER

To turn on the printer, type a Control-P character. If your CP/M has been configured for a printer, all output going to your screen will also be sent to the printer.

Control-P works like a push-on/push-off switch; type it once to turn the printer on; type it a second time to turn it off.

Remember, when you use Control-P to turn the printer on, the printer mimics the screen. Unless someone added a printer interface to your CP/M, you will most likely have to tolerate the following minor inconveniences:

1. Your printer will not paginate; it simply types line after line, oblivious to the end of a page.

2. Any control code imbedded in the text (a clear screen code, for example) may adversely affect the printer. Many computers use the Form Feed character to clear the screen; every time your screen clears, the printer may skip to the next page.

3. Unless you have a high-speed printer, output to your video display will be slowed down. Every time the computer wants to send a character and finds the printer busy, it will wait to send that character.

Some programs will disable the printer automatically, whether or not you have selected it.

Likewise, if you purchased your programs as complete, pre-written (canned) packages, they may turn the printer on and off as necessary. Do not type a Control-P before executing such a program unless directed by the manual; let the computer do this work whenever possible.

If you type a Control-P and double characters appear on your screen but not on your printer, contact the firm that sold you the system.

```
A>DIR^P<cr>
SSTTUUTTTTEERR.TTXXTT
RREEPPEEAATT..DDOOCC
OOVVEERR..AAGGNN
AA>>
```

Control-P is typed, but
a printer driver has not
been installed.

```
A>DIR
STUTTER.TXT
REPEAT.DOC
OVER.AGN
A>
```

Control-P is typed;
printer driver is
properly installed.

```
A> ^PD
```

Control-P is typed, but
printer is off, disconnected,
or "not ready."

Control-P actually turns on the LST: device; while the LST: device is almost always a printer, it can be another device (see the STAT command in Chapter 3).

CONTROL-R — REPEAT THE CURRENT COMMAND LINE

Versions 1.3 and 1.4 of CP/M usually lack true backspace/delete. Instead as you delete characters they are *echoed*, or repeated. Type BLA and then Delete or Rubout; you will see either:

or
BLAA   Deleted characters are echoed

BL   Deleted characters are erased (rubbed out)

Echoed characters may seem a little strange. When CP/M was first designed, the primary console device on most microcomputers was a teletypewriter. This printer cannot backspace. In order to show a character was erased, Digital Research used echoing.

If you are a lousy typist and have a CP/M system that echoes deleted characters, you might find that the command DIR B:BASIC???.* looks more like:

DIBBR BAA:BASIXXC?????.*

If you have to read command lines like that, you may come to hate your computer. Control-R comes to the rescue. Type a Control-R to display a new, correct line below the original command line. This new line deletes all the characters you deleted. Here is an example:

DIBBR BAA:BASIXXC?????.* ^R
DIR B:BASIC???.*

The Control-R command does not work in version 1.3. Users of CP/M version 2.0 or newer will probably not find the Control-R command useful. Almost all implementations of the newer version of CP/M have incorporated true backspace/delete function via the Backspace (or Control-H) key.

CONTROL-S — PAUSE DISPLAY

CP/M can *pause* the video display screen. Like a freeze frame in film, everything stops until you tell it to begin again. Pause the screen by typing a Control-S. Another Control-S resumes the output to your screen (actually, typing any character except a Control-C will resume the output to the screen). Control-S really pauses the computer, and as a result the display pauses.

This is not the best possible answer to handling overflow on the screen, however. Generally, you are surprised by the overflow, or respond too slowly to pause the frame exactly where you want. "Good" programs use formatted screen output and never attempt to put more information on the screen than it can handle. "Good" programs also include an automatic stop at the end of each screen of information and wait for you to press the Carriage Return (or some other key) before resuming output. In short, if you find yourself using the Control-S key while executing a program, you might consider other programs with better *human interfacing*, or ask your vendor to modify your program.

CONTROL-U OR CONTROL-X — CANCEL THE CURRENT COMMAND

If you start typing gibberish, don't worry, it happens to all of us. Perhaps you typed:

DIRG A:THOMKJLSK.SAB=SLIUF

Instead of using the Backspace or Delete key to get back to the first mistake, it may be easier to start over by typing Control-U. CP/M will then ignore what you typed and move to the beginning of the next line. Sometimes CP/M places a number sign (#) at the end of the cancelled line.

With CP/M version 1.3, use Control-U; Control-X does not work. With CP/M version 1.4, use either Control-U or Control-X; they work identically. With CP/M version 2.0 or newer, use Control-X if you want to erase the cancelled command line; use Control-U if you want to keep the cancelled line on the screen.

DELETE OR RUBOUT — CANCEL ONE CHARACTER AND ECHO IT

The Delete function cancels the last uncancelled character in the command line and echoes (repeats) it. Press the key marked DELETE, DEL, RUBOUT, or RUB to do this.

Use Delete or Rubout to correct simple typing errors before pressing the Carriage Return.

Some custom implementations of CP/M versions 1.3 and 1.4 may convert Delete or Rubout to the Backspace function described under "Control-H."

3

CP/M Transient Commands

In the last chapter we introduced CP/M's built-in commands. CP/M also allows you to expand the basic set of commands by having any number of additional programs that *act* like commands. This chapter will describe some of these additional programs, specifically those normally supplied with CP/M.

WHAT IS A PROGRAM?

Recall from Chapter 2 that built-in commands are those words which CP/M can interpret using only the instructions already present in memory, while transient commands (or programs) are invoked by typing a command-like phrase which tells CP/M to get further instructions from the diskette.

How does CP/M know what other instructions are available on the diskette?

If you type something in response to the CP/M command prompt, and CP/M does not recognize it as a command, it searches the diskette directory for a file with the extension COM whose file name matches the first word you type. Suppose you type:

BUY<cr>

After realizing that BUY is not a built-in command, CP/M will look for a file entitled BUY.COM on the current disk drive. If there is no such file, CP/M will issue the error message BUY?. If such a file does exist, CP/M will load that file into memory and transfer control to it.

You should immediately recognize the value of this facility; if the file which matched your "command" contained instructions for the computer to do something, it would seem just like you had typed a CP/M command (although it would require more time since the disk must be accessed before the program starts working).

What is this program which acts like a command? For the time being we will define a *program* in the context of CP/M as follows: A program is a set of instructions stored on diskette in a file with the extension COM and invoked by typing its file name. This program is often called a *transient program* or *transient command*.

This means once a program is loaded from the diskette into the memory of your computer, the computer temporarily ignores CP/M and obeys the instructions in the program. A hypothetical DISPLAY.COM program might instruct the computer to:

1. Ask you for the file name of the file you wish to display.
2. Go to the disk and find the file you requested.
3. Read a character from the file.
4. Display the character on the console display.
5. If there are more characters in the file, go back to Step 3.
6. Return to CP/M.

Invoking a Program

The command line is what you type after the prompt, up to but not including the carriage return. CP/M allows a command line up to 127 bytes long; you could type up to 127 characters for a single command. Does it strike you as strange that the file name is at most eight characters long, but that CP/M would accept 119 more? (Assume the file is a COM file and its name is the first thing typed after the prompt — our definition of a program.)

Just as some commands can have extra refinements added by typing further information, so too can programs be invoked with additional information. With DIR B:*.BAS, for instance, the command is DIR, but B:*.BAS refines the command. For lack of a better name or even an established standard, we will call this additional information *parameters*.

There may be more than one parameter in a command line.

Let us recap briefly. A generalization of the command line format looks like this:

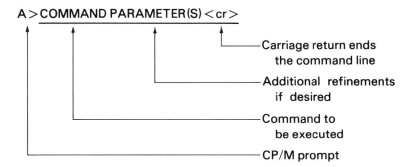

Likewise, we can generalize the way a program is invoked:

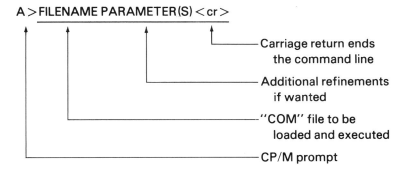

Now, what are the parameters we give the program? There is no simple answer; some programs use no additional parameters, some have optional parameters, while some require parameters. The number of parameters passed to the program may be as few as one or as many as the command line can hold.

This chapter describes transient commands. *Transient* conveys the idea that the commands (programs, actually) are not permanently in memory but are kept on a diskette. We will use the term *transient command* to conform with the Digital Research description of the programs it supplies along with CP/M.

There is a trend to include faster and larger capacity disks in microcomputer systems. These newer disks are constructed of thick, rigid metal platters as opposed to the thin, flexible plastic of diskettes. These newer disks are therefore called *hard disks*, *rigid disks*, or just *disks*. Up to this point in this book, we used the term "diskette" almost exclusively. Since CP/M version 2.0 was designed to accommodate hard disks, and since several commands new to version 2.0 are presented here, we will change our terminology slightly. Throughout the rest of this book, the term "disk" will be used frequently and is usually meant to include both floppy disks and hard disks. References to diskettes earlier in this book are generally applicable to hard disks also.

You now have all the information you need to proceed. While we have exhausted the list of commands that CP/M recognizes, we have barely hinted at the number of programs that may be loaded and executed. In the remainder of this chapter, we will deal with some important transient commands that Digital Research provides with CP/M. Chapter 4 will deal with the remaining Digital Research programs that may be important to you.

FORMAT FOR TRANSIENT PROGRAM DESCRIPTIONS

Just as we used a structured format to describe each command introduced in Chapter 2, we will structure transient programs in this chapter as follows:

PROGRAM NAME and brief description of program
Command line summary:

Command line format	Description
.	.
.	.
.	.
Command line format	Description

Introduction to the transient command
  • Brief discussion with definitions of terms
Uses of the transient command
  • List of specific functions of the transient command
Command Line Descriptions
  • Purpose of command line
  • Example with computer display result
          •
          •
          •
  • Example with computer display result
  • Explanation of display
  • Inputs other than command line
  • Error messages

HOUSEKEEPING UTILITIES

For computer users, *housekeeping* maintains the environment in which a computer program and its data will operate. A well maintained environment ensures proper storage and retrieval of information; we place information so we can easily find it later. Consider a file cabinet. In this cabinet we arrange files for easy access. But what happens when the file cabinet becomes full? If we are in a hurry, do we still maintain everything in the proper order? How do we retrieve an item which temporarily resides on our desk? The answers to all these questions involve any routine housekeeping we undertake to maintain the integrity of the information kept in the cabinet.

Now consider the diskette used to store information (and instructions) as an electronic file cabinet. Just like a regular file cabinet, this electronic one can become full, go out of order, or lack information that is stored elsewhere.

Clearly we need a few housekeeping routines to maintain that electronic cabinet, our disks. These routines must perform the following housekeeping tasks:

- Ascertain the current status of the diskette
- Rearrange the information on the diskette
- Expand the filing capabilities

"Aha," you say, "we already have some commands that perform these tasks." True, we could categorize the commands described in Chapter 2 by function as shown in the following table.

Command	Use		
	Status	Rearranging	Expansion
DIR	x		
ERA		x	
REN		x	
SAVE		x	x
TYPE	x		
USER		x	

However, these commands are not sufficient to usefully alter a diskette or to do major reordering. For instance, while you can see which files are on the diskette, you cannot determine the size of those files.

Fortunately, Digital Research provides a number of housekeeping utilities to help you keep your diskettes in order. These housekeeping utilities include the following transient programs:

STAT
PIP
ED
DUMP
SYSGEN
MOVCPM

As with the built-in commands above, the transient housekeeping commands may be categorized by function.

Command	Use		
	Status	**Rearranging**	**Expansion**
STAT	x	x	x
PIP		x	x
ED	x	x	x
DUMP	x		
SYSGEN		x	x
MOVCPM		x	x

SYSGEN and MOVCPM are described in Chapter 5. STAT, PIP, ED, and DUMP are described in this chapter.

The description of STAT is divided into two sections because of the two distinct uses of this program.

The Statistics on Files section tells how STAT is used in the housekeeping of files. The Statistics on Devices section tells how STAT is used in the housekeeping of devices. Devices were introduced in Chapter 1 and are further explained in the second STAT section.

As with STAT, PIP coverage is divided into separate sections. These three sections reflect the natural differences in the data sources and destinations which may be connected by PIP.

STAT — STATISTICS ON FILES

STAT, short for STATISTICS, provides information about a file or a group of files on a diskette. Uses of STAT relating to devices are described after this section on files. The STAT on files command line summary is as follows:

STAT < cr >
> Displays attributes and amount of free space for all diskette drives accessed since last warm or cold start.

STAT x: < cr >
> Displays amount of free space on the diskette in drive x.

STAT x:filename.typ < cr >
> Displays size and attributes of file(s) filename.typ on drive x. filename.typ may be ambiguous. x: is optional; if omitted, currently logged drive is assumed.

STAT x:filename.typ $atr < cr >
> Assigns the attribute atr to the file(s) filename.typ on drive x (CP/M 2.0 and newer). filename.typ may be ambiguous. x: is optional; if omitted, currently logged drive is assumed.

Introduction to STAT Commands

STAT commands either provide information on the size and attributes of a file or files on a diskette, or change the attributes of a file or files on a diskette. The command line parameters specify which files are to be included. *File size* refers to the amount of space (in bytes) occupied by a file. *Free space* refers to the amount of unused space (in bytes) still available on the diskette for the storage of files. *File* or *diskette attributes* are a specific set of characteristics we can assign to a file or diskette.

Disk Space and File Size

The size of a file or the amount of storage which is currently unused on a diskette will be expressed in bytes. As we discussed in Chapter 1, a *byte* is a memory unit capable of storing a single character. Also recall that 1 Kbyte equals 1024 bytes, a quantity which is universally but incorrectly called a kilobyte.

If STAT tells us that we have 34K of space remaining on our diskette, we can store an additional 34,816 (1024 times 34 = 34,816) bytes of information on that diskette.

Experience is the best guide for interpreting what STAT tells you about your files. If you use STAT often and compare its reports, you will develop a sense of what 34K represents. For your reference, 34 Kbytes is the equivalent of 10 single-spaced pages of typewritten material (assuming 65 characters per line and 54 lines per page).

File Attributes

Users of CP/M 2.0 and newer may assign two pairs of file attributes: R/O or R/W, and DIR or SYS.

R/O — Read-Only File. You may not update an R/O file, nor erase it by using the ERA command. You may not write to or enter information on an R/O file. R/O status protects against accidental erasures of valuable files.

R/W — Read/Write File. You may update or erase an R/W file; it is not protected (unless the diskette is write-protected). This is the normal attribute of a file and is the default attribute (i.e., you do not have to set it explicitly).

SYS — System File. A SYS file does not appear in the display of a diskette directory. You may retrieve information from a SYS file or store new information in it, erase it, or use it in any other normal manner, but it will not appear in any directory. It will appear when you use the command STAT *.*. Also, all SYS files are available to all user areas. (Note: You might consider this a mild security measure, since the file does not appear in the directory.)

DIR — Directory File. A DIR file appears in all directory displays for the current user area. This is the normal attribute given to a file.

The members of each pair of attributes are mutually exclusive; files cannot be both R/W and R/O, nor can they be both SYS and DIR.

If you try to save information on an R/O diskette or write on an R/O diskette, the error message BDOS ERR ON x: R/O will appear (where x is the drive identifier). Even if a diskette is not protected by its notch, it may still appear as an R/O type with STAT; this means you exchanged diskettes without telling CP/M, but CP/M recognized the swap. To restore the new diskette to R/W status, simply type a Control-C.

Uses of STAT on Files

We use the information on file size, file attributes, and disk space to:

- Examine how much space is left on a diskette
- Examine how much space is occupied by a group of files
- Examine how much space is occupied by a single file
- Assign R/O or R/W to a group of files
- Assign R/O or R/W to a single file
- Assign DIR or SYS to a group of files
- Assign DIR or SYS to a single file

To determine which STAT command line to enter for each of the uses listed above, consider the next few pages carefully. Examine each command line, its purpose, and the computer display results. Try these examples at your computer. Try to generate the error messages. Consider how you might use the information displayed, given the uses of STAT we have just listed.

STAT <cr>

Displays the attribute and the amount of free space left on the diskettes in the drives accessed since the last cold or warm start.

```
A>STAT<cr>
A: R/W, SPACE: 2K
A>

A>STAT<cr>
A: R/W, SPACE: 2K
B: R/O,  SPACE: 120K
A>
```

CP/M version 1.3 reports on the currently logged drive only, as follows:

```
A>STAT<cr>
BYTES REMAINING ON A: 170K
A>
```

A:, B:	Diskette Drives
R/W, R/O	Status of diskette write-protection attribute; R/W = Read/Write, R/O = Read-Only
2K, 120K	Amount of free space (number of bytes) remaining on diskette

Input other than Command Line

None

Error Messages

None

STAT x: <cr>

Displays the amount of free space available on the diskette in drive x:

```
A>STAT B:<cr>
BYTES REMAINING ON B: 170K
A>
```

Input other than Command Line

None

Error Messages

BDOS ERR ON x: SELECT

May appear if you specified a nonexistent drive; x: represents
the drive specifier. Press <cr> or Control-C to recover.

The computer may "die" if you specified an empty or
nonexistent drive. Insert a diskette or do a cold start to recover.

FILE NOT FOUND

May appear if you omitted the colon from the drive specifier.

STAT x:filename.typ <cr>

Displays the amount of space occupied by the file(s) filename.typ on
drive x. The file name and extension may be ambiguous. The drive
specifier x: is optional; if omitted, the current drive is assumed.

```
A>STAT JOAN.ARC <cr>
RECS BYTS EX ACC D:FILENAME.TYP
  5    2K   1  R/W B:JOAN.ARC
A>

A>STAT B:JOAN.ARC <cr>
RECS BYTES EX ACC D:FILENAME.TYP
  5    2K   1  R/W B:JOAN.ARC
A>

A>STAT *.COM <cr>
RECS BYTES EX ACC D:FILENAME.TYP
  4    2K   1  R/W A:DUMP.COM
 48    6K   1  R/W A:(ED.COM)
 56    8K   1  R/O A:PIP.COM
 24    4K   1  R/W A:STAT.COM
 10    2K   1  R/W A:SUBMIT.COM
BYTES REMAINING ON A: 218K
A>

A>STAT B:EXAMPLE.?X? <cr>
RECS BYTES EX ACC D:FILENAME.TYP
 48    6K   1  R/W B:EXAMPLE.TXT
BYTES REMAINING ON B: 170K
A>
```

RECS	Number of 128-byte records used by the file. CP/M stores information in 128-byte units.
BYTS or BYTES	Length of the file in bytes. 2K represents 2048 characters of information; a kilobyte is 1024 bytes since computers use the binary number system.
EX	Number of *logical extents* occupied by the file. Each logical extent consists of 16 Kbytes of disk space. Logical extents are another part of the way CP/M maintains files.
ACC	File access attribute, R/W or R/O. Present for CP/M 2.0 and newer.

D:FILENAME.TYP	Heading for the drive and filename column on the display. Heading absent for CP/M 2.0 and newer.
R/O	File access attribute, Read-Only. Present for CP/M 2.0 and newer.
A:218K	Amount of free space remaining on diskette in drive A.
A:(ED.COM)	Parentheses indicate SYS file attribute is set; otherwise DIR attribute is set. Present for CP/M 2.0 and newer.

Input other than Command Line

None

Error Messages

BDOS ERR ON x: SELECT

May appear if you specified a nonexistent drive; x: is the drive specifier. Press <cr> or Control-C to recover.

The computer may "die" if you specify an empty or nonexistent drive. Insert a diskette or do a cold start to recover.

FILE NOT FOUND

May appear if the file you specified does not exist.

May appear if you omitted the colon from the drive specifier.

STAT x:filename.typ $atr <cr>

Assigns the attribute atr (R/O or R/W, DIR or SYS) to the file(s) filename.typ on drive x. filename.typ may be ambiguous. x: is optional; if omitted, the currently logged drive is assumed.

```
A>STAT BROTHER.AND $R/O<cr>
BROTHER.AND SET TO R/O
A>

A>STAT B:BROTHER.AND $SYS<cr>
B:BROTHER.AND SET TO SYS
A>

A>STAT *.* $R/W<cr>
BROTHER.AND SET TO R/W
SISTER.TOO SET TO R/W
A>
```

Input other than Command Line

None

Error Messages

INVALID FILE INDICATOR

Appears if you do not specify R/O, R/W, DIR, or SYS.

BDOS ERR ON x: SELECT

May appear if you specified on a nonexistent drive; x: represents the drive specifier. Press <cr> or Control-C to recover.

The computer may "die" if you specify an empty or nonexistent drive. Insert a diskette or do a cold start to recover.

FILE NOT FOUND

May appear if the file you specified does not exist.

May appear if you omitted the colon from the drive specifier.

STAT — STATISTICS ON DEVICES

STAT on devices provides information on CP/M physical and logical devices. This is the other use of the STAT program. The STAT on devices command line summary is as follows:

STAT DEV: <cr>

Reports which physical devices are currently connected to the four logical devices.

STAT VAL: <cr>

Reports the possible device assignments and partial STAT command line summary.

STAT log:=phy: <cr>

Assigns the physical device phy: to the logical device log: (may be more than one assignment on the line; each should be set off by a comma).

STAT USR: <cr>

(CP/M 2.0 and newer) Reports the current user number as well as all user numbers for which there are files on currently logged disks.

STAT x:DSK: <cr>

(CP/M 2.0 and newer) Reports the characteristics of disk drive x.

STAT x:=R/O <cr>

(CP/M 1.4, 2.0 and newer) Assigns a temporary write-protect status to drive x.

Review of Physical and Logical Devices

In Chapter 1 we briefly introduced physical units as the devices you may choose to make up your microcomputer system. A logical device denotes a general function of your microcomputer, while a physical device is the specific piece of equipment you choose to perform that function. CP/M requires us to select a physical device to perform the function of each logical device. We convey our choices to the computer by using the STAT (on devices) command.

There are four logical devices in CP/M:

    CON: enter commands and display information; operator console function

    RDR: receive information; paper tape reader function

    PUN: send information; paper tape punch function

    LST: list (print) information; list function

There are 12 physical devices possible:

    TTY: slow console (teletypewriter)

    CRT: fast console (cathode ray tube display)

    BAT: batch processor

    UC1: user defined console

    PTR: paper tape reader

    PTP: paper tape punch

    UR1: user reader #1

    UR2: user reader #2

    UP1: user punch #1

    UP2: user punch #2

    LPT: line printer

    UL1: user list device

There are 16 physical to logical device assignments possible:

    The CON: function may be performed by the TTY:, CRT:, BAT:, or UC1: physical device.

    The RDR: function may be performed by the TTY:, PTR:, UR1:, or UR2: physical device.

    The PUN: function may be performed by the TTY:, PTP:, UP1:, or UP2: physical device.

    The LST: function may be performed by the TTY:, CRT:, LPT:, or UL1: physical device.

Your microcomputer must be programmed for each physical device. This programming was most likely performed by the vendor who sold you your CP/M. If you have two printers, one might be programmed to be the LPT: line printer device and the other printer the UL1: user list device. Once made, such arrangements are constant; they reflect the distinct programming required to connect each printer to the microcomputer. In our example, both LPT: and UL1: are physical devices; they are specific pieces of equipment which can perform the list function of the logical device LST:.

The specific pieces of equipment programmed for your system might be:

CRT: CRT Terminal

LPT: Printer

PTR: Modem

PTP: Modem

The paper tape reader and paper tape punch are not widely used; the abbreviations PUN, RDR, PTR, and PTP reflect an earlier time when paper tape was commonly used.

Default Device Assignments

On cold start, the default values of the device assignments are made. These default assignments vary from system to system and are programmed into your CP/M by your vendor. The default values should be the assignments you most often use.

A cold start changes the device assignments to their default values, but a warm start does not affect the assignments in any way.

The BAT: Device

The BAT: device is not really a physical device. If the BAT: device is assigned to the CON: function, then console input will come from the current RDR: device, and console output will go to the current LST: device.

Uses of STAT on Devices

We use STAT on devices to:

- Learn the current device assignments
- Learn the possible device assignments
- Assign physical devices to logical devices.

A few STAT on devices command lines request information on the disk drives. Specifically we use these command lines to:

- Learn the current status of a disk drive.
- Learn the current status of user areas on the disk
- Protect a disk from accidental ''writes''

To determine which STAT on devices command line to enter for each of the uses listed above, consider the following pages carefully. Examine each command line, its purpose and the computer display results. Consider how you might use the information displayed, given the uses of STAT on devices we have just listed.

STAT DEV: <cr>

Displays the current device assignments.

```
A>STAT DEV:<cr>
CON: IS CRT:
RDR: IS UR1:
PUN: IS UP2:
LST: IS UL1:
A>
```

The left-hand entry is the logical device; the right-hand entry is the physical device assigned to the logical device.

**Input other than
Command Line**

None

Error Messages

FILE NOT FOUND
May appear if you omitted the colon.

STAT VAL: <cr>

Displays the possible assignments of physical to logical devices and an abbreviated STAT command line summary.

All lines appear for CP/M version 2.0 and newer; only the last four lines appear for CP/M versions 1.3 and 1.4

```
A>STAT VAL:<cr>
TEMP R/O DISK : D:=R/O
SET INDICATOR: D:FILENAME.TYP $R/O $R/W $SYS $DIR
DISK STATUS   : DSK: D:DSK:
USER STATUS  : USR:
IOBYTE ASSIGN:
CON: = TTY: CRT: BAT: UC1:
RDR: = TTY: PTR: UR1: UR2:
PUN: = TTY: PTP: UP1: UP2:
LST : = TTY: CRT: LPT : UL1 :
```

D:=R/O   Type STAT x:=R/O<cr> to make drive x
                                        a temporary read-only drive.

D:FILENAME.TYP $atr   Type STAT x:filename.typ $atr<cr> to
                                        set file attribute.

DSK: D:DSK   Type STAT x:DSK:<cr> to request
                                        the storage characteristics of disk
                                        drive x.

                                        Type STAT DSK:<cr> to request the
                                        storage characteristics of all drives
                                        accessed since last cold or warm
                                        start.

USR: Type STAT USR:<cr> to request user
                                        status.

IOBYTE ASSIGN: Possible assignments of physical to
                                        logical devices follow.

**Input other than
Command Line**

None

Error Messages

FILE NOT FOUND
May appear if you omitted the colon.

STAT log:=phy: <cr >

Assigns the physical device phy: to the logical device log:.

A>STAT CON:=CRT:,LST:=UL1:<cr>
A>

CON:=CRT: Assigns the physical device CRT: to the
                                        logical device CON:.

LST:=UL1:   Assigns the physical device UL1: to the
                                        logical device LST:.

You may place one or more assignments on the command line.
Separate the assignments with commas, and follow the last assignment
with the carriage return.

**Input other than
Command Line**

None

Error Messages

INVALID ASSIGNMENT
May appear if one of the device names was misspelled or if an
assignment was not one of the 16 allowed assignments.
FILE NOT FOUND
May appear if you omitted one of the colons.

The computer may ''die'' if you assign the wrong device to the CON: function. Do a cold start to recover.

STAT USR: <cr>

Displays the current user number and lists all user numbers for which there are files.

```
A>STAT USR: <cr>
ACTIVE USER :  0
ACTIVE FILES:  0  1  3
A>
```

ACTIVE USER : 0   The currently active user
                          number is zero.
ACTIVE FILES: 0 1 3   The currently logged disk
                          contains files with user
                          numbers 0, 1, and 3.

**Input other than
Command Line**

None

Error Messages

FILE NOT FOUND
May appear if you omitted the colon.

STAT x:DSK: <cr>

Displays information on how data is stored on the disk in drive x.

```
A>STAT B:DSK:<cr>
  B: DRIVE CHARACTERISTICS
4096: 128 BYTE  RECORD   CAPACITY
 512: KILOBYTE  DRIVE    CAPACITY
 128: 32 BYTE    DIRECTORY ENTRIES
 128: CHECKED   DIRECTORY ENTRIES
 128: RECORDS/EXTENT
  16: RECORDS/ BLOCK
  58: SECTORS/ TRACK
   2: RESERVED TRACKS
A>
```

x: is optional; if omitted, information is displayed for all disks accessed since last cold or warm start.

```
A>STAT DSK:<cr>
  A: DRIVE CHARACTERISTICS
4096: 128 BYTE  RECORD   CAPACITY
 512: KILOBYTE DRIVE   CAPACITY
 128: 32   BYTE DIRECTORY ENTRIES
 128: CHECKED   DIRECTORY ENTRIES
```

```
128: RECORDS/ EXTENT
 16: RECORDS/ BLOCK
 58: SECTORS/ TRACK
  2: RESERVED  TRACKS
  B: DRIVE CHARACTERISTICS
4096: 128  BYTE RECORD  CAPACITY
512: KILOBYTE DRIVE  CAPACITY
128: 32  BYTE DIRECTORY ENTRIES
128: CHECKED  DIRECTORY ENTRIES
128: RECORDS/ EXTENT
 16: RECORDS/ BLOCK
 58: SECTORS/ TRACK
  2: RESERVED  TRACKS
A>
```

This information will probably be of little use to you.

128 BYTE RECORD CAPACITY	The maximum number of 128-byte records you may store on the disk.
KILOBYTE DRIVE CAPACITY	The maximum number of Kbytes you may store on the disk.
32 BYTE DIRECTORY ENTRIES	The maximum number of files you may store on the disk.
CHECKED DIRECTORY ENTRIES	Usually the same as "32 BYTE DIRECTORY ENTRIES" for drives with removable media (diskettes); usually "0" for drives with non-removable media (sealed hard disks).
RECORDS/EXTENT	The maximum number of records per directory entry.
RECORDS/BLOCK	The minimum amount of disk space which may be allocated to a file.
SECTORS/TRACK	The number of sectors into which a track is divided (see Chapter 1).
RESERVED TRACKS	The number of disk tracks not available for storage of files.

The most relevant information in the display is "KILOBYTE DRIVE CAPACITY", which is the amount of free space on an empty disk, and "32 BYTE DIRECTORY ENTRIES", which is the maximum number of files you can store on the disk. (The number of files will be smaller if any files are larger than one extent.)

The information in the STAT x:DSK: display will not change unless you modify your CP/M. This static information reflects design decisions about how to arrange data on the disks.

Input other than Command Line

None

Error Messages

BDOS ERR ON x: SELECT

May appear if you specified a nonexistent drive; x: represents the drive specifier. Press <cr> or Control-C to recover.

The computer may "die" if you specify an empty or nonexistent drive. Insert a diskette or do a cold start to recover.

FILE NOT FOUND

May appear if you omitted a colon from a drive specifier or device name.

STAT x:=R/O <cr>

Assigns a temporary write-protect (read-only) status to the disk in drive x.

```
A>STAT B:=R/O<cr>
A>

B:=R/O                          The disk in drive B is to be write-
                                protected.
```

**Input other than
Command Line**

A cold or warm start cancels R/O status.

Error Messages

INVALID DISK ASSIGNMENT

May appear if you follow the drive specifier with anything except =R/O.

BDOS ERR ON x: SELECT

May appear if you specified a nonexistent drive; x: represents the drive specifier. Press <cr> or Control-C to recover.

The computer may "die" if you specify an empty or nonexistent drive. Insert a diskette or do a cold start to recover.

FILE NOT FOUND

May appear if you omitted the colon.

BDOS ERR ON x: R/O

Will appear if you *subsequently* try to write anything on the write-protected disk.

PIP — COPYING FILES

PIP, Peripheral Interchange Program, copies files from one place to another. The PIP (files) command line summary is as follows:

PIP <cr>
>   Loads PIP into memory. PIP then prompts for commands.

PIP x:new.typ=y:old.top [p] <cr>
>   Copies the file old.top on drive y to the file new.typ on drive x, using parameters p.

PIP x:new.typ=y:oldl.top [p] z:old2.tip [q] <cr>
>   Creates a file new.typ on drive x which consists of the contents of file oldl.top on drive y using parameters p followed by the contents of file old2.tip on drive z using parameters q.

File names and extensions can be ambiguous or unambiguous. The drive name (specifier) can be omitted; if omitted, the currently logged drive is assumed. Parameters are optional; if you omit them, also omit the square brackets.

PIP can be invoked in one of two ways. If you want to perform only one operation with PIP, invoke it as follows:

A > PIP pipcommandline <cr>

If you have several operations to perform, use the second way to invoke PIP:

A > PIP <cr>
*pipcommandline <cr>
*pipcommandline <cr>
*pipcommandline <cr>
*

No matter which method you use, there is no significant difference in the way PIP performs the operation specified by pipcommandline. A minor difference is explained under the Q parameter later in this PIP section. Another minor difference is in PIP's response to errors. If the first invocation method is used, errors will cause a return to the CP/M prompt. If the second method is used, errors will cause a return to the PIP prompt.

pipcommandline usually takes the following form:

destination = source

where destination is the name of the new file, and source is the name of the file from which the data is copied.

If there is already a file with the same name as the destination file, then the existing file is erased after successful completion of the copy. The previous contents of the destination file are lost.

The form of pipcommandline is the same with either of the two methods of invoking PIP. The following command line descriptions arbitrarily show the first method.

PIP Parameter Summary

We can append PIP command lines with several parameters:

B	Specifies "block mode" transfer.
Dn	Deletes all characters after the "n"th column.
E	Echoes the copying to the console as it is being performed.
F	Removes form feed characters during transfer.
Gn	Directs PIP to copy files from other user areas.
H	Checks for proper Intel Hex File format.
I	Ignores any ":00" records in Intel Hex File transfers.
L	Converts upper-case letters to lower-case.
N	Adds a line number to each line transferred.
O	Object file transfer (ignores end-of-file markers).
Pn	Issues page feed after every "n"th line.
Qs ^ Z	Specifies end (Quit) of copying after the string "s" is encountered.
R	Directs PIP to copy from a system file.
Ss ^ Z	Specifies start of copying after the string "s" is encountered.
Tn	Sets tab stops to every "n"th column.
U	Converts lower-case letters to upper-case.
V	Verifies copy by comparison after copy finished.
W	Directs PIP to copy onto a R/O file.
Z	Zeros the parity bit on ASCII characters.

These parameters are described in detail at the end of the PIP section.

Parameters are set off by square brackets and follow the file they reference. You may specify more than one parameter in a single command line by placing the parameters one after the other, separated by zero or more blanks, as follows:

or

PIP B:=A:filename.typ[BEF] < cr >

PIP B:=A:filename.typ[B E F] < cr >

Uses of PIP — Copying Files

PIP command lines and special parameters specify the transfer made between two files. In every instance, the original file remains intact; we can duplicate all the files on a diskette or only a portion of a file without changing the original. We can specify that certain characteristics of the new file be changed from the original, without changing the original. Here are some uses of PIP (files):

- Copy a file from one diskette to another
- Create an identical file with a different file name
- Copy several files from one diskette to another
- Copy all files from one diskette to another
- Create one file from the concatenation of several files from one or more diskettes
- Copy a portion of a file
- Copy from a system file
- Copy onto a R/O file
- Display the contents of the copied file, in progress

PIP — Copying Between Devices

PIP also copies data from a file to a device, from a device to a file, or between devices. The PIP (devices) command line summary is as follows:

PIP x:filename.typ=dev:[p] <cr>
   Copies data from device dev: to the file filename.typ on drive x.

PIP dev:=x:filename.typ[p] <cr>
   Copies data from filename.typ on drive x to device dev:.

PIP dst:=src:[p] <cr>
   Copies data to device dst: from device src:.

The variations of the PIP command line for file copying may be used with devices by substituting the device name for a file name. The parameters described for PIP — Copying Files also apply to PIP — Copying Between Devices.

When you read from or write to a device, as opposed to a disk file, make sure you can terminate the copying process. Some devices do not emit an end-of-file marker (^ Z) as CP/M does at the end of every disk file. You can use the Q parameter to terminate the copying session.

Here are some uses of PIP (Devices):

- Send the contents of a file to a device such as a printer.
- Pass the data from a device, such as a paper tape reader or modem, into a file.
- Send the data from one device to another device.
- Print the contents of a file, formatting it for a special printer or paper size.

- Display on the console selected data arriving at an input device.
- Convert upper-case letters to lower-case or vice versa.
- Save in a file all the data arriving at an input device for later examination.

Special PIP Devices

We can further enrich PIP command lines with the following special "device" names:

NUL: A source "device" which sends 40 *nulls* (do-nothing characters — 00_{16}) to the destination specified.

EOF: A source "device" which sends an *end-of-file* marker (Control-Z or $1A_{16}$) to the destination.

OUT: A user-created custom destination device. PIP must be modified to include this device.

INP: A user-created custom source device. PIP must be modified to include this device.

PRN: A special form of the LST: device which expands tabs, numbers lines, and paginates the copy. (Same as LST:[NPT8]).

As with the devices discussed earlier, these device names are used as sources and destinations in the command line.

Here are some uses of special PIP devices:

- Create a file of the data arriving at a special input device
- Send the contents of a file to a special output device
- Print a file in a more convenient format
- Simulate tab stops on a printer which does not have them
- Feed blank leader and trailer at the ends of a paper tape

Examine the following pages. Each PIP command line parameter and option is illustrated with an explanation of the computer display. Explore the possible combination of PIP command lines, parameters, and options and the resulting variations on the uses we have listed.

PIP <cr>

Loads PIP into memory.

A > PIP <cr>
*

```
A > PIP < cr >
* pipcommandline < cr >
*
```

```
A > PIP < cr >
* < cr >
A >
```

```
A > PIP < cr >
* ^ C
A >
```

*	PIP's prompt; PIP is ready for additional commands.
pipcommandline	Command to PIP.

Input other than Command Line

Any PIP command line.

< cr > or ^ C cancels PIP and returns the CP/M prompt.

Error Messages

PIP?

Will appear if the currently logged disk does not have the PIP program (PIP.COM) on it.

PIP x:new.typ=y:old.top[p] < cr >

Copies the file old.top on drive y to the file new.typ on drive x using parameter(s) p.

```
B > PIP LETTER2.DOC=LETTER1.DOC < cr >
B >
```

LETTER1.DOC	Copy the file "LETTER1.DOC" from the currently logged disk...
LETTER2.DOC=	...onto a file, also on the currently logged disk, and assign the new file the name LETTER2.DOC.
B >	Copy completed.

```
B > PIP A:LETTER2.DOC=B:LETTER1.DOC < cr >
B >
```

A:	The destination file is to be placed on drive A.
B:	The source file is on drive B.

```
B > PIP LETTER2.DOC=LETTER1.DOC[V] < cr >
B >
```

[V]	Verify parameter. After copy, compare the new file with the old file to verify that it is an accurate copy.

B>   Copy and verify complete and
                                      successful.

Note: It is always a good practice to include the [V] parameter when
copying files.

A>PIP B:=A:DOCUMENT.LET[V]<cr>
A>

A:DOCUMENT.LET   Copy the file "DOCUMENT" with the
                                      extension LET from the diskette in
                                      drive A...
B:=   ...onto the diskette in drive B: and
                                      assign it the same file name,
                                      DOCUMENT.LET.

Note: When copying from one disk to another when the same file
name is used on both, an abbreviated form of the command can be used
as illustrated above. An equivalent and equally valid command is shown
below:

A>PIP B:DOCUMENT.LET=A:[V]<cr>
A>

A>PIP B:=A:*.BAS[V]<cr>
COPYING-
APRIL.BAS
MAY.BAS
JUNE.BAS
A>

A:*.BAS   Copy all files with the extension BAS
                                      from the diskette in drive A...
PIP B:=   ...onto the diskette in drive B and
                                      assign the same file names.
COPYING-   Displays the name...
APRIL.BAS   ...of each file...
MAY.BAS   ...as it is being...
JUNE.BAS   ...copied.
A>   All copying completed

Note: This PIP command is frequently used to copy groups of files
from one diskette to another.

A>PIP B:=A:*.*[V]<cr>
COPYING-
DOCUMENT.ONE
DOCUMENT.TWO
LET.ONE
A>

A:*.*   Copy all files on the diskette in drive
                                      A...
PIP B: ...onto the diskette in drive B and
                                      assign the same file names.

COPYING-	Displays the name of. . .
DOCUMENT.ONE	. . .each file. . .
DOCUMENT.TWO	. . .as it is being. . .
LET.ONE	. . .copied.
A>	All copying completed.

Note: This PIP command is frequently used to copy all files from one diskette to another.

PIP x:new.fil=y:oldl.fil[p],y:old2.fil[p] <cr>

Creates a file new.fil on drive x which consists of files old1.fil and old2.fil, respectively, from drive y.

```
A>PIP B:DOC=A:JUNE[V], A:JULY <cr>
A>
```

A:JUNE,A:JULY	Copies the file JUNE, then the file JULY from the diskette in drive A. . .
B:DOC=	. . .onto a file on the diskette in drive B, and assigns it the file name DOC.
A>	Copy completed.

Note: See the [V] parameter for instructions for verifying the correct concatenation of files.

PIP dev:=x:filename.typ[p] <cr>

Sends the contents of the file filename.typ on drive x to device dev:.

```
B>PIP LST:=B:LAFFERTY.RT <cr>
B>
```

B:LAFFERTY.RT	Copies the file LAFFERTY.RT on the diskette in drive B. . .
LST:=	. . .to the list device (printer).
B>	Copy completed.

```
B>PIP LST:=B:*.DOC <cr>
COPYING-
LETTER.DOC
BROCHURE.DOC
MEMO.DOC
WHATSUP.DOC
B>
```

B:*.DOC	Sends each file with extension DOC on drive B. . .
LST:	. . .to the LST: device (printer).

Note: This is a handy way to print several files with only one command.

Acceptable PIP destination devices are the following:

CON:	PUN:	LST:	Logical devices
TTY:	PTP:	LPT: ⎫	
CRT:	UP1:	UL1: ⎬	Physical devices
UC1:	UP2:	⎭	
	OUT:	PRN:	Special PIP devices

PIP x:filename.typ=dev:[p] <cr>

Copies input from device dev: to file "filename.typ" on drive x.

```
B>PIP B:DOCUMENT.MAY=CON:<cr>
B>
```

CON:	Copies input from console device...
B:DOCUMENT.MAY	...to a file DOCUMENT.MAY on the diskette in drive B.
B>	Copy completed.

Input other than Command Line

Control-Z terminates the transfer and signifies the end of the file. Control-S pauses PIP.

Acceptable PIP source devices are the following:

CON:	RDR:	Logical devices
TTY:	PTR: ⎫	
CRT:	UR1: ⎬	Physical devices
UC1:	UR2: ⎭	
	NUL: ⎫	
	EOF: ⎬	Special PIP devices
	INP: ⎭	

If the source is the PTR: device, then PIP will monitor the console during the transfer. If a Control-Z is received from the console, the transfer will be terminated.

PIP dst:=src:[p] <cr>

Copies data from input device src: to output device dst:.

```
A>PIP PTP:=PTR:[EU]<cr>
THIS IS A PAPER TAPE
A>
```

PTR:	Copies input from the PTR: paper tape reader...
PTP:=	...to the PTP: paper tape punch,...
[EU]	...converts lower-case letters to upper-case (U), and displays the data as it is copied (E).

| THIS...TAPE | Data echoed to the console during copying. |

PIP Parameter Descriptions

This section describes each of PIP's optional parameters. You will probably use one or two of these parameters frequently; you may never use some of the others.

[B] PIP Parameter

Specifies block mode transfer of information.

Notes on [B]

[B] designates the "block mode transfer." In block mode, PIP transfers information from the source to a buffer until the ASCII character DC3 (equivalent to hexadecimal 13 and Control-S, and sometimes called *x-off* or *reader off*) is received. Once this character is received, PIP takes the information it has received so far and sends it to the destination specified. Then PIP returns to the source for more data. We use [B] for those source devices which transfer data continuously and would fill up PIP's buffer area (where it stores information before processing to the specified file or device) if the buffer were not periodically purged. For normal file-to-file operations, [B] is not necessary.

[B] is normally used to read a paper tape into a file. Whatever the source device, it must send the DC3 character often enough to avoid filling the buffer, and then wait for PIP to empty the buffer.

[Dn] PIP Parameter

Deletes all characters after the "n"th column.

Notes on [Dn]

[Dn] tells PIP to delete any character received that extends past a column number, which is specified immediately following the D ([D20] for example). This type of transfer will work only for line-oriented data (i.e., data which is terminated periodically with the carriage return character). After each carriage return is detected, PIP counts and processes characters up to and including the column number specified and then ignores all remaining characters sent until the next carriage return is received. (Note: line feed characters are interpreted the same as carriage returns for this operation.)

This parameter is primarily used to send wide-lined output to a device which handles only narrow lines (like a printer or CRT terminal). For file-to-file transfers, this option is rarely used.

The value ''n'' is a decimal integer number in the range 1 through 255, inclusive.

Input lines longer than 255 characters are not truncated properly by the [Dn] option.

[E] PIP Parameter

Echoes the copying to the console as it is being performed.

```
A>PIP B:DOC=A:LET[E]<cr>
LET ME
LET YOU
LET HE, SHE, OR IT
A>
```

A:LET	Copy the file LET from the diskette in drive A. . .
B:DOC=	. . .onto the diskette in drive B and assign it the file name DOC.
[E]	Display the file contents as the file is copied.
LET. . .IT	The contents of the file as it was copied.
A>	Copy completed.

[F] PIP Parameter

Filters form feed characters from the original file; the destination receives no form feed characters.

```
A>PIP LST:=*.DOC[F]<cr>
COPYING-
AMERICAN.DOC
THEODORE.DOC
MAILER.DOC
A>
```

*.DOC	Send all the DOC files from the diskette on drive A (the currently logged drive). . .
PIP B:=	. . .to the printer (the LST: device).
[F]	Send no form feed characters.

Notes on [F]

The [F] option ''filters'' form feeds from the data flow; PIP ignores the ASCII-defined character for form feeds and copies without it. Form feeds are often embedded in files to correctly paginate the printed output. You may wish to eliminate form feeds to conserve paper, to display a file on your console screen, or to use a printer which improperly interprets the form feed character.

The ASCII form feed character is called "FF" and is equivalent to hexadecimal 0C and Control-L.

The form feed character is a *format effector* character that controls the layout or positioning of information in printing or display devices. Thus a printer would normally respond to this character not by printing it, but by advancing the paper to the top of the next form or page.

Use [F] if your printer does not respond properly to form feed characters.

See parameter [Pn] and device PRN:.

[Gn] PIP Parameter

Directs PIP to copy files from other user areas.

```
A>STAT USR:<cr>
ACTIVE USER : 2
ACTIVE FILES: 0 2 4
A>PIP A:=A:*.STH [G4]<cr>
COPYING-
PWDRMKR.STH
WELTY.STH
FAULKNER.STH
A>
```

A:*STH	Copy all the files on drive A with the extension STH...
[G4]	...from user area 4...
A:=	...to the currently active user area (2) on the same drive (A).

Notes on [Gn]

The [Gn] option allows PIP to copy files from another user area to the current one. A decimal number (between 0 and 15) representing the source user area should immediately follow the G in the command line. This option is helpful in setting up a user area with files that may be needed later.

The [Gn] parameter is available in CP/M versions 2.0 and newer.

[H] PIP Parameter

Checks for proper Intel Hex Format.

```
A>PIP PUN:=PROGRAM.HEX[H]<cr>
A>
```

PROGRAM.HEX	Copy the file PROGRAM.HEX, which contains hex format records, on the currently logged drive...
PUN:	...to the PUN: device...
[H]	...and check for proper Intel Hex Format.

Notes on [H]

[H] specifies that the data to be transferred is in the special *Intel Hex Format* rather than in the normal ASCII or binary format. The Intel format is usually used with paper tape punch and reader devices. Most end users do not use this option.

In case errors are detected in the Hex format, PIP will display prompt messages for corrective action on the console.

See the [I] parameter.

[I] PIP Parameter

Ignores any null records in Intel Hex Format transfers.

```
A>PIP PUN:=PROGRAM.HEX[I]<cr>
A>
```

Notes on [I]

The [I] option also applies to Intel Hex Format records (see [H]). In this case the [I] parameter tells the PIP program to ignore any data which appears in a null record (":00" in Intel format). Again, this option is rarely of use to end users, as it applies primarily to paper tape reader and punch devices.

If the [I] option is specified, then the [H] option is automatically set by PIP. Thus the command line

```
PUN:=PROGRAM.HEX[I]
```

is equivalent to

```
PUN:=PROGRAM.HEX[HI].
```

[L] PIP Parameter

Converts upper-case letters to lower-case letters.

```
B>PIP B:FEMALE.WTR=A:LESSING,C:WOOLF,D:SONTAG[L]<cr>
B>
```

A:LESSING	Copy the file LESSING from drive A. . .
C:WOOLF	. . .then the file WOOLF from drive C. . .
D:SONTAG	. . .then the file SONTAG from drive D. . .
B:FEMALE.WTR=	. . .onto the diskette in drive B and assign the name FEMALE.WTR to the new file.
[L]	Convert upper-case letters to lower-case letters.

Notes on [L]

Only the characters A through Z are affected.

[N] PIP Parameter

Adds line numbers to each line transferred during the copying process.

```
A>PIP TEST1.ASM=TEST.ASM[N]<cr>
A>

A>PIP TEST2.ASM=TEST.ASM[N2]<cr>
A>
```

Notes on [N]

The [N] option adds a line number to each line transferred. Each time a carriage return (or line feed) is detected by PIP, the line number counter is incremented. [N] is of particular use when transferring a file to the printer.
If the old lines from file TEST.ASM looked like this:

Text   (First line)
    •
    •
    •
More text   (Tenth line)
    •
    •
    •
Still more text   (Hundredth line)
    •
    •
    •
More?   (Thousandth line)

then the new lines in file TEST1.ASM would look like this:

Column Number: 1   7 9

                      1: Text
                          •
                          •
                          •
                     10: More text
                          •
                          •
                          •
                    100: Still more text
                          •
                          •
                          •
                   1000: More?

If the [N2] parameter is specified, leading zeros are included, and the colon is replaced by a space.

The new lines in file TEST2.ASM would look like this:

```
Column Number: 1      6      9
                   000001   Text
                            .
                            .
                            .
                   000010   More text
                            .
                            .
                   000100   Still more text
                            .
                            .
                   001000   More?
```

[O] PIP Parameter

Transfers object files or other non-ASCII files.

```
B>PIP B:=A:DATA.BIN[O]<cr>
B>
```

DATA.BIN   Copy the binary data file DATA.BIN. . .
[O]   . . .and do not interpret Control-Z as the end-
                                of-file marker.

```
B>PIP B:=A:PROGRAM.COM<cr>
B>
```

PROGRAM.COM   Copy the object program file PROGRAM.COM and
                                do not interpret Control-Z as the end-of-file
                                marker because the file extension is COM.

Notes on [O]

Use the [O] parameter when copying from non-ASCII files (such as program, object code, or binary data files) or from devices sending non-ASCII data.

Specifying the [O] parameter is not necessary when copying from files with the extension COM, because PIP assumes that COM-type files are non-ASCII files.

Use of [O] tells PIP to treat Control-Z ($1A_{16}$, also called SUB or Substitute) just like any other character it receives from a source device or file; PIP would otherwise interpret Control-Z as signalling the end of the transfer from that source.

The following paragraphs contain more detailed information about ASCII files, non-ASCII files, and end-of-file markers. Read on if you are interested in these details.

PIP assumes that a Control-Z character received from an ASCII source (device or file) is an end-of-file marker or data terminator, meaning that all the data has been transferred.

PIP sends a Control-Z character to an ASCII destination (file or device) to indicate that all the data has been sent.

The difference in handling non-ASCII data is necessary because CP/M uses different methods for marking (and detecting) the end of ASCII and non-ASCII files.

CP/M marks the end of an ASCII file by placing a Control-Z character in the file after the last data character. Use of this character as the end-of-file marker is possible because Control-Z is seldom used as data in ASCII files.

In a non-ASCII file, however, Control-Z is just as likely to occur as any other character. Therefore it can not be used as the end-of-file marker. CP/M uses a different method to mark the end of a non-ASCII file. CP/M assumes it has reached the end of the file when it has read the last record (basic unit of disk space) allocated to the file. The disk directory entry for each file contains a list of the disk records allocated to that file. This method relies on the size of the file, rather than its content, to locate the end of the file.

[Pn] PIP Parameter

Issues form feed after ''n''th line: [Pn].

A > PIP LST:=LEGAL.DOC[P78] < cr >
A >

LST:=LEGAL.DOC	Print the file LEGAL.DOC. . .
[P78]	. . .on 14 inch long paper (14 inches times 6 lines per inch less 6 lines for top and bottom margins leaves 78 lines for text).

A > PIP LST:=B:PROGRAM.PRN[FP] < cr >
A >

LST:=B:PROGRAM.PRN	Print the file PROGRAM.PRN from drive B.
[FP]	Remove form feed characters and print 60 lines per page.

Notes on [Pn]

Use [Pn] when the destination is the LST: device and the current LST: device (usually a printer) does not print the source data as follows:

1. There should be a blank top margin,
2. There should be a blank bottom margin,

3. The top and bottom margins should together total six
    lines; and
4. Text should fill the space between the top and bottom
    margins.

Deviation from these conditions usually occurs when the current LST:
device:

1. Does not understand the form feed character (see parameter
    [F]),
2. Does not insert top and bottom margins, or
3. Is printing on a different length page than that assumed
    by the source data.

[Pn] tells PIP you want it to insert a form feed after each "n" lines of
data. Enter the desired number of lines in place of "n" in the [Pn]
parameter. "n" is an integer decimal number in the range 1 through 255
inclusive. If you do not enter a number or if the number is 1, PIP assumes
you want a page eject after each 60 lines.

If [F] is also present, all form feeds detected during the transfer will be
removed, and PIP will then insert new form feeds as specified by [Pn]. In
other words, [F] and [Pn] used together will override the paging implied
by the presence of form feed characters in the source data.

A printer which understands the form feed character responds to it by
immediately advancing the paper to the top of the next page, whether or
not the current page is full.

See the section on the PIP PRN: device.

[Qstring ^ Z] PIP Parameter

Copies a portion of a file by specifying the final characters to be copied.

```
A>PIP B:=A:ALLEN.ANN[Qdeath. ^ Z] <cr>
A>

A>PIP <cr>
*B:=A:ALLEN.ANN[QDEATH. ^ Z] <cr>
* <cr>
A>
```

A:ALLEN.ANN	Copy the file ALLEN.ANN from drive A from the first character. . .
[QDEATH. ^ Z]	. . .up to and including the characters "DEATH.". . .
PIP B:=	. . .onto the diskette in drive B and assign the same file name.

Notes on [Q]

Select the terminating string of characters carefully; they must be unique to ensure you are copying the exact portion of the file desired. Q marks the beginning of the string, and " ^ Z" marks the end of the string: [Qstring ^ Z].

See the parameter [Sstring ^ Z].

The string following the S parameter is converted to upper case if the command line is typed after the CP/M prompt (A >) as in the first example above. If the command line is typed after the PIP prompt (*), as in the second example, then the automatic conversion does not occur. Thus the two examples are equivalent, and the quit string is "DEATH.".

To include lower-case letters in the string, your command line must follow the PIP prompt, as illustrated by this example:

```
A > PIP < cr >
*B: = A:ALLEN.ANN[Qdeath. ^Z] < cr >
```

[R] PIP Parameter

Directs PIP to copy a system file.

```
A > PIP B: = A:*.* [R] < cr >
COPYING—
NOWON.NOS
SECRET.ONE
SECRET.TWO
A >
```

A:*.*	Copy all files from the diskette in drive A.
[R]	Copy system files as well...
PIP B: =	...onto the diskette in drive B and assign the same file names.

Notes on [R]

Only by appending the command line with [R] can we copy system files; they are not assigned to any user area, and PIP copies only from the current user area. The system file attribute, if present, is copied. This parameter applies to CP/M versions 2.0 and newer.

[Sstring ^ Z] PIP Parameter

Copies a portion of a file by specifying the initial characters to be copied.

```
A > PIP < cr >
*B: = A:GENESIS.ALL[SIn the begin ^ Z] < cr >
```

A:GENESIS.ALL	Copy the file GENESIS.ALL from the diskette in drive A...
[SIn the begin ^ Z]	...beginning with the characters "In the begin"...
B: =	...onto the diskette in drive B and assign the same file name.

Notes on [S]

Just like the [Q] option, the [S] option specifies that you wish to copy only a portion of a file using PIP, this time beginning at the point where PIP detects the string of characters specified immediately following the S [Sstring ^ Z] where "string" is the sequence of characters to search for and " ^ Z" is a Control-Z used to terminate the string. Both the [S] and [Q] options may be present in the same command line.

See the important explanation of automatic lower-case to upper-case conversion under the [Q] option.

[Tn] PIP Parameter

Sets tab stops at every "n"th column.

```
A>PIP LST:=COLOMSOF.NUM[T10]<cr>
A>
```

LST:=COLOMSOF.NUM	Print the file COLOMSOF.NUM. . .
[T10]	. . .and replace each tab character with enough spaces to reach the next column which is a multiple of 10.

Notes on [Tn]

[Tn] tells PIP to expand any *tab* character it detects to the number of spaces necessary to reach the next tab stop. This is useful as some editor programs do not save tabs as spaces, but as tab characters, and not all printers or terminals are set up to detect tab characters and expand them to the number of spaces they represent. Use [Tn] to change the standard tabbing from eight characters (or whatever your console or printer defaults to) to a number you define.

The ASCII tab character is called HT or Horizontal Tab and is equivalent to 09_{16} or Control-I.

[V] PIP Parameter

Verifies the copy is correct by comparing the original source(s) with the newly created file(s).

```
A>PIP B:RADIO.STA=A:EZROCK.93[V]<cr>
```

A:EZROCK.93	Copy the file EZROCK.93 from the diskette in drive A. . .
PIP B:	. . .onto the diskette in drive B. . .
RADIO.STA=	. . .and assign the file name RADIO.STA. . .
[V]	. . .then verify the copy is correct.

```
A>PIP B:RADIO.STA=A:EZROCK.93[V],A:JIVE.95,A:KIOI.101<cr>
A>
```

Notes on [V]

The destination must be a disk file; if it is not, V is ignored. After the transfer is complete, a second transfer occurs where both source and destination are read and compared character by character.

When concatenating several sources as shown in the second example above, the [V] parameter must follow the first source name. Only one [V] is necessary.

[W] PIP Parameter

Directs PIP to copy into a R/O file.

    A>PIP B:WEATHER=A:STORM[W]<cr>
    A>

| A:STORM | Copy the file STORM from the diskette in drive A... |
| B:WEATHER | ...onto the R/O file WEATHER on drive B. |

Notes on [W]

Since [W] permits you to write in an R/O file, verifying this attribute is no longer required before proceeding.

If B:WEATHER is an R/O file and you did not include [W], the following dialog would occur:

    A>PIP B:WEATHER=A:STORM<cr>
    DESTINATION FILE IS R/O, DELETE (Y/N)? Y
    A>

If you decided not to write into it, then the dialog would look like this:

    A>PIP B:WEATHER=A:STORM<cr>
    DESTINATION FILE IS R/O, DELETE (Y/N)? N
    NOT DELETED
    A>

Finally, if you know you want to write into the file even if it is an R/O file, then you can include the [W] parameter as shown in the first example above to skip the question-and-answer session.

The [W] parameter is available in CP/M versions 2.0 and newer.

[Z] PIP Parameter

Zeros the parity bit on each ASCII character received from the source.

    A>PIP SEVENBIT.TXT=RDR:[Z]<cr>
    A>

| RDR: | Send each character received from the current RDR: device... |

SEVENBIT.TXT=	...to the file SEVENBIT.TXT...
[Z]	...after setting the high-order (parity) bit to zero.

Notes on [Z]

Use the [Z] parameter to set the unused eighth bit of a character to zero when receiving ASCII characters from a device.

Each ASCII character uses seven of the eight bits which are processed by the computer. The eighth bit is sometimes called the *parity bit*. To avoid mysterious problems when processing ASCII data, it is usually wise to set the unused bit to zero.

NUL: PIP Device

Sends 40 null (do-nothing) characters to the destination specified.

```
A>PIP PUN:=NUL:,FILE.HEX,NUL:<cr>
A>
```

PUN:=	Punch a paper tape consisting of...
NUL:	...a four-inch blank leader...
FILE.HEX	...followed by the contents of file FILE.HEX...
NUL:	...followed by a four-inch blank trailer.

NUL: was originally used to terminate punched output with a blank section of paper tape; it provided a *header* or *trailer* to the actual information, useful for threading purposes. NUL: will produce a four-inch length of blank paper tape.

The ASCII null character is called "NUL" or "Null" and is equivalent to 00_{16} or Control-@ on some computers.

EOF: PIP Device

Sends an end-of-file marker (^ Z) to the destination device.

When copying between two ASCII-type disk files, an end-of-file marker is automatically sent to the destination device. In some special instances, EOF: can be used to terminate the transfer. You use it to terminate an entry from keyboard or a remote machine as in PIP A:filename = RDR:, EOF:

PRN: PIP Device

Specifies additional instructions to the LST: device. Expands tabs, numbers lines, paginates the copy.

```
A>PIP PRN:=TEXT.DOC<cr>
A>
```

TEXT.DOC	Print the file TEXT.DOC...

PRN:=   . . .with the current LST device; set tab stops at
                                              every eighth column; replace tab characters with
                                              spaces; number lines; print 60 lines per page.

Tab stops are assumed at every eighth column. Every time a tab
character is detected, PIP inserts spaces instead; all lines are numbered
(beginning at 1 and continuous throughout the transfer); page ejects are
sent to the printer every 60 lines (giving you a margin of three lines at the
top and bottom of a normal 11-inch high piece of paper). PRN: is used for
program development and for listing the contents of an ASCII-type file;
the line numbers provide recognizable reference points within the file.
The example shown above is equivalent to the following:

A>PIP LST:=TEXT.DOC[N P T8]<cr>
A>

INP: and OUT: PIP Devices

INP: retrieves information from a special user-created PIP input source.
OUT: sends information to a special user-created output destination.
You can add special input and output routines (in machine language) to
PIP. Hexadecimal locations 103, 104, and 105 are reserved for a *jump
instruction* to your special input routine. PIP CALLs location 103_{16} to
input a character and, upon return, expects to find the character in
location 109_{16}. Hexadecimal locations 106, 107, and 108 are reserved
for the jump to your special output routine. PIP loads Register C with the
character to transmit and then CALLs location 106_{16}. In addition, the area
from $10A_{16}$ to $1FF_{16}$ is free for you to insert your routines. It is rare for an
end user to use this option.

ED — CONTEXT EDITOR

ED is program with a number of built-in commands used to edit text files.
The ED command line summary is as follows:

ED x:filename.typ<cr>
Invokes the editor, which then searches for filename.typ on
drive x and creates a temporary file, x:filename.$$$, to store
the edited text. filename.typ is unambiguous. x: is optional; if
omitted, the currently logged drive is assumed. ".typ" is
optional.

Editing a File

How do you put something new onto the diskette? Use an editor. CP/M includes an editor; you will find it saved in the file ED.COM.

The editor is a program which takes characters from the keyboard and puts them in a disk file. Since you might make entry errors or wish to make changes, the editor also includes a number of built-in commands which display, modify, delete, and add to the information you have typed.

The CP/M editor (called *Context Editor* by Digital Research) is both character- and line-oriented; commands operate on text either a character at a time or a line at a time. A *line* is a block of characters ending in a carriage return.

To edit the file filename.typ, type the following:

A > ED filename.typ < cr >

Once the editor program is loaded into memory, it will create a new file with the name filename and the extension $$$, and wait for your command. You may now use ED's built-in commands to:

- Delete or change any part of the existing file
- Insert new information into the file from the keyboard or from another file

For example, suppose the file DOCUMENT.MAY requires editing. To invoke ED type:

A > ED DOCUMENT.MAY < cr >

ED creates the temporary file DOCUMENT.$$$ on the diskette. This file contains no information; it contains only the structure of the file to be written.

In order to make changes to the original file DOCUMENT.MAY, you must be able to see the text and to manipulate it. ED's commands permit you to move text from the original file into memory, to view the text that you have moved into memory, to make the required changes, and to move the text from memory back to the file. You can only edit a file then, while it is in memory. The area of memory ED sets aside to hold text is called the *edit buffer*.

As you progress in your editing, you will move more text from the original file into the edit buffer for editing. The edit buffer holds a limited amount of text; as it becomes full you must move the edited text to the temporary file, DOCUMENT.$$$.

When you complete your editing session, some text may remain in the original file DOCUMENT.MAY, some in the edit buffer, and some in the temporary file DOCUMENT.$$$. To end the edit, ED first moves the edit buffer contents to the temporary file DOCUMENT.$$$. Then ED moves remaining text from the original file to the temporary file. Finally the original file, DOCUMENT.MAY, is renamed DOCUMENT.BAK, and

DOCUMENT.$$$ is renamed DOCUMENT.MAY. This may be illustrated
as follows:

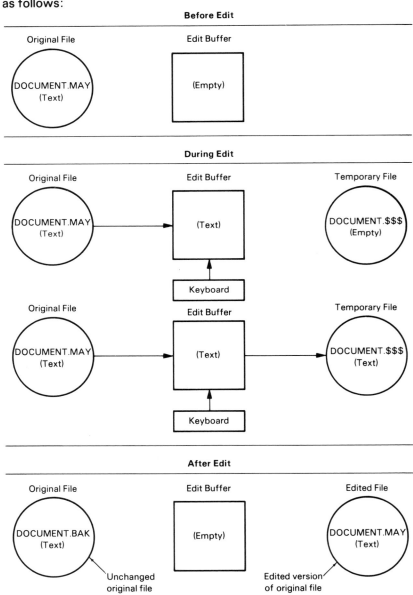

You now have a copy of the original input in DOCUMENT.BAK, and
your newly edited version exists on your diskette in file
DOCUMENT.MAY.

Since movement through the entire text may require shifting bodies of text in and out of the edit buffer in the direction shown by the arrows above, you can only move forward through the text. This will be explained in more detail later. Examine the ED commands on the following pages to learn how to perform the tasks we have described.

ED Command Summary

nA	Append lines. Moves ''n'' lines from original file to edit buffer. OA moves lines until edit buffer is at least half full.

+/−B	Begin/Bottom. Moves CP:
	    +B moves CP to beginning of edit buffer
	    −B moves CP to end of edit buffer

+/−nC	Move by characters. Moves CP by ''n'' character positions:
	    + moves forward
	    − moves backward

+/−nD	Delete characters. Deletes ''n'' characters before or after the CP in the edit buffer:
	    + deletes after the CP
	    − deletes before the CP

E	End. Ends edit, closes files, and returns to CP/M; normal end.
nFstring ^ Z	Find string. Finds the ''n''th occurrence of ''string,'' beginning the search after the CP.
H	Move to head of edited file. Ends edit, renames files, then edits former temporary file.
I<cr>	Enter insert mode. Text from keyboard goes into edit buffer after the CP; exit with Control-Z.
Istring ^ Z	Insert string. Inserts ''string'' in edit buffer after the CP.
Istring <cr>	Insert line. Inserts ''string'' and CRLF in the edit buffer after the CP.
nJfindstring ^ Zinsertstring ^ Zendstring ^ Z	
	Juxtaposition. Beginning after the CP, finds ''findstring,'' inserts ''insertstring'' after it, then deletes all following characters up to

	but not including "endstring"; repeats until performed "n" times.
+/−nK	Kill lines. Deletes "n" lines: + Deletes after the CP − deletes before the CP
+/−nL	Move by lines. Moves the CP to the beginning of the line it is in, then moves the CP "n" lines forward or backward: + moves forward − moves backward OL moves the CP to the beginning of the line it is in
nMcommandstring ∧ Z	Macro command. Repeats execution of the ED commands in "commandstring" "n" times; if n=0, n=1, or n absent, repeats execution until error occurs.
nNstring ∧ Z	Find string with autoscan. Finds the "n"th occurrence of "string", automatically appending from original file and writing to temporary file as necessary.
O	Return to original file. Empties edit buffer, empties temporary file, returns to beginning of original file, ignores previous ED commands.
+/−nP	Move CP and print pages. Moves the CP forward or backward one page, then displays the page following the CP; displays "n" pages, pausing after each.
Q	Quit edit. Erases temporary file and block move file, if any, and returns to CP/M; original file is not changed.
R < cr >	Read block move file. Copies the entire block move file X$$$$$$$.LIB from disk and inserts it in the edit buffer after the CP.
Rfilename < cr >	Read library file. Copies the entire file "filename" with extension LIB from disk and inserts it in the edit buffer after the CP.
nSfindstring ∧ Zreplacestring ∧ Z	Substitute string. Starting at the CP, repeats "n" times: finds "findstring" and replaces it with "replacestring."

+/−nT   Type lines. Displays "n" lines:

+ displays the "n" lines after the CP

− displays the "n" lines before the CP

If the CP is not at the beginning of a line:

OT displays from the beginning of the line to the CP

T displays from the CP to the end of the line

OTT displays the entire line without moving the CP

+/−U   Upper-case conversion. After +U command, alphabetic input to the edit buffer is converted from lower case to upper case; after −U, no translation occurs.

0V   Edit buffer free space/size. Displays the decimal number of free (empty) bytes in the edit buffer and the total size of the edit buffer.

+/−V   Verify line numbers. After +V, a line number is displayed with each line displayed; ED's prompt is then preceded by the number of the line containing the CP. After −V, line numbers are not displayed, and ED's prompt is *.

nW   Write lines. Writes first "n" lines from the edit buffer to the temporary file; deletes these lines from the edit buffer.

nX   Block transfer (Xfer). Copies the "n" lines following the CP from the edit buffer to the temporary block move file X$$$$$$$.LIB; adds to previous contents of that file.

OX deletes the contents of X$$$$$$$.LIB

nZ   Sleep. Delays execution of the command which follows it. Larger "n" gives longer delay, smaller "n" gives shorter delay.

n: Move CP to line number "n." Moves the CP to the beginning of line number "n" (see +/−V).

:m   Continue through line number "m." A command prefix which gives the ending point for the command which follows it. The beginning point is the location of the CP (see +/−V).

+/−n   Move and display one line. Abbreviated form
                              of +/−nLT.

ED Commands

To use ED commands, invoke ED, and follow ED's prompt (∗) with the
proper command and a carriage return <cr>, as follows:

A >ED x:filename.typ<cr>
∗edcommand<cr>

We will use several abbreviation conventions in this section. Whenever
a plus or minus sign can be typed, you will see the symbol +/−; if you
type neither + nor −, ED assumes you mean +. Whenever a number can
be typed to give the command further information, you will see the
symbol "n." "n" can be any decimal integer number in the range 0
through 65535, inclusive. Do not use a comma between digits. If you
omit the number, ED assumes a value of 1. Typing a zero (0) has a special
meaning for some commands. If you type a number sign (#), ED
substitutes 65535.

For the purposes of ED, a line of text is a sequence of zero or more
characters followed by a carriage return character and a line feed
character. We will represent this character pair by the symbol CRLF.
When you type a line of text for ED and then press carriage return, ED
adds the line feed character so that the line ends with CRLF.

We can separate ED commands into four functions:

1. Transferring Text. Transfer by line or by blocks of text:

    · From the original file into the edit buffer
    · From the edit buffer into the temporary file
    · From the original file to the temporary file
    · From the edit buffer into another file (not original or
      temporary but a distinct file on the disk)
    · From another file (not original or temporary but a distinct file
      on the disk) into the edit buffer.

2. Working in the Edit Buffer. An imaginary character pointer (CP)
    locates the text in the edit buffer. These editing commands:

    · Manipulate text within the edit buffer in relation to the CP
    · Direct movement of the CP.

3. Searching and Changing Text. Works within the edit buffer to:

    · Search for a particular set of characters
    · Substitute a set of characters

- Switch placement between sets of characters
- Move text from the original file through the edit buffer to the temporary file automatically while searching.

4. Combining Commands. A string of ED commands can be entered in one command line ending with a <cr> to permit a variety of sequential editing functions and to repeat a command string a specified number of times.

Commands for Transferring Text

nA	Append (copy) a number of lines from the original file to the edit buffer. Each append session is distinct; the line counting begins again with each A command. To move a single line, enter only A; 1 is the default number of lines to move. To move the maximum number of lines into the edit buffer, include the number sign (#A). The A command will move lines until the original file is exhausted, the edit buffer is full, or 65535 lines have been moved. To move a portion of the text into the edit buffer, enter 0A; text will move from the original file until the edit buffer is at least half full. Once appended, lines in the original file are ignored by subsequent commands which read from the original file.
nW	Write a number of lines from the edit buffer into the temporary file:

W   Write a single line
#W   Write the maximum number of lines
0W   Write until the edit buffer is at least half empty

W always begins with the first line in the edit buffer and writes it in the temporary file after the line most recently placed there. Lines are deleted from the edit buffer as they are written in the temporary file.

E	End the edit. Text is transferred and files are renamed as follows:

1. All text remaining in the edit buffer moves

to the temporary file, as by the W command.

2. All text remaining in the original file moves to the temporary file.

3. The extension of the original file becomes BAK.

4. The extension of the temporary file is changed to the former extension of the original file.

5. The block move file X$$$$$$$.LIB, if present, is erased.

6. The CP/M prompt returns.

Use the "E" command as the normal ending of an editing session.

H　　　　　　　　　Move to the beginning of the edited file. Text is transferred and files are renamed as follows:

1. All text remaining in the edit buffer moves to the temporary file, as by the W command.

2. All text remaining in the original file moves to the temporary file.

3. The extension of the original file becomes BAK.

4. The extension of the temporary file is changed to the former extension of the original file.

5. A new, empty temporary file is created.

6. You are now ready to edit the new original file.

The H command has two uses:

1. Since the A, N, and W commands can move only forward, not backward, through the original and temporary files, use the H command to save the editing done so far and return to the beginning of the file for more editing.

2. Use the H command every few minutes during editing to save your results on the disk. Text left in the edit buffer is easily

lost if an operator error or equipment malfunction occurs, but text saved in the temporary file is easily recovered from it.

Frequent use of H is especially important when inserting a lot of text or making numerous changes.

O   Erase the edited file. Text is transferred as follows:

1. Delete the contents of the edit buffer and the temporary file.
2. Return to the beginning of the original file.

ED asks "O-(Y/N)?" before it proceeds since all changes made to the text will be erased. Press Y to return to the original file or N to continue editing.

Use O if you made incorrect changes and you want to start the edit over.

Q   Quit editing; do not institute any changes. Type a Q, answer Y to the question "Q-(Y/N)?", and you are returned to the CP/M prompt. Use O if you want to start an edit over; use Q if you want to cancel the editing session completely.

R < cr >   Reads the file created by the X command into the edit buffer. R < cr > inserts the entire contents of the transfer file X$$$$$$$.LIB into the edit buffer immediately after the CP. The transfer file is not affected; you can read it as many times as you want during an edit session. The transfer file is automatically erased when you leave ED with the E, Q, or Control-C commands.

Rfilename < cr >   Reads the library file filename.LIB into the edit buffer. This command inserts the entire contents of the specified file into the edit buffer immediately after the CP. The library file is not affected.

nX   Write (Xfer) lines from the edit buffer to a temporary file X$$$$$$$.LIB. You may later transfer these lines back to the edit buffer by using the R < cr > command. With the X,

R<cr> command combination you can
move blocks of information. The file
X$$$$$$$.LIB will be erased (with an E, Q,
or Control-C command) when the editing is
completed. The X command copies the "n"
lines which follow the CP in the edit buffer
into the transfer file. The lines are not deleted
from the edit buffer, and they are added to
any previous contents of the transfer file.

Commands for Working in the Edit Buffer

+/−B   Move the CP to the beginning or end of the
                 edit buffer. The sign indicates a direction; +
                 means move to the beginning, − means
                 move to the end. The command moves the
                 CP and allows us to quickly view the text in
                 memory. Notice that the direction implied by
                 the sign with the B command is the opposite
                 of that for all other commands.

+/−nC   Move the CP by plus or minus "n"
                 characters. Count CRLF as two separate
                 characters. Type +5C to move the CP five
                 characters toward the end of the edit buffer.

+/−nD   Delete the "n" characters immediately
                 before (−) or after (+) the CP.

                     100: NOW IS THE TIME FOR ACTION
                     100: *−3D<cr>

                 If the CP were between the T and the I in
                 TIME, −3D would request: NOW IS THIME
                 FOR ACTION.

I<cr>   Enter the insert mode. ED accepts all
                 characters you type and inserts them into the
                 edit buffer after the CP. With certain
                 exceptions, every character you type goes
                 into the buffer until you press Control-Z.
                 Control-Z terminates the insert mode and
                 returns the ED prompt.

The exception characters are:

                 ^ H or BACKSPACE
                     Deletes last character typed (CP/M versions
                     2.0 and newer).

^ L

   Inserts CRLF.

^ M or RETURN

   Inserts CRLF.

^ R

   Redisplays the current line (CP/M versions
   1.4 and newer).

^ U

   Deletes the current line.

^ X

   Deletes the current line.

RUBOUT or DELETE

   Deletes the last character typed and
   redisplays (echoes) it.

   The "current line" consists of the
characters which follow the last < cr >
typed while in insert mode.

   Use insert mode to type in a new file or to
add several lines to an existing file.
Remember to exit the insert mode and use
the save command H often.

Istring ^ Z   Insert a string. This command inserts the
                     character sequence "string" into the edit
                     buffer following the CP. Use this command
                     to insert short strings.

Istring < cr >   Insert a line. This command inserts the
                     character sequence "string" into the edit
                     buffer following the CP. A CRLF pair is
                     inserted after the string. This CRLF is the
                     difference between this command and
                     "Istring ^ Z." Use this command to insert a
                     single line.

+/−nK   Kills (deletes) those lines from the edit buffer
                     which you do not wish to appear in the final
                     edited version; they are not transferred to
                     the temporary file, but remain in the original
                     file which later becomes the backup file. You
                     may remove any number of lines from the
                     edit buffer in either direction from the CP. +K
                     or K erases all characters after the character
                     pointer in the line. −K erases all characters in
                     the line before the character pointer. If you

still have some characters remaining in a line which you thought you had deleted using the K command, this is because the CP was not at the beginning of the line.

+/−nL   Move the CP forward or backward (+ or −) "n" lines in the edit buffer. First the CP moves to the beginning of the current or next line, respectively, if the CP is not at the beginning of the line when you issue the command. Subsequent moves will encompass full lines; the CP moves "n" lines forward or backward. 0L moves the CP to the beginning of the current line.

+/−nP   Move the CP by one page and print (display) the page following the CP; repeat for a total of "n" pages. P is a convenient method for scrolling through the text in the edit buffer. A *page* is a fixed number of lines which varies with the version of CP/M. Common page sizes are 15 and 23 lines. +nP scrolls forward through the edit buffer and −nP scrolls backward. P operates by first moving the CP backward or forward one page and then displaying the page which follows the CP. 0P displays a page without moving the CP.

+/−nT   To see lines of text that are in the edit buffer, use the T (type) command. To see the three lines before the CP, type −3T. To see the three lines after the CP, type +3T or just 3T, since the + sign is optional. If the CP is positioned at the beginning of a line, type T to see that line. If the CP is positioned within a line, type 0T to see the part of the line before the CP, type T to see the part of the line after the CP, or type 0TT to see the whole line.

     The T command does not move the CP; it displays lines of text in relation to the CP and provides the exact location of the CP.

+/−U   Sometimes you might want to translate lower-case letters to upper-case ones (some assemblers require upper-case only; others do not care). +U begins translating characters; −U ends the translation.

Ordinarily ED does not translate characters. After being given the command U or +U, however, ED will translate characters which enter the edit buffer either from the keyboard or from the original file. The lower-case letters a through z will be translated to the corresponding upper-case letters A through Z. This translation will continue until ED receives the −U command or the edit session is ended.

+/−V   Verify line numbers. Once you type V, each displayed line will begin with n:, where n indicates the current line number. Type −V to suppress the line numbers. The line numbers are very useful in identifying text and moving the CP.

0V   A special function of the V command indicates how much of the edit buffer is in use and how much is free (still available). Type a 0 before the V:

      *<u>0V</u> < cr >
      33706/33719
      *

The first number is the amount of ''free,'' currently available bytes in the edit buffer; the second is the maximum possible size of the edit buffer. Subtracting the first from the second, we find that 13 characters of the file being edited are currently in the buffer.

n: Move the CP to line number n. When line numbers are being displayed (see +/−V), you can use this command to move the CP directly to the beginning of a specific line.

:m   Start at the CP and continue through line number m. This is not really a command by itself, but a prefix to a command. Suppose you type the command line:

      55:*<u>:75T</u> < cr >

ED will type lines (T) beginning at the CP (line 55) and ending at line 75.

Notice that you can use this command together with the previous one (n:) to perform an operation on a specified range of lines. For example, to delete lines 20 through 30, no matter where the CP is, type the command line:

87:*20::30K<cr>

+/−n Move forward or backward and display one line. This is an abbreviated form of the command +/−nLT, where the CP is moved forward or backward by "n" lines, whereupon the line then at the CP is displayed. The simplest form of this command is just a carriage return:

11:*<cr>
12:LINE OF TEXT
12:*

This is equivalent to LT, which moves the CP to the next line and displays it.

Commands for Searching and Changing Text

nFstring ∧ Z Find a particular unique sequence of characters. The usual format is:

*Fstring of characters ∧Z

This means: press F, type the unique string to search for, and press Control-Z.

In addition, you may specify the number of times ("n") to find the string. If the search is successful (i.e., the string is found the specified number of times), the CP will be placed immediately following the "n"th matching string. If you were searching for the first chorus of "Row, Row, Row Your Boat" with the command 3FRow<cr>, the character pointer would come to rest between "w" and the space preceding "Your" if its original position was before the first letter of the first "Row." If the search cannot satisfy the command given, the character pointer will not move.

The search begins at the location of the

CP, so be sure it is positioned well before the string to be found when using the F command.

Also remember that the F command searches only within the text in the edit buffer. See the "N" command below. Use Control-L to represent the CRLF pair if it is part of the string.

J   See below, after command S, for command J.

nNstring ∧ Z   Looks for the string in the edit buffer and on the diskette; it automatically loads the next portion of the original file into the edit buffer and writes lines from the edit buffer to the temporary file as necessary. The N command (autoscan) acts on the entire document, beginning at the CP, even if portions of it are still in the original file, while F looks only in the edit buffer for the string.

Remember to position the CP properly before issuing the N command.

See the F command above.

Use Control-L to represent the CRLF pair if it is part of the string.

nSfindstring ∧ Zreplacestring ∧ Z

Substitute information in the edit buffer.

The substitute command finds one string and replaces it with another. As shown, the command would search for "findstring" and replace it with "replacestring." The searching begins at the CP and ends at the last character in the edit buffer. The substitution is performed a total of "n" times.

As in all substitution commands, be sure the strings you want to replace are unique.

Use Control-L to represent the CRLF pair in the strig.

nJfindstring ∧ Zinsertstring ∧ Zendstring ∧ Z

Juxtapose two or more unique strings, one or more times. It combines the insertion and deletion operations.

This command works like this: First find

"findstring." Immediately following
"findstring" insert "insertstring," then delete
all characters from the end of "insertstring"
to the beginning of "endstring." Repeat a
total of "n" times. The CP, assuming that the
operation was successful, is placed at the
end of the final "insertstring."

For example, suppose the following line
appears in the document:

> WHEN IN ROM DO AS THE ROMANS
> DO, AND BE ROMANTIC...

If you wanted to replace one occurrence of
the letters DO with DON'T, you could use the
J command as follows:

> JDO ^ZN'T ^Z ^Z < cr >

The result would look like this:

> WHEN IN ROM DON'T AS THE
> ROMANS DO, AND BE ROMANTIC...

Be careful when using multiple repetitions of
the juxtaposition command (as in 2J, 3J,
etc.). In the example above, if you had used a
2J instead of just J, you would have added
more than one N'T to the first occurrence of
DO. Can you figure out what would appear?.

Combining Commands

ED lets you group commands in one command line to save typing time.
You can cascade ED commands one after the other and follow the last
command with the carriage return. For example:

> 1:*0A < cr >
> 1:*B < cr >
> 1:*T < cr >
> 1:LINE 1
> 1:*

can be typed as:

> 1:*0ABT < cr >
> 1:LINE 1
> 1:*

There are a few simple rules to follow when typing several commands on one line:

1. Some commands must be typed alone in a command line in CP/M versions 1.4 and newer; these commands are E, H, O, and Q. This is done to prevent the disastrous consequences of certain typographical errors.

2. When typing commands which use strings, use Control-Z, rather than <cr>, to end the strings. Commands which use strings are F, I, J, N, and S. Use <cr> only at the end of the command line.

nMcommands remembers a frequently used command sequence (Macro command). The format is:

    *nMcommand1command2command3 <cr>

For example, type:

    *MFROM ^Z-3DIRAM ^ZOTT <cr>

The command line says to repeatedly perform the following sequence of steps:

1. Find ROM (the CP is placed after the M),
2. Delete the three previous characters (ROM),
3. Insert RAM, and
4. Show each line as it is changed (OTT).

    The macro command will change all occurrences of ROM to RAM. If used on the example in the J commands, the resulting line will read: WHEN IN RAM DO AS THE RAMANS DO, AND BE RAMANTIC...

If "n" is absent, or if n = 0 or n = 1, the command sequence will be repeated until an error condition develops.

DUMP — DISPLAYING THE CONTENTS OF A FILE

DUMP presents the contents of a file in hexadecimal form. The DUMP command line summary is as follows:

DUMP x:filename.typ <cr>
    Displays the hexadecimal representations of each byte stored in the file filename.typ on drive x.

DUMP x:*.* <cr>
    Displays the hexadecimal representations of the first file which matches the *.* parameters.

    DUMP operates like the TYPE command discussed earlier. Instead of presenting the ASCII representations of the file, DUMP presents the contents of a file in hexadecimal form.

Uses of DUMP

Assembly language programmers use the DUMP command to check the contents of a program file, a binary data file, or any non-ASCII file.

DUMP x:filename.typ < cr >

Displays the hexadecimal representations of each byte stored in the file filename.typ on drive x.

A > DUMP B:PROGRAM.COM < cr >

```
0000   3A  07  00  FE  C8  DA  AC  03  21  00  00  39  22  25  07  31
0010   00  C8  3E  11  D3  FD  21  27  07  7D  D3  FD  7C  D3  FD  CD
0020   3B  02  11  13  04  CD  28  02  CD  3B  02  11  55  04  CD  28
```

A >

DUMP B:PROGRAM.COM	Display the hexadecimal representation of each byte stored in the file PROGRAM.COM on the diskette in drive B.
0000 0010 0020	The four-digit number at the left of each line is the relative address of the first byte on that line.
3A	Each hexadecimal digit represents four bits of each byte.
3A 07...07 31	Each display line consists of 16 pairs of hexadecimal numbers, one pair for each byte in the file.
A >	Display completed.

Input other than Command Line

∧ S pauses DUMP.

Strike any key to interrupt DUMP and return to A >.

Error Messages

NO INPUT FILE PRESENT ON DISK

The file you requested does not exist.

Batch Processing Utilities

Your computer is far more sophisticated than the mammoth beasts used in the 1960s. Almost all of the original computers operated primarily in the *batch mode*. A *batch* is a group of things; in the case of computers, it's a sequence of commands and/or data.

Most microcomputers in use today are *interactive* machines. This means that you input something, the computer responds, you input something else, the computer responds again, and so on. Interactive processing is appropriate for small business accounting, word processing, and other tasks for which microcomputers are used.

However, it is sometimes more efficient to submit a group of commands to be processed sequentially without your presence. The SUBMIT and XSUB commands fulfill these functions for CP/M.

SUBMIT — COMMAND LINE AUTOMATION

Directs the sequential entry and execution of a number of CP/M commands, without additional operator response. The SUBMIT command line summary is as follows:

SUBMIT filename < cr >

Creates a file $$$.SUB which contains the commands listed in filename.SUB; CP/M then executes commands from this file rather than the keyboard.

SUBMIT filename parameters < cr >

Creates a file $$$.SUB which contains commands from the file filename.SUB; certain parts of the command lines in filename.SUB are replaced by parameters during creation of $$$.SUB. CP/M then gets commands from this file rather than the keyboard.

To utilize SUBMIT, you must first create a file with the extension SUB, using the CP/M Editor or another editor. This file contains the list of CP/M commands to be executed, in the order you wish them performed, one to a line.

Uses of SUBMIT

SUBMIT can provide a linkage to the BACKUP or DISKCOPY program every time you finish using a program. First, create a SUBMIT file named ORREPENT.SUB which has only two commands in it:

RUN YOURPROG.RAM < cr >
BACKUP < cr >

Then, run YOURPROG.RAM by typing SUBMIT ORREPENT < cr > instead of RUN YOURPROG.RAM < cr >; be assured that your information is duplicated every time you finish using the program.

SUBMIT can also prepare diskettes with ready-to-run programs.

Program developers often use a *compiler* rather than an *interpreter* to write programs. A compiled program requires an extra process: the compilation. In small business packages there may be five, ten, or more related program modules, all of which need compiling. The compilation process could take as much as an hour; the SUBMIT facility can perform this function and free the programmer.

SUBMIT sequences can be chained by including a normal SUBMIT command line as the last line in a SUB file.

SUBMIT filename <cr>

Creates a file $$$.SUB which contains the commands listed in filename.SUB and executes commands from this file rather than from the keyboard.

Suppose you have created a file named NUCLEAR.SUB which contains the following:

    STAT *.BAS
    ERA *.BAS
    DIR *.BAS

When you submit this file for execution, the dialog will look like this:

```
A>SUBMIT NUCLEAR<cr>
A>STAT *.BAS

RECS        BYTS        EX        D:FILENAME.TYP
2           4K          1         A:PORGY.BAS
4           8K          1         A:PORKY.BAS
8           17K         2         A:PORTLY.BAS

BYTES REMAINING ON A: 151K

A>ERA *.BAS
A>DIR *.BAS
NO FILE
A>
```

The commands following SUBMIT are not underlined, since CP/M is doing the typing, not you. The only thing you type is SUBMIT NUCLEAR <cr>.

Input other than Command Line

Press Rubout, Delete, Backspace or Control-H to stop the execution of the $$$.SUB file while CP/M is reading the file; then wait patiently.

SUBMIT filename a b c <cr>

Creates a file $$$.SUB which contains the commands listed in filename.SUB and executes commands from this file rather than from the keyboard. This form of the SUBMIT command differs from the previous one in that you may include incomplete CP/M command lines in filename.SUB when you create it. SUBMIT will fill in the missing information using the parameters a, b, c, etc., which you supply in the SUBMIT command line. These parameters can be file names or any other information needed by the commands in filename.SUB. The symbols $1, $2, $3, etc. are used to hold the place of the missing parameters in filename.SUB.

Suppose you are editing a file on drive A and you want to copy it to drive B, then check disk space each time you finish an edit session. Without SUBMIT, you would have entered the following command lines in the course of your work (intervening ED commands and other dialog are omitted for clarity):

A > ED MYFILE.DOC < cr >
A > PIP B:=A:MYFILE.DOC[V] < cr >
A > STAT B:MYFILE.* < cr >

Suppose you use this method with every file you edit, not just with MYFILE.DOC. To get help from SUBMIT, first create a SUB file named WORKON.SUB (for example) containing the incomplete commands listed:

ED $1.$2 < cr >
PIP B:=A:$1.$2[V] < cr >
STAT B:$1.* < cr >

Now, to use this SUB file, type the command line below:

A > SUBMIT WORKON MYFILE.DOC < cr >

SUBMIT will create $$$.SUB from WORKON.SUB by substituting the first parameter, MYFILE, for $1 each time it appears, and the second parameter, DOC, for $2 each time it appears. SUBMIT then initiates a warm start, and CP/M looks for the file $$$.SUB. It then executes the commands listed in $$$.SUB.

XSUB — USER INPUT AUTOMATION: A SUBSET OF SUBMIT

It is possible to put more than commands in a SUB file. In fact, it can respond to questions a program might ask or add other variables when you invoke SUBMIT. This is done using the XSUB command (CP/M 2.0 or newer).

XSUB must be the first command in your SUB file in order to function properly. When SUBMIT encounters the XSUB command, a special set of instructions is loaded into memory with CP/M, and whenever a program requests console information, the SUBMIT file will be used to input it.

As with a SUBMIT file, you may use the $1, $2, etc. symbols to indicate last-minute submissions of information via the SUBMIT command line; the symbols are replaced with the parameters you type in the actual SUBMIT command.

You should note that XSUB is a subset of SUBMIT; you do not ever type XSUB in response to a CP/M prompt. XSUB may appear only in a SUB file.

XSUB is most often used in program and system development. But you might find that programs you purchase will use XSUB for a portion of their input.

You might also use XSUB to provide another automatic backup system. For example:

&BEFREE.SUB contains: 2BCNTIUD.SUB contains:
RUN YOURPROG.RAM < cr >   XSUB < cr >
SUBMIT 2BCNTIUD < cr >   BACKUP < cr >
A < cr >
B < cr >

The following process occurs when you run the program:

```
A > SUBMIT &BEFREE < cr >
A > RUN YOURPROG.RAM < cr >
       .
       .
       .
(Program executes until completion)
       .
       .
       .
A > SUBMIT 2BCNTIUD < cr >
       .
       .
       .
(xsub active)
A > BACKUP < cr >
DRIVE FOR SOURCE DISKETTE (A,B,C,D)? A < cr >
DRIVE FOR DESTINATION DISKETTE (A,B,C,D)? B < cr >
PUT A BLANK DISKETTE IN DRIVE B
AND PRESS RETURN WHEN YOU ARE READY TO BEGIN < cr >
```

From the time execution of the program YOURPROG.RAM stops to the time you put a blank diskette in the second drive and press the carriage return, the BACKUP process has been automated. This standardizes the completion of each computing session, and assures a proper backup of information.

4

Assembly Language Utilities

Despite CP/M's simplicity, the computer novice will find a lot to learn about it, certainly more than an end user requires. The information in this chapter has limited application for end users who primarily use packaged programs. If you are not developing or modifying programs in assembly language, skip this chapter.

This chapter covers the CP/M assembly language programming aids ASM, DDT, and LOAD. ASM is an assembler. It converts a source program written in assembly language into an object program in Intel Hex Format. This product of the assembler is an intermediate step to a true machine language program which the computer can use. LOAD performs the final conversion step by creating a machine language program file from the Intel Hex Format file. DDT is a debugging program used to locate and correct errors in machine language programs. The DUMP program described in Chapter 3 is another useful assembly language programming aid. DUMP displays the contents of a file as hexadecimal numbers.

WHY 8080 ASSEMBLY LANGUAGE IS USED

Assembly language is two steps removed from the action in the computer. Remember, the computer uses 1's and 0's as the basic elements of data. These *bits* can be either data or instructions to the computer, depending upon the context in which the CPU receives them.

Since it is inconvenient to think in terms of 10001010 and
10010010, we use hexadecimal notation to refer to eight bits at a time.
We call these eight-bit groups *bytes* of information. Some hexadecimal
representations of bytes are: C3, 45, and 0D. Remember that the
computer itself always uses binary notation (1's and 0's), but we use the
hexadecimal representation to help us recognize the patterns.

Since the hexadecimal representations are also awkward, we assign
names to the machine instructions and data they represent. The names
are the components of the language known as *assembly language*. We
call the names which represent instructions *mnemonics*. A mnemonic is
the assembly language representation of one CPU machine instruction.
Other names are used to represent other elements of a program; these
names are all described in the section on ASM.

Generally, any machine language program for the 8080 CPU will run
correctly on an 8085 CPU or a Z80 CPU. Since CP/M was written for the
8080, it also runs on the 8085 and Z80. This book uses only the 8080
instruction mnemonics designated by Intel, as they represent the
assembly language instructions available to all users of CP/M.

The assembly language mnemonics for the 8085 CPU are nearly
identical to those of the 8080. Those of the Z80 CPU are completely
different, however, even though the same machine language instructions
are often intended. ASM and DDT understand only Intel 8080
mnemonics, assembly language, and machine language.

This chapter assumes you understand assembly language
programming. If you do not, but want to learn, see the bibliography in
Appendix F for an appropriate book on the subject.

ASM Assemble an 8080 Program

The assembler converts an 8080 assembly language source program
into object code, executable by a computer. The assembler also provides
a listing showing each line from the source program together with the
corresponding object code it has created.

ASM Command Line

Once you have obtained or created the source file, you invoke ASM as
follows:

A > ASM filename.opt < cr >

The file name must be a valid CP/M file with the extension ASM; otherwise an error message will be displayed. The options opt in the above command line are not the file extension. ASM BSM.CCC <cr> does not mean assemble the program with the file name BSM.CCC, but assemble the program BSM.ASM with the options CCC.

The option letters after the file name represent (in order):

1. The drive which contains the source (original) file "filename.ASM."
2. The drive which should receive the *hex* (assembled program) file "filename.HEX."
3. The drive which should receive the *print* (listing of the program with error messages) file "filename.PRN."

You can use the standard CP/M drive specifiers A through P as option letters, subject to the existence of those drives on your computer.

Also, the option letters X and Z have special meanings; they do not mean drives X and Z.

Use Z for either the HEX or PRN file option to skip generation of that file. Use X as the PRN file option to display the listing on the console instead of storing it in a file.

If you type:

A > <u>ASM BSM.AAZ</u> <cr>

you are telling CP/M to assemble a file named BSM.ASM, found on drive A, into a HEX (object program) file named BSM.HEX, also on drive A, and to skip generation of the print file. The assembled program file always has the extension HEX; the *print* file always has the extension PRN.

Note: If all files are to be on the currently logged drive, you need not specify anything after the file name; i.e., no options or period. After assembling the program BSM.ASM in such an assembly, you have the following files:

BSM.ASM	Original (source) file
BSM.HEX	Assembled program file
BSM.PRN	Listing file

Files Used by ASM

What does this multiplicity of files do for you? The ASM file contains the assembly language source program. You created the ASM file with ED or another editor.

The assembler creates the HEX file. It contains the hexadecimal representations of the instructions in the ASM file. The format for the HEX file is known as Intel Hex Format. Intel first used the format for storing the hexadecimal characters on paper tape devices, and the disk format is equivalent. Here is an example of a short HEX file:

```
:0001000003E00BF
:0000000000
```

Not particularly enlightening, is it? Here is the assembly language program which created that information:

```
ORG    0100H                ; program starts at
                            address 0100 hex
MVI    A,0                  ; move a 00 hex into Register A
END                         ; end of program
```

The PRN file combines both files. We see both the program we originally typed and what the assembler created:

```
0100              ORG   0100H        ; program starts at address
                                      0100 hex
0100   3E00   MVI     A,0            ; move a 00 hex into
                                      Register A
0102              END                ; end of program
```

This type of listing is particularly useful when you use many *labels* and *symbols*.

Of what use are the HEX and PRN files? The HEX file is used to create an executable program. The PRN file is useful in the process of *debugging* a program (ridding it of errors). The listing in the PRN file is also an important part of the program documentation.

SOURCE PROGRAM FORMAT

The assembler expects the source file to be in a very specific form. The source file is a sequence of ASCII-coded statements or lines. Each line ends with the carriage return/line feed character pair.

Assembly Language Statements

Each assembly language statement is composed of between one and five *fields*. A field is a group of characters, and the fields are separated from one another by spaces or tab characters. Tab characters create a more readable source program because the fields are aligned at the tab stops. ASM sets the tab stops at columns 1, 9, 17, 25, 33 and so on every eight columns. The general format of the assembly language statement is:

line#   label   mnemonic   operand   ;comment

Each of the five fields in the statement is discussed below.

Line Numbers (line#)

The line number is an optional integer decimal number at the beginning of the line. Some editors insert these line numbers; ED does not. ASM ignores the line number.

Labels

A label is an identifier used to represent an address or value. A label is 1 to 16 characters long. The first character must be a letter; the others can be letters or numbers. Lower-case letters are treated as if they were upper-case. A colon may follow a label when it is used in the label field. The dollar sign ($) may be inserted in labels to improve readability. The assembler ignores the dollar signs, and they do not count toward the 16-character length limit. The label is optional for all statements except the EQU and SET directives. Generally, a particular label should appear in the label field of only one statement, but it can appear in the operand field of many statements.

There are certain reserved words which must not be used in the label field, because they have predetermined meanings. The reserved words are:

- All the 8080 instruction mnemonics
- All the ASM directive names: DB, DS, DW, END, EQU, IF, ENDIF, ORG, and SET
- All the 8080 register names: A, B, C, D, E, H, L, M, SP, and PSW.

Mnemonics

The mnemonic field is the only field which is not optional; it must be included in every statement. This field contains either an 8080 instruction mnemonic or the name of an assembler directive. Most of the assembly language programming books listed in Appendix F contain a list of the 8080 instruction mnemonics.

Operands

Some assembly language instructions require one or two operands or none at all. Assembler directives generally require one or more operands.

An operand can be a constant, a label, or an expression. Constants and expressions are described below.

Comments

The comment field begins with a semicolon. It is optional, and it is ignored by the assembler. However, you should always include comments because they are essential program documentation.

Constants and Expressions

The operand field of an assembly language instruction or directive can be occupied by a label, a constant, or an expression. Labels were explained above. Constants and expressions, and the rules for forming them, are described here.

Constants

A *numeric constant* is a fixed number in one of four number bases which is used as an operand.

A *binary constant* is a sequence of the digits 0 and 1 followed by the letter B.

An *octal constant* is a sequence of the digits 0 through 7 followed by the letter O or Q.

A *decimal constant* is a sequence of the digits 0 through 9 optionally followed by the letter D. If no letter suffix follows a constant, ASM assumes the constant is decimal.

A *hexadecimal constant* is a sequence of the digits 0 through 9 and A through F followed by the letter H. A hexadecimal constant must begin with a number; this requirement can be satisfied by preceding the constant with the number 0.

You can insert the dollar sign within a numeric constant to make it easier to read. ASM ignores the dollar signs. The following three constants are equal:

11010101=1101$0101=11$010$101

A *string constant* is a sequence of characters which is enclosed between apostrophe (') symbols. A string constant is limited to 64 characters. Only printable characters are allowed. Lower-case letters are *not* converted to upper-case. You can include an apostrophe within a string by typing two apostrophes instead of one. ASM computes the value of a string by adding a high order bit of 0 to the seven-bit ASCII code for each character.

Expressions

You can use expressions in place of operands. An expression is a combination of constants, labels, arithmetic operators, logical operators, and parentheses. During assembly each expression is evaluated and reduced to a single value.

Arithmetic Operators

The assembler can perform simple arithmetic when it evaluates an expression to determine its value. You can use the following arithmetic operators to join labels and constants into expressions:

A+B is the sum of A and B
A−B is B subtracted from A
+B is the same as B
−B is the same 0−B
A*B is A multiplied by B
A/B is the quotient of A divided by B
A MOD B is the remainder of A divided by B

The assembler performs the operation on 16-bit unsigned values and produces a 16-bit unsigned result, modulo 2^{16}.

Logical Operators

The assembler can perform Boolean (logical) operations as well as arithmetic operations. The following operators can be used:

NOT B is the bit-by-bit complement of B

A AND B is the bit-by-bit logical AND of A and B

A OR B is the bit-by-bit logical OR of A and B

A XOR B is the bit-by-bit logical exclusive OR of A and B

A SHL B is A shifted left B bit positions; shifted-out high-order bits are discarded, and vacated low-order bits are replaced with zeros

A SHR B is A shifted right B bit positions; shifted-out low-order bits are discarded, and vacated high order bits are replaced with zeros

Logical operations are performed on 16-bit unsigned values and result in a 16-bit unsigned value.

Precedence of Operators

When the assembler evaluates an expression containing several operators, it does not simply proceed from left to right applying each operator in sequence. Instead it applies certain operators before others. This hierarchy is called the *precedence* of the operators. The hierarchy used by ASM is shown below. Operators shown on the first line are always used first if they exist in an expression. Those on the fifth line are used last. Within a line below, the operators have equal precedence and are used left to right as they are encountered in an expression. ASM's precedence of operators is:

      * / MOD SHL SHR (highest)
      − +
      NOT
      AND
      OR XOR (lowest)

You can use sets of parentheses in an expression to override this hierarchy or to make the expression easier to read.

ASSEMBLER DIRECTIVES

You can include a number of "special" instructions to the assembler which are not part of the 8080 assembly language set. These *assembler directives* control the assembly process and affect the resulting machine code. You place assembler directive statements in the source program in roughly the same form as assembly language statements. The directive name goes in the mnemonic field of the statement.

DB, DW, and DS Assembler Directives

Use these three directives to initialize storage areas in memory.

      DB — Define Byte. Initializes an area byte by byte.
      DW — Define Word. Initializes an area two bytes at a time.
      DS — Define Storage. Reserves an area of a specified size.

Operand expressions in the DB statement are evaluated and stored as 8-bit values in successive memory locations. Expressions in the DW statement are evaluated and stored as 16-bit values in successive pairs of memory locations; within a pair, the low-order byte is stored first, followed by the high-order byte. The expression in the DS directive is evaluated, and the number of memory locations given by the resulting

16-bit value are reserved. These reserved locations are not filled.

```
label DB    exp1,exp2,exp3        ;comment
label DW    exp1,exp2,exp3        ;comment
label DS    exp1                  ;comment
```

The label is optional; if used, ASM assigns it the value of the address of the first byte defined or reserved by the DB, DW, or DS directive.

exp1, exp2, and exp3 are any valid expressions, including labels, numeric or string constants, etc. Any number of expressions, separated by commas, can be used with the DB and DW directives. Only one expression can be used with the DS directive, however.

The comment field is optional.

END Assembler Directive

The END directive tells the assembler that it has reached the end of the source statements. The form of the directive is:

```
label   END   expression       ;comments
```

The END directive is optional; if present it should be the last statement in the source program.

The optional label is assigned the value of the assembler's location counter at that point in the program. The optional expression is evaluated and used as the program starting address in the Intel Hex Format file. If expression is omitted, a starting address of 0000_{16} is used.

The comment field is optional.

EQU Assembler Directive

The EQUate statement assigns values or expressions to a label. The format is:

```
label   EQU   expression       ;comments
```

where expression may be any valid number, address, constant or expression. The label and the expression are required in an equate statement. You may use other labels (if previously defined) in the expression. Thus:

```
TAB   EQU   IT+1
```

is a valid equate, and TAB would now equal one plus the value of IT.

IF and ENDIF Assembler Directives

Define a section of assembly language code which will be assembled only if the condition listed in the IF statement is true. The form of these directives is:

IF expression
    •
    •
    •
Assembly Language Statements
    •
    •
    •
ENDIF

The assembler evaluates the expression in the IF statement. If the value of the expression is zero, the assembler ignores the statements between the IF and the ENDIF. If the value of the expression is non-zero, the statements are assembled.

Using IF statements is called *conditional assembly;* the assembly takes place only if certain conditions are met.

The IF statement may be used in assembly language programming in a number of ways. Here is one of the most frequent:

```
HAVE$TERMINAL       EQU       0FFFFH
NO$TERMINAL         EQU       NOT HAVE$TERMINAL
IF HAVE$TERMINAL
    •
    •
    •
assembly language statements to be used when there
is a terminal
    •
    •
    •
ENDIF
IF NO$TERMINAL
    •
    •
    •
assembly language statements to be used when there
is no terminal
    •
    •
    •
ENDIF
```

In the example given, you can change the program to reflect the presence of a terminal by changing only the HAVE$TERMINAL equate. Note that HAVE$TERMINAL (a label) is assigned a value which is all ones; NO$TERMINAL (another label) is assigned the complement value of HAVE$TERMINAL. The operator NOT changes each one to a zero.

ORG Assembler Directive

The ORG directive gives the assembler the memory address to use for the sequence of statements which follow it. The form of the ORG statement is:

    label   ORG   expression   ;comments

The value of the expression is used by the assembler as the memory address of the next program instrucion or define directive. The optional label is assigned the value of the expression. Comments are optional. You can use more than one ORG in a program.

SET Assembler Directive

The SET directive assigns a value to a label and allows you to change the value of a label. EQU allows you to set the value of a label only once. If you use SET, you may do so several times. The format is like the EQU command:

    label   SET   expression   ;comments

The label and expression are required. The comments are optional.

ASSEMBLER PROGRESS MESSAGES

The assembler will display a message when it starts and when it finishes. After you enter the ASM command line, you will see a message like:

    CP/M ASSEMBLER — VER 2.0

This may be followed by error messages if there are errors.
    When the assembler has finished its job, it displays a three-line message:

    xxxx
    yyyH USE FACTOR
    END OF ASSEMBLY

Interpret this as follows: xxxx is the hexadecimal address of the first *free* (unused) location following the assembly language program. yyyH is a rather perplexing indication of the portion of the symbol table area which has been used; the assembler has a finite amount of room in which to store the values of labels. yyy is a hexadecimal number between 000 and OFF. This number divided by OFF_{16} is the fraction of the symbol table used. If yyy is 080 for example, then about half $(80_{16}/FF_{16} = 128_{10}/255_{10})$ of the symbol table has been used. The END OF ASSEMBLY message means that ASM is finished; it does not mean that the assembly language program was necessarily created successfully.

ASSEMBLER ERROR MESSAGES

The assembler gives two kinds of messages. The first is a terminal error message; conditions prevented the assembler from completing its job.

Problems with disks or files typically cause terminal error messages. The second kind or error message arises when ASM cannot properly assemble a source code statement, but can continue the assembly in spite of the error.

Terminal Error Messages

NO SOURCE FILE PRESENT

The assembler could not find the file you specified. Are the drive specifying letters in the command line you used to invoke the assembler correct? Did you type the file name correctly? Does a file with that name and extension ASM exist?

NO DIRECTORY SPACE

The disk directory is full. Erase some files to make room for your PRN and HEX files. This is distinct from lacking space on a diskette. The directory can usually hold only 64 file names.

SOURCE FILE NAME ERROR

You cannot use the * and ? characters in a file name to be assembled. Only one file may be assembled at a time.

SOURCE FILE READ ERROR

The file containing the assembly language program has information the assembler cannot understand. Portions of another file may have been written over your assembly language file, or information was not properly saved on the diskette. Use the TYPE command to locate the error. Assembly language files contain the letters, symbols and numbers appearing on your keyboard; if you see something else or if the screen starts doing "funny things," you have found the spot where some computer instructions have sneaked into your file.

OUTPUT FILE WRITE ERROR

You have specified a write-protected diskette as the destination for the PRN and HEX files, or the diskette has no more space left. Either problem must be solved before you can assemble your program.

CANNOT CLOSE FILE

CP/M found the file but could not write anything to it. This usually occurs when the disk is write-protected.

Source Program Error Messages

The assembler provides the second set of messages during program assembly. If no messages appear, then the assembler is proceeding and has encountered nothing it cannot understand (this is much, much different from saying the program is correct!). If the assembler encounters something it does not understand, it will display a line in the following format:

a bbbb cccc   label   mnemonic   operand   ;comment

The "a" represents one of the following error codes:

D   Data Error. The value of the expression does not fit into the data area you indicated; it may be too long.

E   Expression Error. You formed the expression improperly, or its value is too long to fit the specified data area.

L   Label Error. You used the label incorrectly. This normally occurs when you use the same label in the label field of more than one statement in a program.

N   Feature Not Implemented. Digital Research also has an assembler known as MAC, which accepts directives that ASM cannot handle. When ASM encounters something that only MAC can recognize, the N error message is given.

O   Overflow Error. Your expression is so complicated that the assembler cannot handle it in its present form. Separate the expression into smaller pieces or simplify it by reducing the number of operators.

P   Phase Error. The label changes value during

assembly. If you must reassign a value, use the the SET directive. Can also be caused by a duplicate label.

R   Register Error. You specified a register that is not compatible with the mnemonic given. For instance, POP B is a valid assembly language statement, but POP A is not. POP A would trigger the R error message.

U   Undefined Symbol. You used a label in an expression without assigning a value to it. For example:

U 0102 0600   MVI   B,ONE

will appear if ONE has not been defined.

V   Value Error. The operand (expression) encountered is not correct. This usually occurs with typing errors, where you forget to include a comma or certain letter.

The bbbb in the format of the error message is the hexadecimal memory address of the statement at which the error was encountered, and the cccc is the hexadecimal representation of the machine language created by the assembler. When an error occurs, some or all of the machine code is set to zeros because the assembler did not know what to put there. In the U example above, note that the first portion of the cccc area is filled with 06 to indicate that the assembler recognized that the instruction was Move Immediate to Register B. But ASM could not calculate the value of the immediate operand because the value of ONE had not been assigned.

DDT

The Dynamic Debugging Tool (DDT) is used to test and debug machine language programs. The DDT command line summary is as follows:

DDT < cr >
    Loads the Dynamic Debugging Tool program and waits for further instructions

DDT x:filename.typ < cr >
    Loads DDT into memory and also loads filename.typ into memory for examination, modification, or exension. typ must be COM or HEX.

USES OF DDT

You use DDT to:

- Load an assembled program into memory
- Make simple changes to a machine language program
- Help locate errors in machine language programs
- Make corrections or updates to your software
- Install a special *driver* routine (a program that drives a peripheral, like a printer)
- Examine and modify the contents of memory
- Enter assembly language code one line at a time
- *Disassemble* a section of a program (i.e., turn machine language back into assembly language instructions)
- Examine and modify the contents of the internal registers of the CPU
- Set *breakpoints*; these are locations to stop program execution and allow you to check what has happened so far
- *Trace* the execution of a program; follow what is happening to memory and the internal registers of the CPU

DDT COMMANDS

There are twelve basic commands you may give the DDT program once you load it into memory.

Assss	Enter assembly language statements beginning at hexadecimal address ssss
D	Display the contents of the next 192 bytes of memory
Dssss	Display the contents of 192 bytes memory beginning at hexadecimal address ssss
Dssss,ffff	Display the contents of memory starting at hexadecimal address ssss and finishing at hexadecimal address ffff
Fssss,ffff,cc	Fill memory with the 8-bit hexadecimal constant cc starting at hexadecimal address ssss and finishing with hexadecimal address ffff

G	Begin execution at the address contained in the program counter
Gssss	Begin execution at hexadecimal address ssss
Gssss,bbbb	Set a breakpoint at hexadecimal address bbbb, then begin execution at hexadecimal address ssss
G,bbbb	Set a breakpoint at hexadecimal address bbbb, then begin execution at the address contained in the program counter
G,bbbb,cccc	Set breakpoints at hexadecimal addresses bbbb and cccc, then begin execution at the address contained in the program counter
Ifilename.typ	Set up the default file control block using the name filename.typ
L	List the next eleven lines of assembly language program disassembled from memory
Lssss	List eleven lines of assembly language program disassembled from memory starting at hexadecimal address ssss
Lssss,ffff	List the assembly language program disassembled from memory starting at hexadecimal address ssss and finishing at hexadecimal address ffff
Mssss,ffff,dddd	Move the contents of the memory block starting at hexadecimal address ssss and ending at hexadecimal address ffff to the block of memory starting at hexadecimal address dddd
R	Read a file from disk into memory (use I command first)
Rnnnn	Read a file from disk into memory beginning at the hexadecimal address nnnn higher than normal
Sssss	Display the contents of memory at hexadecimal address ssss and optionally change the contents
Tnnnn	Trace the execution of (hexadecimal) nnnn program instructions

Unnnn	Execute (hexadecimal) nnnn program instructions, then stop and display the CPU registers' contents
X	Display the CPU registers' contents
Xr	Display the contents of CPU register or flag r and optionally change it

DDT <cr>

Loads the Dynamic Debugging Tool program from disk into memory.

```
A>DDT<cr>
DDT VERSION x.x
-
```

DDT VERSION x.x	DDT sign-on message
-	DDT prompt; DDT is waiting for commands

DDT x:filename.typ <cr>

Loads an assembled program into memory.

```
A>DDT x:filename.typ<cr>
DDT VERSION x.x
NEXT  PC
nnnn  mmmm
-
```

DDT VERSION x.x	DDT identifies itself
NEXT	Identifies NEXT free memory location which follows the loaded file
PC	Identifies program counter setting
mmmm	The program you loaded into memory begins at this hexadecimal location
nnnn	Program ends just before this hexadecimal location
-	DDT prompt

Assss <cr>

Enter assembly language instructions beginning at hexadecimal address ssss.

```
-A0100<cr>
0100 MOV A,C<cr>
0101 <cr>
-
```

–	DDT waiting for input
A0100<cr>	Enter assembly language code beginning at memory location 0100_{16}
0100	DDT affirms location
MOV A,C <cr>	You enter a valid Assembly language instruction
0101	DDT presents location for next instruction
<cr>	You terminate the assembly session.
–	DDT waiting for command

Error Messages

?

DDT does not understand the assembly language instruction.

Notes on Assss

There is no space between the command letter and the address you specify; this applies to all DDT commands. You may enter only 8080 mnemonics and operands; you may not use labels or assign a value to a label. All numeric operands must be hexadecimal numbers; you must know the value when you enter the statement. DDT will print the current address (the one you specified) in the left margin and wait for you to type an instruction. Mnemonic and operand should be separated by a space. Each instruction is terminated by a carriage return; the entire session is terminated by typing just a carriage return. ssss is a one- to four-digit hexadecimal address.

D <cr>

Displays a 192 byte section of memory as 12 lines of 16 bytes each.

```
-D<cr>
0100   3A 07 00 FE C8 DA AC 03 21 00 00 39 22 25 07 31   : . . . . . . . ! . . 9 " % . 1
0110   00 C8 3E 11 D3 FD 21 27 07 7D D3 FD 7C D3 FD CD   . . > . . . ! ' . } . . | . . .
0120   3B 02 11 13 04 CD 28 02 CD 3B 02 11 55 04 CD 28   ; . . . . . ( . . ; . . U . . (
0130   02 1E 07 0E 02 CD 05 00 0E 01 CD 05 00 FE 1B CA   . . . . . . . . . . . . . . . .
0140   A1 03 FE 0D C2 28 01 11 91 04 CD 28 02 3E 4D 32   . . . . . ( . . . . . ( . . > M 2
0150   2A 07 21 1D 07 36 0B 7E D6 0D D3 FF 3E 07 32 1E   * . ! . . 6 . . . . . . > . 2 .
0160   07 21 2A 07 35 3E 01 32 2B 07 11 AE F9 CD AB 02   . ! * . 5 > . 2 + . . . . . . .
0170   3E 04 32 20 07 CD 65 02 21 27 07 36 21 CD 2E 02   > . 2 . . . e . ! ' . 6 ! . . .
0180   FA D6 02 CD C5 02 C2 6A 01 21 1E 07 35 C2 61 01   . . . . . . . j . ! . . 5 . a
0190   3E 02 32 24 07 CD 65 02 3A 2A 07 C6 07 32 2A 07   > . 2 $ . . e . . * . . . 2 .
01A0   36 07 21 2A 07 35 3E 02 32 21 07 CD 65 02 21 27   6 . ! . . 5 . . 2 ! . . e . ! '
01B0   07 36 32 CD 2E 02 FA E9 02 3E 01 32 2B 07 11 AE   . 6 2 . . . . . . > . 2 + . . .
-
```

D<cr>	Display the next 192 bytes
0100	Initial address (location in memory) for the memory contents displayed in the first line
07	Hexadecimal digit pair represents bit pattern at memory location 0101
01B0	Address of the first byte in the 12th line of the display

Notes on D

The D command displays 192 bytes of memory. Each successive use of the D command displays the next 192 bytes of memory. The starting address for the first use of D depends on the file, if any, loaded with DDT. Common starting values are 0100_{16} and 0000_{16}.

The ASCII representation of each byte is displayed at the right end of each line. Non-graphic characters are represented by a period (.).

Dssss < cr >

Displays the contents of the 192 bytes of memory beginning at hexadecimal address ssss.

```
–D500 < cr >
0500   52 52 4F 52 20 20 20 44 52 3E 42 24 52 45 41 44   R R O R       D R = B $ R E A D
0510   20 45 52 52 4F 52 20 20 20 20 44 52 3D 42 24 56     E R R O R       D R = B $ V
0520   45 52 49 46 59 20 45 52 52 4F 52 20 20 42 4C 4F   E R I F Y   E R R O R     B L O
0530   43 4B 3D 2D 2D 24 20 20 54 52 4B 3D 2D 2D 20 20   C K = - - $   T R K = - -
0540   53 43 54 52 3D 2D 2D 24 20 20 53 54 53 57 44 3D   S C T R = - - $   S T S W D =
0550   2D 2D 2D 2D 2D 2D 2D 2D 20 20 24 AE 05 C1 05 D5   - - - - - - - -   $ . . . . .
0560   05 E5 05 F5 05 08 06 1A 06 9B 05 2F 06 3F 06 58   . . . . . . . . . . . / . ? . X
0570   06 9B 05 9B 05 9B 05 9B 05 9B 05 71 06 83 06 95   . . . . . . . . . . . q . . . .
0580   06 A7 06 BE 06 D4 06 EB 06 FF 06 9B 05 9B 05 9B   . . . . . . . . . . . . . . . .
0590   05 9B 05 9B 05 9B 05 9B 05 9B 05 4E 4F 20 45 52   . . . . . . . . . . . N O   E R
05A0   52 4F 52 20 4D 53 47 20 46 4F 55 4E 44 24 44 52   R O R   M S G   F O U N D $ D R
05B0   49 56 45 20 4E 4F 54 20 4F 50 45 52 41 42 4C 45   I V E   N O T   O P E R A B L E
```

See D < cr > for explanation of display.

Notes on Dssss

If you start a display command with an address which is not a multiple of 16 (does not end with a 0), the first line of the display will not have 16 locations represented; DDT likes nice round numbers, and round numbers to it mean multiples of 16. The first line in our example would show only fifteen bytes if we had typed D501 < cr >.

ssss is a one- to four-digit hexadecimal number.

The ASCII representation of each byte is displayed at the right end of each line. Non-graphic characters are represented by a period (.).

A subsequent D < cr > command will resume where Dssss < cr > left off.

Dssss,ffff < cr >

Displays the contents of memory starting at hexadecimal address ssss and finishing at hexadecimal address ffff.

```
-D101,137<cr>
 0101   07  00  FE  C8  DA  AC  03  21  00  00  39  22  25  07  31      . . . . . . . . . ! . . 9 " % . 1
 0110   00  C8  3E  11  D3  FD  21  27  07  7D  D3  FD  7C  D3  FD  CD   . . > . . . . ! ' . | . . | . .
 0120   3B  02  11  13  04  CD  28  02  CD  3B  02  11  55  04  CD  28   ; . . . . . . ( . . ; . . U . . (
 0130   02  1E  07  0E  02  CD  05  00  . . . . . .
 -
```

See D < cr > for explanation of display.

Notes on Dssss,ffff

If you start a display command with an address which is not a multiple of 16 (does not end with a 0), the first line of the display will not have 16 locations represented; DDT likes nice round numbers, and round numbers to it mean multiples of 16. The first line in our example shows only fifteen bytes because we typed D101,.

ssss and ffff are one- to four-digit hexadecimal numbers.

The ASCII representation of each byte is displayed at the right end of each line. Non-graphic characters are represented by a period.

A subsequent D command will resume where Dssss,ffff < cr > left off.

Fxxxx,yyyy,z < cr >

Fills a portion of memory with a constant value.

```
-F0100,01F0,00<cr>
 -
```

F	Fill a portion of memory...
0100	...beginning at location 0100_{16}...
01F0	...and ending at location $01F0_{16}$...
00	...with the constant value 00_{16}.

Notes on F

You can use this command to set a portion of memory to a known value (like 00_{16}) before placing and/or modifying any information in that area.

If you suspect memory errors, use the F command followed by the D command to isolate any blatant memory problems. Hint: do not use just one pattern of bits; try 00, 55, AA, and FF in consecutive fills. Be careful, however, not to fill memory used by CP/M or DDT (generally the first 256 memory locations and the last 4K to 8K memory locations).

G < cr >

Executes instructions beginning at the address contained in the program counter.

Notes on G

You will seldom use this form of the G command when debugging a program because DDT will have no control over execution. After the G command you will usually have no way of stopping the program and returning to DDT.

You can display the contents of the program counter with the X or XP commands.

Gssss <cr>

Executes instructions beginning at the hexadecimal address ssss.

Notes on Gssss

This command places the hexadecimal value ssss into the program counter and then lets the CPU begin execution at that address. As with the G command, DDT may never regain control.

Gssss,bbbb <cr>

Executes instructions beginning at hexadecimal address ssss and ending at hexadecimal address bbbb.

Notes on Gssss,bbbb

This command first sets a breakpoint at address bbbb by storing an RST 7 instruction there. Then execution is started at address ssss. If the CPU executes the breakpoint at bbbb, execution of the program stops, and DDT prompts for another command.

Gssss,bbbb,cccc <cr>

Executes instructions beginning at hexadecimal address ssss and ending at hexadecimal address bbbb or cccc.

Notes on Gssss,bbbb,cccc

This command is the same as Gssss,bbbb except that it sets two breakpoints instead of one. If either breakpoint is executed, DDT prompts for another command.

G,bbbb <cr>

Executes instructions beginning at the address contained in the program counter and ending at hexadecimal address bbbb.

Notes on G,bbbb

This command starts execution at the address in the program counter. It is otherwise the same as Gssss,bbbb. It is useful for continuing after a previous breakpoint.

G,bbbb,cccc < cr >

Executes instructions beginning at the address contained in the program counter and ending at hexadecimal address bbbb or cccc.

Notes on G,bbbb,cccc

This command starts execution at the address in the program counter. It is otherwise the same as Gssss,bbbb,cccc. It is useful for continuing after a previous breakpoint.

Ifilename.typ < cr >

Identifies the file you wish to load into memory using the R command.

```
-IPCOPY.COM < cr >
-R < cr >
NEXT PC
1400 0100
-
```

I	Set up a file control block...
PCOPY.COM	...for the file PCOPY.COM
R	Read the file using the R command

```
-IPCOPY.COM < cr >
-S5C < cr >
005C 00 02 < cr >
005D 50 . < cr >
-R < cr >
NEXT  PC
1400 0100
. -
```

S5C	Change file control block drive specifier...
00	...from currently logged drive...
02	...to drive B.

Notes on I

The I command, called Input or Identify, prepares a file control block so that you can use the R command to read a file from disk into memory. I sets up the default file control block (FCB) at location $005C_{16}$ with the unambiguous file name and extension you specify. It does not actually load the file nor perform a disk access to verify that the specified file exists.

The I command always sets up the file control block for accessing the currently logged disk drive. You may *not* include a drive specifier, such as B:, with the I command; an error message will result if you do. You can specify another drive, however, by modifying the file control block after using the I command. Use the S command to change the byte at memory location $005C_{16}$ from 00 to the value which corresponds to the desired drive. Choose one of the values from Table 4-1.

L < cr >

Disassembles a portion of memory; lists the contents of memory in assembly language, beginning after the last listed address.

```
−L < cr >
0151 MOV D,A
0152 MVI E,00
0154 PUSH D
0155 LXI H,0200
0158 MOV A,B
0159 ORA C
015A JZ  0165
015D DCX B
015E MOV A,M
015F STAX D
0160 INX D
−
```

L < cr >	List memory beginning after the last listed address
015A	Address of the first byte of the instruction
JZ	Instruction mnemonic
0165	Instruction operand

Error Messages

aaaa ?? = dd

The ?? = indicates DDT did not know how to represent the hexadecimal value dd encountered at address aaaa in 8080 assembly language. In other words, dd is not an 8080 machine instruction opcode.

Notes on L

Each successive use of L disassembles the next eleven instructions. When ?? = appears in the mnemonic field, display the corresponding area of memory with the D command to find out why.

Operands which are numeric values are always displayed as hexadecimal numbers; labels and symbols are not displayed.

TABLE 4-1. Values for Disk Drive Specifier
in Default File Control Block

Contents of Location $005C_{16}$ (Hexadecimal)	Disk Drive Selected
00	Currently Logged Drive
01	Drive A
02	Drive B
03	Drive C
04	Drive D
05	Drive E
06	Drive F
07	Drive G
08	Drive H
09	Drive I
0A	Drive J
0B	Drive K
0C	Drive L
0D	Drive M
0E	Drive N
0F	Drive O
10	Drive P

Lssss < cr >

Lists (disassembles) eleven instructions beginning at ssss, a one- to four-
character hexadecimal memory address.

```
−L13D <cr>
013D LXI SP,0200
0140 PUSH B
0141 PUSH B
0142 LXI D,0130
0145 MVI C,09
0147 CALL 0005
014A POP B
014B LXI H,0007
014E MOV A,M
014F DCR A
0150 SUB B
−
```

L   Disassemble machine instructions into
                                  assembly language instructions. . .

13D   . . .beginning at hexadecimal memory address 013D

Error Messages

aaaa ??= dd

The ??= indicates DDT did not know how to represent the
hexadecimal value dd encountered at address aaaa in 8080
assembly language. In other words, dd is not an 8080 machine
instruction opcode. You may have instructed DDT to
disassemble at a location which contained data or the operand
of an instruction.

Lssss,ffff <cr>

Lists (disassembles) instructions beginning at ssss and ending at ffff.
ssss and ffff are one- to four-digit hexadecimal memory addresses.

```
-L151,154<cr>
0151 MOV D,A
0152 MVI E,00
0154 PUSH D
0155
-
```

| L | List assembly language instructions. |
| 151,154 | . . . beginning at address 0151 and ending at address 0154. |

Error Messages

aaaa ??= dd

The ??= indicates DDT did not know how to represent the
hexadecimal value dd encountered at address aaaa in 8080
assembly language. In other words, dd is not an 8080 machine
instruction opcode. You may have instructed DDT to
disassemble at a location which contained data or the operand
of an instruction.

Mssss,ffff,dddd <cr>

Moves a portion of memory from one location to another, where ssss is
the first memory location to be moved, ffff is the last memory location to
be moved, and dddd is the first memory location of the destination. ssss,
ffff, and dddd are one- to four-digit hexadecimal addresses.

**Input other than
Command Line**

None

Error Messages

None

Notes on M

There are a number of considerations to keep in mind with the move command. Do not specify a destination within the block of memory to be moved.

The move command does not *relocate* a program. A program usually contains references to other locations within the program. The move command does a literal move; each byte in the original block will be moved exactly as is to the new location. If a program is moved away from its normal location, it will most likely not work at its new location.

Rnnnn <cr>

Reads a file from the diskette, if preceded by an I command which identifies the file. nnnn is an optional one- to four-digit hexadecimal address offset.

Input other than Command Line

None

Error Messages

None

Notes on R

The optional nnnn is an *offset* or *bias* as Digital Research refers to it. If omitted, an offset of zero is assumed. The offset is added to the normal load location, and the file is loaded at the resulting address.

Any address which would exceed $FFFF_{16}$ will *wrap around* to 0000. Thus a file that would load at 8000_{16} with an offset of zero would load at 0100_{16} if loaded with an offset of 8100_{16} (R8100 <cr>). Also, you may not load a file so that it resides in the portion of memory between 0000 and 0100 hex or so that it overlays DDT.

You should generally not load a file which would load into any part of memory used by CP/M. The forbidden areas are 0000_{16} to 0100_{16} and the CP/M area below $FFFF_{16}$. The address of the start of this area can be found by entering the command L105,107 <cr>; the address shown after the JMP mnemonic is the lowest address used by CP/M and DDT.

If you entered a file extension of COM with the I command, then loading will begin at 0100_{16}+nnnn. If you entered any other extension, including HEX, the R command assumes the file will be in Intel Hex Format, and it will add the offset to the addresses contained in the Hex Format file to determine load addresses.

Sssss <cr>

Display and optionally change (set) the contents of memory, beginning at location nnnn, where nnnn is a one- to four-digit hexadecimal address.

```
-S0100<cr>
0100 C3 3D<cr>
0101 28 4F<cr>
0102 38 <cr>
0103 C3 .<cr>
-
```

–	DDT waiting for input
S0100<cr>	Change the contents of memory location 0100...
C3	...from C3...
3D<cr>	...to 3D
0101	Next address...
28	...contains 28...
4F<cr>	...change to 4F
0102	Next address...
38 <cr>	...contains 38, but do not change it.
0103	Next address...
.<cr>	...no more changes.

Input other than Command Line

cc<cr> To change the contents of the memory location just displayed, enter the new value cc as a one- or two-digit hexadecimal value, then press Return.

<cr> To leave a memory location unchanged and examine the next location, press Return.

.<cr> When finished making changes, press period, then Return.

Error Messages

None

Tnnnn <cr>

Selectively traces program execution. Displays CPU registers before each program instruction.

```
-T5<cr>
COZOMOEOIO    A=00    B=0FB6    D=0000    H=0000    S=0100    P=013D    LXI     SP,0200
COZOMOEOIO    A=00    B=0FB6    D=0000    H=0000    S=0200    P=0140    PUSH    B
COZOMOEOIO    A=00    B=0FB6    D=0000    H=0000    S=01FE    P=0141    PUSH    B
COZOMOEOIO    A=00    B=0FB6    D=0000    H=0000    S=01FC    P=0142    LXI     D,0130
COZOMOEOIO    A=00    B=0FB6    D=0130    H=0000    S=01FC    P=0145    MVI     C,09*0147
```

T5 <cr>	Trace execution of next five program instructions; display CPU registers before each instruction is executed
P=013D	Contents of Program Counter Register is $013D_{16}$ before first instruction is executed
LXI SP,0100	The instruction at address $013D_{16}$
C0	The value of the Carry flag is 0
Z0	The value of the Zero flag is 0
M0	The value of the Minus flag is 0
E0	The value of the Even Parity flag is 0
I0	The value of the Intermediate Carry flag is 0
A=00	The Accumulator contains 00
B=0FB6	Register B contains 0F and Register C contains B6
D=0000	Registers D and E both contain 00
H=0000	Registers H and L both contain 00
S=0100	The Stack Pointer Register contains 0100
*0147	Tracing stopped; the next instruction is at location 0147_{16}

Input other than Command Line

Any key stops tracing and returns control to DDT.

Notes on T

The program being traced runs about 500 times slower than normal because many DDT instructions simulate each program instruction.

nnnn is a one- to four-digit hexadecimal number; it is the number of instructions to trace. If you omit nnnn, DDT will trace one instruction.

After you use the T command, DDT sets the default starting address for the display command (D) to the contents of register pair H and L. It similarly sets the default starting address for the list command (L) to the address of the next instruction to be executed.

The trace command enables interrupts. This can be a problem if your program requires that interrupts be disabled.

Unnnn

The U (untrace) command is like the trace command, except you see only one line representing the CPU registers after the completion of all nnnn program steps. It is similar to setting a breakpoint nnnn program steps away and following this with an X command. The U command thus differs from the T command in that only the final values of the registers are given, where T would display the CPU registers for each instruction traced.

Using U is faster than using T but slower than using G. Using U is preferable to using G without breakpoints because you can interrupt execution by pressing a key on the keyboard.

Input other than Command Line

Any key stops execution and returns control to DDT.

X < cr >

Examines the *current state* of the CPU. Each CPU status flag and register is displayed.

```
−x<cr>
C0Z0M0E0I0 A=00 B=0FB6 D=0130 H=0000 S=01FC P=0145 MVI C,09
−
```

C0	The value of the Carry flag is 0
Z0	The value of the Zero flag is 0
M0	The value of the Minus flag is 0
E0	The value of the Even Parity flag is 0
I0	The value of the Interdigit Carry flag is 0
A=00	The Accumulator contains 00.
B=0FB6	Register B contains $0F_{16}$ and Register C contains 6_{16}
D=0130	Register D contains 01 and Register E contains 30_{16}
H=0000	Registers H and L both contain 00
S=01FC	The Stack Pointer Register contains $01FC_{16}$
P=0145	The Program Counter Register contains 0145_{16}
MVI C,09	The instruction at address 0145_{16}

Input other than Command Line

None

Error Messages

?

DDT does not understand your input.

Xr < cr >

Displays the contents of a single CPU register or flag and optionally changes it.

r represents the register or flag to be displayed and possibly modified; use one of the following values:

Xr Command	Register or Flag Affected	Register or Flag Size (Bits)
XC	Carry Flag	1
XZ	Zero Flag	1
XM	Minus (Negative) Flag	1
XE	Even Parity Flag	1
XI	Interdigit Carry Flag	1
XA	Accumulator (Register A)	8
XB	Register Pair B and C	16
XD	Register Pair D and E	16
XH	Register Pair H and L	16
XS	Stack Pointer Register	16
XP	Program Counter Register	16

**Input other than
Command Line**

$<cr>$ Leave register or flag unchanged.

$nnnn<cr>$ Change register or flag contents to nnnn. For nnnn
use 0 or 1 for the flags; use $0\text{-}FF_{16}$ for the Accumulator;
use $0\text{-}FFFF_{16}$ for the 16-bit registers.

Error Messages

?
      DDT does not understand your input.

LOAD — Create an Executable Program

The LOAD command has only one function: it takes a file with the extension HEX and converts it into an executable file with the extension COM.

A HEX file s created by the CP/M assembler. A HEX file contains Intel Hex Format machine code ready to be tested using DDT or converted into an executable file. LOAD creates a COM file, which begins at 0100_{16} and contains executable machine code.

LOAD x:filename < cr >

Creates an executable program file.

```
A >LOAD B:POX < cr >
FIRST   ADDRESS      0100
LAST    ADDRESS      0234
BYTES   READ         0135
RECORDS WRITTEN       02
A >
```

LOAD B:POX	LOAD the file POX.HEX on Drive B
0100	First address in the program
0234	Last address in the program
0135	Number of bytes in the program
02	Number of 128-byte records written by LOAD into file POX.COM

**Input other than
Command Line**

None

Error Messages

ERROR: CANNOT OPEN SOURCE, LOAD ADDRESS xxxx
   Displayed if LOAD cannot find file specified or if no file name
   is specified.

Notes on LOAD

x: is optional; if omitted, the currently logged drive is used.
   The Intel Hex Format records must be in ascending order by address;
otherwise the COM file will be incorrect.

5

Other Transient Programs and CP/M

You will use many different types of programs in conjunction with CP/M. Digital Research provides a number of support programs to help you develop your own software, but Digital Research does not market end user application programs. Remember, CP/M is not the entire solution. Application programs contribute significantly to the solution.

The four classes of "solution" programs this chapter addresses are:

- Utilities
- High level languages
- Application programs
- Word processors

In Chapter 2 we used the term housekeeping to describe programs that help you keep your disk files clean. We can refer to another class of related programs as *utilities*. A *utility disk* contains programs which maintain your disk collection. Such utility programs are:

- Editors
- Disk copy programs
- Disk formatters
- CP/M system generators
- Disk viewers

Editors differ in degree of sophistication; a pencil, scissors, tape, typewriter and copy machine each add information to paper. An editor or a word processing program adds, deletes, or modifies information on a disk.

You may add information on a disk using the Digital Research Context Editor, ED, or by using a powerful word processing program (such as WordStar). In this chapter we describe several popular editors and explain how to use them with CP/M.

Assembly language is one of several layers of software existing between the computer and the user. Historically, software was frequently designed to make subsequent development of microcomputer programs easier. In this way, layers of software exist; each layer is directly dependent on an earlier development.

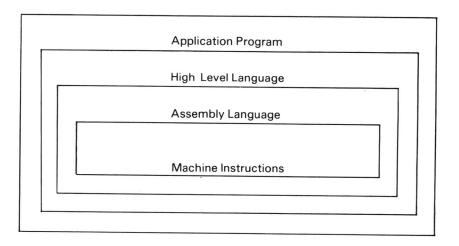

At the core of programming are *machine instructions*. These are the binary 1's and 0's the CPU interprets. Each different pattern of 1's and 0's causes the CPU to perform a unique task. Each CPU model has a particular set of instructions it understands. To program (instruct) a computer at this level you need a way of entering the machine instructions. CP/M does not provide this facility directly, but you may do this indirectly with DDT (see chapter 4). There are two conceptual problems with machine instructions.

1. A machine instruction (such as 11000011) bears little resemblance to the operation which the computer performs in response to it. This is true of any code or language which does not use hieroglyphics. While the 1's and 0's represent various on and off states to the computer, we must translate the 1's and 0's further. In human languages, number strings do not form basic components of meaning. The series of numbers may represent something, but we require an intermediary translation. Thus,

11000011 translates to a jump execution to the memory location specified next.

2. Instructions perform operations that are firmly rooted in computer architecture and terminology. The task you wish to perform may be difficult to describe using the selected computer's machine instructions. Suppose you want to place a character on a piece of paper using a printer; the necessary instructions might be:

Hexadecimal Representation	Binary Machine Instruction
3E	00111110
58	01011000
DB	11011011
03	00000011
E6	11100110
01	00000001
C2	11000010
00	00000000
00	00000000
D3	11010011
02	00000010

Assembly language moves one step away from the computer, providing an English-like mnemonic to describe the action of each machine instruction. Using the above example (sending a character for the printer to type), we now have:

```
MVI   A,58H
IN    03
ANI   01
JZ    0000
OUT   02
```

If you know what MVI, IN, ANI, JZ, and OUT mean, then the instruction is now represented in a shorthand which is more easily translated into human-readable language. Unfortunately these five assembly language program lines convey only the meaning of each single instruction. What do the five lines together, as a program, accomplish?

One step further removed from machine instructions, the computer interprets a *high level language*. Here assembly language instructions are combined into larger building blocks. Our program now becomes:

```
LPRINT "X"
```

which sends a character X to the printer. The concept of what the program does is now evident. LPRINT ''X'' may actually trigger the execution of several (or even several hundred) machine instructions, but by LPRINT ''X'' we immediately understand the function of the program. As we get closer to understanding the task the computer accomplishes, we get further from the machine instructions the CPU actually executes. The first high level languages were created using the next most sophisticated method: in this case, assembly language. And the first assembly language programs were written in machine instructions.

The last level we will consider is the *application program*. An application program causes a computer to execute a specific task, for example, to create and maintain a list of names and addresses. Most computer users run application programs unaware of any lower level of program interface.

Now that we have introduced the levels of program instructions, let us look in more detail at each of the four types of programs we may use with CP/M.

Utility Programs

We will present several useful utility programs in a general fashion. Each supplier of CP/M may also provide some utility programs which are similar to, but not the same as, the programs described here. It is important to be aware of these utilities, and to learn how to use them. This is particularly true of the disk formatting and copying programs. As you read the following sections, consult the manual(s) which accompanied the CP/M you purchased. Compare the material in your manuals with our discussion, to determine how to use your CP/M utility programs.

FORMAT — PREPARING A DISKETTE FOR USE

How does the computer know where to put information on a disk? We discussed how the disk is laid out in sectors and tracks, but how does the computer distinguish between sectors or tracks? How does it assign information within a sector or track? Part of the job is done by the hardware (equipment) and CP/M, but another part requires you to prepare the disk.

Almost any CP/M package will include a *format* or *initialization* type of program. Among others, the following names have been given to initialization programs:

FORMAT
INIT
IN
DSKFMT
FMT
CREATE
INITDSK
FORMT#
FORMTHD
MFORMAT

The exact name of your formatting program depends on your CP/M source. In some rare instances, there may be no initializing program; instead the accompanying documentation describes how to initialize a disk.

Every blank disk must be formatted before you can put data onto it. This is a good practice even if your diskette vendor claims to have formatted the disks for you.

Assume your initialize disk program is called FORMAT. A FORMAT program session might look like this:

```
A>FORMAT<cr>
DISK TO FORMAT? (A,B,C,D) B<cr>
PRESS RETURN TO BEGIN INITIALIZATION<cr>
DISK FORMATTED. MORE? (Y/N) N<cr>
A>
```

While the exact syntax of the messages may differ, these steps will occur:

1. Run the program (type its name, then press return).
2. Tell the program which drive contains the disk to initialize.
3. If your system runs both single and double density disks, then you must specify a density.
4. Tell the program whether you want to quit or format another disk.

The program may also direct you to remove any disk you are not formatting, to prevent accidental formatting.

The format program may or may not obey the write-protect notch on the disk. To determine this, try to format a protected disk. If the format program ignores the write-protect mechanism, then you must be extra careful not to inadvertently format a disk containing useful information.

Initializing a disk only prepares it for use. If you ask for a directory of the disk after initializing it, messages like NO FILE or NOT FOUND will appear, since files are not on it. Also, initializing a disk does not mean the disk can now start or *boot* the system; the disk does not contain the CP/M system (see SYSGEN below).

The format program moves the magnetic head of the disk drive to the first sector of the first track. Then the program writes some known dummy information and moves on. Each sector of a track is written into, then the head moves to the next track. Most programs fill the disk with the hexadecimal byte E5. You probably do not care what is done, or how, so long as the disk is properly prepared.

COPY — TRANSFERRING INFORMATION FROM ONE DISK TO ANOTHER

Suppose you want to copy an entire disk. You could use PIP as described in Chapter 3, but it is slower and will not initialize a blank disk. Instead you could use a COPY program.

Like initialization, the name of the program used to copy entire disks will vary depending on your CP/M implementation. Names vary because Digital Research included neither an initialize nor copy program with CP/M. Efficient initialize and copy programs must be written specifically for each hardware system; manufacturers and distributors generally provide custom versions of these two programs. Among the various copy program names you may encounter are:

```
COPY
DISKCOPY
COPYDISK
DSKCPY
BACKUP
COPYATOB (Copy Disk A to Disk B)
COPY1D  (Copy with one Drive)
SDCOPY
MCOPY
```

Using any of these programs is similar to using the formatting program we discussed:

```
A > DISKCOPY < cr >
SOURCE DRIVE? A < cr >
DESTINATION DRIVE? B < cr >
PRESS RETURN TO BEGIN COPYING < cr >
COPY COMPLETE.  MORE? (Y/N) N < cr >
A >
```

Again, most copy programs function similarly, but may not conform exactly to the prompts in our example. The following steps will occur:

1. Type the command to load and execute the copy program.
2. Indicate which drive contains the original disk (the one to be copied from; known as the *source*).
3. Indicate which drive contains the disk you want the copy put on (the *destination*).
4. Begin the copy by pressing carriage return.
5. When the copy is complete, indicate whether you wish to quit or do another copy.

Check the manuals you received with your CP/M to determine whether or not the copying program requires an initialized disk as the destination disk. Most do not, but a few do. If you try using the copy program with blank disks and you get a BDOS ERROR ON x: message, try initializing the disk first. Most good copy programs initialize the disk.

MOVCPM — ADJUSTING CP/M TO MEMORY CAPACITY

When you first receive your CP/M disk, it is usually ready to operate in a 16K or 24K computer. This means you only need 16 or 24 Kbytes of RAM memory to use CP/M. You will quickly find this is not enough memory to execute most programs, especially when using a higher level language like BASIC or Pascal. In this case, you need to make CP/M aware of the maximum amount of memory available in your system. If you have 48 Kbytes of memory and you receive a CP/M expecting only 16K, you will waste 32 Kbytes of memory.

The MOVCPM command summary:

MOVCPM < cr >
Prepare a new copy of CP/M which uses all of memory; give control to the new CP/M, but do not save it on disk.

MOVCPM nn < cr >
Prepare a new copy of CP/M which uses "nn" Kbytes of memory; give control to the new CP/M, but do not save it on disk.

MOVCPM * * < cr >
Prepare a new copy of CP/M, which uses all of memory; to be saved with SYSGEN or SAVE.

MOVCPM nn * < cr >
Prepare a new copy of CP/M, which uses "nn" Kbytes of

memory; to be saved with SYSGEN or SAVE.

"nn" is a two-digit integer decimal number.

"nn" can be 16 through 64 for CP/M 1.3 or 1.4.

"nn" can be 20 through 64 for CP/M 2.0 and newer

The MOVCPM command provides a simple solution. Changing CP/M to expect a different quantity of memory is called *moving* it. There are two ways you can use the MOVCPM command:

1. Move CP/M and immediately execute it, but not save it on disk, or
2. Move CP/M and save the new configuration on disk.

The first possibility is perfect for the day you borrow an extra 8 Kbytes of memory from another system to learn what you can do with more memory.

To move CP/M and immediately execute (use) it, type:

MOVCPM <cr>   makes use of all existing memory

or

MOVCPM nn <cr>   where "nn" is the decimal number of
                             Kbytes of memory you want CP/M to
                             recognize. Use this command when
                             you want to reserve some room for a
                             special program or utility above CP/M.

For example, if you want to create and execute a 48K CP/M system (i.e., one that makes use of 48 Kbytes of your available memory), type: MOVCPM 48 <cr>, or just MOVCPM <cr> if you have only 48 Kbytes of RAM memory. After a few moments, you will see a message followed by the A > prompt; you are now using the 48K CP/M system you created.

Most of the time, however, you will want a more permanent solution. To move CP/M and then save it on disk, type:

MOVCPM * * <cr>   makes use of all possible memory

or

MOVCPM nn * <cr>   where "nn" is the number of Kbytes of
                             memory you want CP/M to recognize.

The "nn" in the above examples must be:

1. A decimal number between 16 and 64 inclusive for CP/M versions 1.3 and 1.4, or
2. A decimal number between 20 and 64 inclusive for CP/M versions 2.0 and newer, and
3. Less than or equal to the number of Kbytes of memory in your computer.

Saving a new size CP/M system on disk is a little more difficult. You must perform one additional step; MOVCPM prompts you for this step by displaying:

READY FOR "SYSGEN" OR
"SAVE 32 CPMnn.COM"

This cryptic message means that, in order to save the CP/M just created, you must type SYSGEN < cr > or SAVE 32 CPMnn.COM < cr >. "nn" is the size of the new CP/M system given in the MOVCPM message above. Unless you are an experienced CP/M user or a brave soul you should immediately execute the SYSGEN program by typing SYSGEN < cr >.

MOVCPM is sometimes called CPM.

MOVCPM will not affect any files on the disk.

SYSGEN — PLACING THE CP/M SYSTEM ON A DISK

SYSGEN is short for system generation. System refers to the CP/M operating system. Placing a copy of the operating system on a disk is called *system generation*. This is the purpose of SYSGEN.

Why not copy the system just as you would copy a file? Because the system is not stored as a file. The details of this oddity are explained at the end of this SYSGEN section. For now, remember that SYSGEN copies the CP/M operating system from one disk to another.

System generation is accomplished in one of three ways:

1. By using SYSGEN alone to copy the system, without change, from one disk to another.
2. By using MOVCPM, then SYSGEN to place a new size system on a disk.
3. By using DDT, then SYSGEN to place a modified system on a disk.

Modifying the system is described in Chapter 7. Here we will first describe the use of SYSGEN alone, and then describe the use of SYSGEN with MOVCPM. SYSGEN will not affect any file on either the source or the destination disk.

When copying the system from one disk to another, your dialog with the computer will look like this:

```
A >SYSGEN < cr >
SYSGEN VER x.x
SOURCE DRIVE NAME (OR RETURN TO SKIP) A
SOURCE ON A:, THEN TYPE RETURN < cr >
FUNCTION COMPLETE
DESTINATION DRIVE NAME (OR RETURN TO REBOOT) B
```

```
DESTINATION ON B:, THEN TYPE RETURN <cr>
FUNCTION COMPLETE
DESTINATION DRIVE NAME (OR RETURN TO REBOOT) <cr>
A>
```

Let us examine each step a little more closely. First you type
SYSGEN <cr> in order to load and execute the SYSGEN program. It
requests the source location; you type the letter A. That tells SYSGEN to
get the system from the disk in drive A.

Next SYSGEN asks where to put the system; you specify drive B.
SYSGEN then tells you to put a disk in drive B (DESTINATION ON B:) and
press the carriage return when you are ready. After you press the carriage
return, the drives whirr and clack for a few moments while the system is
written onto the disk in drive B, then the process starts over
(DESTINATION DRIVE NAME...). A carriage return ends the process.

If you want to save the larger CP/M system which you created on the
disk in the A: drive, you could specify this drive instead of the B: drive.
But when you press the carriage return at the end of the program you
may discover something wrong. Usually *you must exit from SYSGEN
using the disk with which you first started the system*. With CP/M
versions 2.0 and newer you may see a message like SYSTEM ERROR or
SYNCHRONIZATION ERROR on rebooting from a different CP/M
system disk.

When saving the new size system you created with MOVCPM, your
dialog with SYSGEN differs slightly. Assume you type MOVCPM
** <cr> or MOVCPM nn * <cr>, and now MOVCPM is ready for a
SYSGEN or a SAVE. Proceed as follows:

```
READY FOR "SYSGEN" OR
"SAVE 32 CPMnn.COM"
A>SYSGEN <cr>
SYSGEN VER x.x
SOURCE DRIVE NAME (OR RETURN TO SKIP) <cr>
DESTINATION DRIVE NAME (OR RETURN TO REBOOT) B
DESTINATION ON B:, THEN TYPE RETURN <cr>
FUNCTION COMPLETE
DESTINATION DRIVE NAME (OR RETURN TO REBOOT) <cr>
```

As the example shows, SYSGEN will continue to ask for a destination
disk until you respond with a carriage return only; you can update many
disks in one session.

Why SYSGEN is Necessary

The step-by-step procedure requires further clarification.

The first two tracks, tracks 0 and 1, of every CP/M disk do not contain
files. Instead, this (normally) 6656-byte space is reserved for bootstrap
(cold start) loader and the CP/M operating system. These programs are

not stored as files, they do not appear in the file directory, nor are they accessible as files. However, it is occasionally necessary to read or write to these tracks.

Disk tracks 0 and 1 are always set aside, whether or not they contain the loader and system programs. It is not necessary to keep these programs on every disk. They are required on a disk only if you do a cold or warm start with it.

Most disk copy programs will copy the system, or lack of it, from one disk to another.

That is why a special program, SYSGEN, is needed to place a new or modified operating system on the disk. Only by using SYSGEN can you save your changed CP/M.

One last word on the subject of system generation: MOVCPM moves only the raw, bare bones of the CP/M operating system. Any additional special printer drivers or other changes you have made to the BIOS section of CP/M (see Chapter 7) will not be moved by MOVCPM. If you use MOVCPM and then the printer (or any other special device you may be using) refuses to work, you might need to re-add the special drivers for those devices. SYSGEN, on the other hand, always copies the entire operating system, including all of BIOS. In fact, SYSGEN copies all of tracks 0 and 1.

High Level Languages

As we mentioned earlier in this chapter, high level languages are one of the building blocks that program developers use. They write computer programs in a high level language for many reasons. The most frequently mentioned reasons are:

1. High level languages are easier to use since one high level instruction conveys the meaning of many machine language instructions. Programming is faster and programs are easier to understand.

2. It is easier to conceptualize the executed process when the command resembles human communication. For example, PRINT is understandable in both human and computer languages.

3. There are high level languages that have been designed for particular computerized tasks (e.g., computer control of machines, emphasis on numerical calculations, etc.).

Inclusion in or exclusion from this chapter of a particular language does not reflect an endorsement or condemnation of the software by the author or publisher. The relative merits of any given package are not to be inferred from any discussion within this chapter.

HISTORY OF HIGH LEVEL LANGUAGES FOR CP/M

Before describing the details of several popular high level languages, a brief history of the development of high level languages using CP/M is necessary.

CP/M became a quasi-standard operating system because it was one of the first operating systems available. An operating system acts as the scheduler and arbitrator of the various tasks a computer must perform. In other words, to use disk drives you must have a disk operating system, but the disk operating system is only a go-between, it is not an end in itself.

Soon after CP/M became available to the general public, Gordon Eubanks, Jr. released a high level language called EBASIC which he developed as part of his Ph.D. dissertation. (EBASIC is sometimes called BASIC-E.) EBASIC was written using another high level language called PL/M. While other languages could be used with CP/M, EBASIC became available relatively early and made good use of CP/M logical and physical device handlers (see the section on devices in Chapter 3). EBASIC was written using some government facilities, which automatically placed the software in the public domain; no copyright privileges could accrue to Eubanks, nor could EBASIC be sold for more than a "reasonable copying charge." In fact, the PL/M instructions (called *source code*) which comprise EBASIC are available from the CP/M Users' Group (see Appendix G).

EBASIC is a type of compiler BASIC. You enter BASIC language instructions using an editor, then EBASIC creates an intermediate file of instructions. But let us back up a step and describe what happens inside the computer when a program or high level language is executed.

The computer executes only machine language instructions, those ones and zeros that keep popping up throughout this book. BASIC is a computer language developed at Dartmouth to help beginners use computers; it has instructions like:

    PRINT
    GOTO
    LET
    IF

How do these instructions translate into 1's and 0's? In EBASIC, when you have entered a set of BASIC instructions with an editor, you have a file of text. We call this file the program *source code*. The source code consists of recognizable letters and numbers. Using other CP/M programs you can manipulate the source code text. For example, you can use PIP to copy the text to a device like a printer and thus create a printed copy of the text.

On a disk you will have a file named EBASIC.COM (assuming that you own a copy of EBASIC). Use that file to create an intermediate code file from the source code file. If you have a BASIC program in a file named SOURCE.BAS, type:

EBASIC SOURCE < cr >

The conversion from text to a more compact form the computer will use occurs automatically. When complete, your diskette has a file named SOURCE.INT. This new file contains no text; instead, each BASIC instruction has been compacted into a one-byte representation. For instance, a PRINT instruction from the source code file (SOURCE.BAS) is stored as hexadecimal 1A in the intermediate code file (SOURCE.INT). A number of advantages result from this compacting process (often called *compiling*, although a true compiler generates real machine instructions, not representations of high level language instructions). The most significant advantages are a reduction in the file size, and faster execution speed. It takes less time to interpret one byte, such as 1A, than it does to interpret a series of letters, as in the PRINT instruction.

To execute a program written in EBASIC, you use another portion of EBASIC called RUN.COM. This program interprets compact instructions in the file SOURCE.INT. RUN.COM is loaded into memory and begins execution, then SOURCE.INT is loaded into memory and is interpreted by RUN.COM. While it sounds confusing, EBASIC takes care of the details, while you:

1. Write (or purchase) an EBASIC program.
2. Use EBASIC to create the intermediate file.
3. Use RUN to execute the intermediate file.

EBASIC is not well suited to business software. Nevertheless, as one of the first high level languages available on CP/M, and because of the low cost, EBASIC was quickly adopted by those supplying CP/M with systems. While EBASIC is actually an extension of the standard Dartmouth BASIC, it lacks several features of a suitable business processing language.

Fortunately, Eubanks did not stop with EBASIC, but using his experience in writing and developing EBASIC he formed a small firm and developed CBASIC (and later, CBASIC2). CBASIC is an upward enhancement of EBASIC; many EBASIC programs will run using CBASIC, but not necessarily vice versa. Many program developers have used CBASIC and CBASIC2 to write programs, and you may find application programs that require CBASIC in order to run. (CBASIC, by the way, uses the same three-step process we described for EBASIC. The program used to run the CBASIC intermediate file is named CRUN.)

While EBASIC/CBASIC was developing as one primary high level language for CP/M, a New Mexico company named Microsoft began supplying another version of BASIC. Microsoft clients included MITS, Radio Shack, Apple, Texas Instruments, Exidy, Ohio Scientific and other microcomputer manufacturers. What began as a cassette-based BASIC interpreter of modest size has grown into a comprehensive, disk-based language. The primary versions of Microsoft BASIC have been:

> 8K BASIC. Usually for cassette; used in various forms by MITS, Ohio Scientific, Apple, Radio Shack, and Exidy.

> Disk BASIC. Originally developed for MITS, also modified for both Radio Shack and CP/M systems.

> Extended Disk BASIC. The current version of the interpreter; used with CP/M, 8086, and Z8000 systems.

Until 1980, all versions of Microsoft BASIC were interpreter high level languages, as opposed to compiler languages like CBASIC. Rather than using an editor to enter programs, with an interpreter BASIC you enter programs directly into the computer's memory. The interpreter BASIC has a built-in line editor; type a command to load BASIC into memory (e.g., MBASIC <cr>), and the interpreter BASIC accepts valid statements immediately. These statements are interpreted as soon as you enter them. (Actually they are interpreted once you press a carriage return.) Each line is processed when completed.

Again, a compacting scheme saves both space and time in the actual execution of a program. The statement is compacted as soon as it is entered, for immediate execution.

Unlike compilers, an interpreter language allows you to develop and test each piece of a program individually. You may at any time stop entering instructions and begin executing the partial program by typing RUN <cr>. If an instruction error is present, the line on which it occurs is identified and a message details the type of error encountered. You can immediately edit the offending line, correct the error and run the program again.

Compare this to the method of program development you must use with a compiler. You must leave BASIC, return to CP/M, invoke the editor, edit the program file, then re-compile it, all before you get another chance to run it. An interpreter performs these same tasks, but the interpreter handles most of the details for you. Microsoft BASIC became popular, even though it largely duplicated features and instructions available from EBASIC and CBASIC.

In 1980 Microsoft released a compiler version of their Extended Disk BASIC. A unique advantage of the Microsoft compiler BASIC allows you to use the interpreter for program development, then compile the final version. Many people believe Microsoft's compiler BASIC provides the fastest execution of any BASIC currently available.

Computers existed long before CP/M became available, and a number of high level languages preceded CP/M; some for specific tasks, others simply to improve on previous languages. The following languages all existed before CP/M.

ALGOL
APL
BASIC
C
COBOL
FORTH
FORTRAN
LISP
Pascal
PL/1
PL/M
RPG

Many programs written in these languages could be adapted to microcomputers, and a strong demand for CP/M-compatible versions of these languages arose.

Microsoft versions of COBOL and FORTRAN became available fairly soon after CP/M appeared. These are the two most popular high level language among programmers of the large computers. For a year or two, CP/M users could choose among EBASIC, CBASIC, Microsoft BASIC, COBOL and FORTRAN.

But just as dialects of English exist, subtle modifications of many computer languages developed and became popular. Individuals "enhanced" languages to compensate for deficiencies or to add new features.

While all high level languages create instructions that perform tasks, the approaches of each are so disparate you may not know how to compare them. We will deal with this problem in three ways:

1. By discussing reasons to choose one language over another.

2. By providing a short profile of the more popular languages.

3. By giving detailed information on how the most popular languages are used with CP/M.

HOW TO CHOOSE A LANGUAGE

The language you choose for your microcomputer must be the language of your application programs.

If you purchase an accounting system written in CIS COBOL, you must purchase CIS COBOL in order to run those accounting programs.

Therefore rule 1 in choosing a language is: *you must purchase any language required by programs you acquire from other sources.* Occasionally a program vendor provides the necessary language, but usually this is not the case.

When you choose a language, consider your level of computer expertise. If you use larger computer systems in your work (i.e., minicomputers or mainframes), it may make sense to choose a familiar language. Luckily, some of the more popular languages are "standardized." (Pascal, Forth, COBOL, and FORTRAN all have standards followed by most language developers.)

Rule 2 is: *If you are already familiar with a high level language, choose a similar one to be your first CP/M language.* Why relearn everything?

If you have read this far without obeying a rule, if you are interested in acquiring another language to satisfy your curiosity, or if you plan to expand your knowledge, you need more information. Read the next section carefully, and investigate any other available sources of information.

A SHORT DICTIONARY OF LANGUAGES

The following are capsule descriptions. Summaries tend to oversimplify and overgeneralize, so do not take them as absolutes. They do, however, provide a starting place for language comparison.

The languages we describe are the most popular languages, according to an October 1980 survey of *BYTE* magazine readers. They represent all but one of the languages which 10 percent or more of *BYTE* readers use currently, or anticipate using. The exception is ALGOL, which is not a popular microcomputer language; it is similar to Pascal and does not warrant a separate description here.

BASIC

BASIC stands for Beginner's All-purpose Symbolic Instruction Code. This language was developed by Dartmouth College in the 1960s to teach computer use and programming. Though BASIC was partially derived from FORTRAN, it has a simpler syntax; BASIC is slightly more understandable to the casual program reader.

Unfortunately, it is difficult to generalize about BASIC. There is an American National Standards Institute (ANSI) definition of the BASIC instruction set, but this standard was defined after the language had established itself as the most popular microcomputer programming language. By the time the standards were set, almost every extant version of BASIC deviated from the standards. In fact, language developers frequently add instructions from other languages to BASIC (most notably from Pascal) to overcome deficiencies.

Reduced to simplest terms, here are some advantages of BASIC:

1. It is widely available; almost every microcomputer uses a version of BASIC.

2. It is easy to learn. Hundreds of books provide introductions to programming using BASIC. Many schools use BASIC for introductory programming courses, and most computer retailers offer instruction using BASIC.

3. It is simple to understand; BASIC uses English-like words and phrases. As Radio Shack, Commodore, and Apple have shown in computer sales to grade schools, with proper instruction children can learn the commands and write programs.

4. A great number of the programs published in computer magazines are written in BASIC, providing samples of programming style and logic to the BASIC user.

5. Most BASICs are interpreters; you can type in instructions and immediately see the results. That makes BASIC an excellent learning tool.

6. There are more BASICs available than any other language (at least for CP/M systems). You will probably find one dialect which suits your style and personality.

Some of the disadvantages of BASIC are:

1. There is no standardization. While the frequently used instructions remain essentially constant in all BASICs, there are many extensions and added instructions. Extensions may please individual programmers, but they frustrate standardization.

2. BASIC programs execute slowly in comparison to other languages. Occasional compiler versions of BASIC notwithstanding, the fact that most BASICs are interpreters immediately adds an extra level of execution (the

interpretation). Even BASIC compilers generate programs that execute slowly. The structure of the language and the resulting program do not make good use of memory space.

3. You can write a very sloppy BASIC program and still have the program work. BASIC does not impart much structure on programs. Unfortunately, the slack BASIC allows in programming style encourages programming off the top of the head.

4. Standard BASIC has not kept pace with other developments in the computer industry. BASIC is over 20 years old, and computers have changed radically in that time. The versions of BASIC which do accommodate these changes inevitably suffer from not being standard.

Overall, BASIC is probably the most approachable language available to CP/M users. The number of programs written in BASIC, the number of books written about it, and its wide application all suggest you will find help, if you need it, in understanding the language.

C

Bell Laboratories developed C. It is an integral part of the Bell operating system, UNIX. Currently there are a few C's available for CP/M, and more will be developed as the language becomes more popular.

Several languages are relatively close cousins: C, ALGOL, PL/M, and Pascal. These four languages all require *structured programming techniques*. In terms of instruction execution order, structured programs are easy to trace, and are not easily written off the cuff.

C differs from its cousins in a number of ways. C often uses abbreviations or shorthand instructions where Pascal and the others use complete words and phrases. For instance, C uses the instruction:

INT X;

Pascal expands that same concept in an instruction like:

X: INTEGER;

C demands more understanding and memorization by its users, but requires less typing.

Despite being exact, C is not difficult to learn. C clearly excels over other languages in the instruction set extensions which make it capable of many tasks normally reserved for assembly language.

C also allows users to develop modules that can be used repeatedly, without reentering instructions. This can be done both internally in a program (using user-defined "procedures") or externally (using the "include" function built into C). Repetitive tasks do not require the same amount of programming effort each time they occur.

C is very transportable. Having been specified and created by Bell Laboratories, it does not suffer from innumerable versions. Your C programs are more likely to run on a larger variety of microcomputers than programs written in any other language.

Among its other advantages, C executes programs extremely quickly and creates extremely compact program code (it is, in fact, a compiler). Its features allow easy access to peripheral devices at a machine language level.

C's primary disadvantage lies in its youth. Few resources are available for learning C. C is so new to the CP/M environment that no application programs are presently commercially available in C, nor have any of the primary computer magazines presented more than a few examples of C programs.

COBOL

COBOL is an acronym for COmmon Business-Oriented Language. COBOL program statements are much like spoken English. In fact, programmers refer to COBOL statements as *sentences*, and use a number of predefined words.

A short section of COBOL program code looks like this:

```
PROCEDURE CALCULATION.
DETERMINE-COST.
    COMPUTE OUR-COST=LIST-PRICE - 10.05
    IF OUR-COST > ZERO
        SET PRICE-TO-US TO OUR-COST
        MOVE "OK" TO VALID-PRICE-CODE
    ELSE
        MOVE "NO" TO VALID-PRICE-CODE.
```

Notice how the sentences end with a period. By reading the sentences aloud, you learn what the program does. COBOL has very little unintelligible computer code built into the language.

The origin of COBOL is unique in the computer world. COBOL is a committee-designed computer language. A group named CODASYL (Conference On DAta SYstems Languages) established the COBOL language and also defined a standardized database structure for business computing. Unlike the other languages described in this book, COBOL is extremely standardized; a program written in ANSI COBOL (the standardized definition) should run on any computer utilizing the language. The United States government recognizes the standard

COBOL version, and periodically will officially recognize COBOL versions as meeting the accepted minimum standards. At present COBOL is one of the only languages the U.S. government checks to assure that a standard definition is met.

Since COBOL was developed with business applications in mind, you would expect it to be used primarily by businesses. This is true for the larger computer environment, but several factors have minimized COBOL's impact in the microcomputer world.

First, COBOL is a large language. COBOL uses full sentences to indicate the task to be performed, and it is a carefully structured language. Statements must appear in a certain order, and a number of system-specific statements must also be included. In consequence, COBOL is not well suited to microcomputers. This was especially true when memory was a relatively expensive component of microcomputer systems. With the decrease in memory prices, 48K and 64K equipped microcomputers are commonplace, and several microcomputer versions of COBOL have appeared.

COBOL is not very efficient; a microcomputer CPU consumes much time deciphering its lengthy program statements. This applies primarily to compilation rather than program execution. In addition, processing usually makes COBOL a relatively slow language compared to others. On larger computer systems, there was plenty of execution speed to spare, and tasks were often handled in a batch mode as opposed to interactive processes. Microcomputers, however, are often taxed by the number of internal manipulations COBOL makes.

COBOL was designed at a time when interactive computing was relatively unknown; it cannot efficiently utilize the console device in a CP/M system. Both Microsoft COBOL and CIS COBOL, the two most popular microcomputer versions of the language, include extra (and thus non-standard) instructions to utilize the high speed console devices featured on most available microcomputers.

FORTH

FORTH is one of the more misunderstood microcomputer languages. A relatively new language (invented in the early 1970s by Charles Moore), FORTH has been described as everything from "an assembly language-like BASIC" to "a religion."

A FORTH program is not easily deciphered. It is a *threaded* language; you use its basic building blocks to make larger ones. In fact, it is extremely difficult to describe just how to program in FORTH. Consider the following program (reprinted from *BYTE*, August 1980, page 158).

```
0 (BREAKFORTH/MMSFORTH, BY ARNOLD SHAEFFER, PART 5 OF 6)
1
2 :CLR
3 XPOS @ 2-124 AND 2+ DUP 4 + SWAP DO YPOS @ I DCLR LOOP
4 YPOS @ 27 - ABS SCORE+! 0 32 PTC SCORE ?  BOP
5 YDIR @ MINUS YDIR !
6 ;
7
8 : BALLCHK  YDIR @ YPOS+ ! XDIR @ XPOS +! XCHK YCHK PCHK
9           YPOS @.XPOS @ D? IF CLR THEN
10 ;
11
12 : BALL YPOS @ XPOS @ DCLR
13        BALLCHK DUP 0= IF YPOS @ XPOS @ DSET THEN ;
14
15 : GAMECHK SCORE @ 1800 MOD 0= IF 191 15616 320 FILL THEN;
```

Pretty intimidating, right? FORTH includes many aspects a beginner prefers not to find in a computer language. It frequently uses abbreviations; numeric manipulations are done in Reverse Polish Notation (the same as some pocket calculators); and FORTH allows the user to invent new commands. (BALLCHK is one such invention in our small sample.)

If FORTH has so many apparent disadvantages, why does it exist? First, it is fast, and well suited to applications which require quick screen or disk manipulations. Second, the machine language code created by FORTH is generally much smaller than other languages (another factor in its speed advantage). And finally, FORTH is the language you make it. The fact that the programmer can extend the language at will is a strong asset; programs can be tailored to the task.

FORTH is probably not a wise choice if you are intimidated by computers, nor is it a wise choice if you want to understand programs quickly.

FORTRAN

FORTRAN is another acronym, this time for FORmula TRANslator language. It was designed for complex numerical calculations where speed is the primary factor. FORTRAN is not good at manipulating characters like letters of the alphabet, does not handle input/output devices efficiently, and is not designed for interactive use (although this can be modified).

In many ways FORTRAN is the parent of BASIC; many BASIC statements are FORTRAN descendants. The primary differences lie in BASIC's efficient input and output to the console, and its ability to manipulate strings. In FORTRAN, the FORMAT statement, which is difficult to understand, must be used to prepare information for transfer to the console or other devices.

FORTRAN, like C and COBOL, is a true compiler. Programs are input using an editor, then reduced to machine instructions. The FORTRAN compiler most often used with microprocessors is the Microsoft version, which is a subset of FORTRAN IV. New programs are rarely written in FORTRAN; it is primarily used to run existing programs in the microcomputer environment.

Pascal

Like C and COBOL, Pascal is a structured language. Programs must follow a particular structural concept. Statements must be executed in order, and blocks of program code are identified to make the block easy to use elsewhere. The same block may used in several programs. BASIC, FORTRAN, and several other languages allow the programmer to jump program execution from one set of statements to another set in an entirely different area. Logical grouping of program statements into *subroutines* (sections of code which perform one function and then return control to the calling statement) are possible in BASIC, but not with the flexibility offered in Pascal.

Developed in Switzerland in 1968 by Nicklaus Wirth, Pascal relates directly to ALGOL. A number of extensions were designed to improve on ALGOL. A typical section of a Pascal program might look like this:

```
VAR HOUR, MINUTES, SECONDS: INTEGER;
BEGIN
  HOURS:=1;
    MINUTES:=1;
    SECONDS:=15;
    REPEAT
      WRITELN('TIME LEFT = ')
      WRITE(HOUR,':')
      WRITE(MINUTES,':')
      WRITE(SECONDS,':');
      WHILE SECONDS >=0 DO
          SECONDS:=SECONDS-1;
      END;
      IF SECONDS=-1 THEN
```

```
                    SECONDS:=59;
                    MINUTES:=MINUTES-1;
                    IF MINUTES=-1 THEN
                         MINUTES:=59;
                         HOURS:=HOURS-1;
               UNTIL (HOURS=0) AND (MINUTES=0) AND (SECONDS=0);
               WRITELN('TIME UP!');
          END.
```

Consider a Pascal program's appearance. First, it has a definite structure. The indentations are not required, but they are strongly suggested to reflect the structure of the program. Next, like COBOL, Pascal uses "sentences" whose meanings are immediately apparent. Unlike COBOL, however, Pascal has relatively few predefined statements, and the sentences formed tend to be shorter. This means Pascal programs are not quite as unwieldy as COBOL in terms of length, but remain readable.

Pascal also has an attribute known as *recursiveness*. To varying degrees, so do ALGOL, PL/I-80, FORTH and C. This means a block within the program may call itself, or pass execution back to itself. This is a useful feature for complex procedures which occur repeatedly within a program. Long division, that awful mathematical tool we all struggled with at some point in our elementary education, employs a recursive function; you apply the same concept repeatedly until you get a zero or repeating pattern. Pascal is well suited to tasks which encompass a number of repeated procedures due to its recursive nature.

Programmers like Pascal because the way they conceive of a program, and the way it works, fits directly into the structural constraints of Pascal. In fact, many programmers use a pseudo-Pascal language to describe the flow of program execution:

```
               WHILE RESULT NOT ZERO DO
                    COMPUTE NEW VALUE
                    IF NEW VALUE > OLD
                         THEN PERFORM FUNCTION X
                    ELSE
                         PERFORM FUNCTION Y
               END WHILE
```

The portion of a Pascal program that accomplishes the above logic might be:

```
               WHILE RESULT NOT 0 DO
                    FIRSTNUM:=SECONDNUM-OFFSET;
```

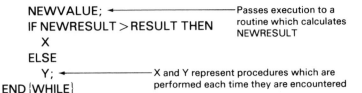

NEWVALUE; ◄─────────────────── Passes execution to a
IF NEWRESULT > RESULT THEN   routine which calculates
   X   NEWRESULT
ELSE
   Y; ◄─────────────── X and Y represent procedures which are
END {WHILE}   performed each time they are encountered

We have discussed the appearance of a Pascal program for a number
of reasons. Pascal is frequently hailed as the language of the future,
partially due to its easily understood structure. Also, Pascal is a good
beginner language because it is straightforward. If you do not try to write
Pascal programs off the top of your head, you will be able to create
working programs. Of course, learning to program any microcomputer
requires a good deal of dedicated effort and time, so seek expert
instruction (many universities offer free or inexpensive courses for
beginners in Pascal programming).

PL/I-80

With the introduction of PL/I-80 in mid-1980 by Digital Research, almost
every major programming language is now available to microcomputer
users. PL/I-80 combines the structure of Pascal and the simplicity of
Pascal and BASIC, and has the ability to perform complex operations
with various peripheral devices.

PL/I-80 and its cousin Intel PL/M are frequently described as *system
development* languages, or languages used by computer manufacturers
and systems integrators to create other software. In fact, EBASIC and a
good portion of CP/M were written in PL/M, as were several other high
level languages.

The primary difficulty with PL/I-80 and the reason it does not interest
end users lies in its wide range of statements and combinations of
instructions; it takes a long time to learn all of the specifics. Many
programmers only use a subset of PL/I-80 instructions, wasting much of
its power and superiority over other high level languages.

Other Languages

RPG (Report Program Generator) was originally developed by IBM for
non-programmers. It is less a language than a way of selecting and
outputting data from a disk file. The only readily available RPG is
marketed by Cromemco; it runs only with the CDOS operating system
(see Chapter 6). If RPG has been recommended to you, or you wish to
find an easy way to create, maintain, and select information from a data

base, consider some of the more sophisticated data management systems like Selector (from MicroAp), Pearl (from Computer Pathways Unlimited) or HDMS (from Micro Data Base).

LISP (LISt Processing) is an interpretive language developed in conjunction with artificial intelligence research at Stanford University. LISP's primary application is string processing, and it is not particularly well suited for numeric applications.

APL, believe it or not, stands for A Programming Language. Its modest name does not properly reflect the immense power this language possesses. Rather than use words to express a given programming concept, APL uses graphic characters to represent certain commands. This APL program calculates the average of a list of numbers and demonstrates APL's conciseness:

```
Vaverage
"Enter the numbers you want averaged"
NUM < - [ ]
SUM < - +/NUM
ANS < - SUM -:- pNUM
"The sum of your numbers is ";ANS
```

Note the use of symbols (V, [ ], < -) to represent a concept. One statement, such as NUM < - [ ], specifies a number of computer operations. The number typed is moved to the variable NUM for each number typed, as opposed to representing each operation with a statement. BASIC and other languages sometimes eliminate this limitation through statements which repeat the execution of another statement.

HOW TO USE SOME POPULAR
HIGH LEVEL LANGUAGES

The following pages describe how to use the more popular high level languages which are available for CP/M. The specific programs discussed are:

BASCOM	CIS COBOL
CBASIC	F80 Microsoft FORTRAN
CRUN	L80 Microsoft Linking Loader
XREF	MBASIC
C	Pascal Z

Each program is described in terms of how to use it and how it relates to overall use of the high level language. For CP/M users, this section should prove to be an invaluable condensed reference.

In general, use the summaries presented here as follows:

1. Read the description of your language.
2. Try using the information here to run your programs.
3. If you have difficulties in understanding the summaries presented here, read the appropriate sections of the manual which accompanied your language.
4. Once you are using a language frequently, the capsule descriptions may serve as your primary reference when you need a quick reminder of a command's exact syntax.

BASCOM — Microsoft BASIC Compiler, Microsoft, Inc.

BASCOM is a compiler for Microsoft Extended Disk BASIC. Using source code that runs with Extended Disk BASIC, BASCOM reduces this to machine language, speeding execution time and reducing the amount of memory needed. The BASCOM command line summary is as follows:

BASCOM < cr >
General form to initialize compiler.
BASCOM destination,listing=source/options < cr >
General form for running compiler with only one command.

The use of BASCOM can be quite complex, as you can define the types of files created by the compiler, and a number of other options. In the command example above, the following definitions pertain:

listing	BASCOM writes assembly language source code for the program being compiled into this file. The original source code file uses BASIC commands and format, and the listing file contains an interpretation of the BASIC program in assembly language.
source	This is the original BASIC program file.
destination	The file which will contain the executable machine code.

Note: you may specify different names for each of the three file types in the BASCOM command. For example, BASCOM OBJECT,LIST=SOURCE < cr > would create a compiled program file called OBJECT.REL and a listing file named LIST.PRN, both based on source code in SOURCE.BAS.

The options are the last entry in the BASCOM command line. Preface each single-letter option with a space and a slash (/); you may specify more than one option.

The options include:

/E	Indicates program contains an ON ERROR GOTO statement.
/X	Indicates program contains a RESUME or RESUME NEXT statement.
/N	Prevents listing of the generated code in symbolic notation.
/D	Turns on the debugging mode (allows TRON and TROFF statements for tracing program flow).
/Z	Tells compiler to use Z80 code wherever possible (instead of usual 8080 code).
/S	Changes how system stores long literal strings of characters.
/4	Tells compiler to use Microsoft BASIC version 4.0 or 4.5 syntax as opposed to version 5.0 (default).
/C	Relaxes line numbering constraints (lines do not have to be numbered or in order).

CBASIC — CBASIC Compiler, Compiler Systems, Inc.

CBASIC is a variation of a compiler language. A program is written with an editor (such as ED or WordStar), then compiled and run in CBASIC. The programs to compile (CBASIC) and run (CRUN) the source program are separate. We will discuss the compiler first.

After the source code of a program has been created, the CBASIC compiler program converts it into a form the computer recognizes. The CBASIC compiler command line summary is as follows:

CBAS filename < cr >
    General form.
CBASIC filename < cr >
    General form on some systems.
CBAS2 filename < cr >
    General form for version 2.
CBAS2 filename $BCDEFG < cr >
    Special form for CBASIC2: The letters following the dollar sign indicate special commands.

In order for CBASIC to compile a program correctly, the source code must be saved in a file which is named using a BAS file extension. If this file exists, invoke the compiler with the command as illustrated above.

In addition to normal compilation, you may give CBASIC some special instructions in your command line, as shown in the last command line. There are six letters following a dollar sign; these follow the file name and are separated from the file name by a space. Any one of the letters, or any combination up to all six, may be typed. Here are the meanings for each special letter command:

B
No listing of the program is to appear on your console device as the compilation occurs. If you do not type B, the listing will appear.

C
You do not wish to create an intermediate file (filename.INT) that can be executed using CRUN. Normally you do create this file, but on long programs it is sometimes wise to go through the compilation process to check for errors before saving the program in a run-time form. To create the intermediate file do *not* type C.

D
The compiler is to differentiate between upper- and lower-case letters. Normally, when D is not indicated, the compiler will treat an upper-case letter (A) and lower-case letter (a) as one and the same. Thus, when the letter "D" appears on the command line, variables named "dummy" and "DUMMY" are treated as a different variable. Note: this instruction has nothing to do with literal strings text that appears in PRINT statements, it refers only to BASIC *instructions*.

E
CBASIC prints the line number of any error it encounters during program execution. This is useful when debugging programs, but slows program execution speed and requires more memory space. Purchased programs should not require this option.

F
Provides a printed program listing. F sends a program listing to the printer even if the B option is used to suppress the listing on the console device.

G
Write a copy of the compiled program listing filename.PRN onto disk. To specify a drive other than the default drive, follow the letter G with the drive name in parentheses:

CBAS2 GOTCHA $BG(A:) < cr >

This command will suppress the console listing
and write a disk file listing of GOTCHA.PRN on
the disk in drive A.

Error Messages

CBASIC reports error messages when an error is encountered. In all but
one case, the program stops when the error is detected. Needless to say,
if you purchased a program, you should never see these messages
(unless you changed the program).

The following are file and disk errors:

NO SOURCE FILE: filename.BAS
OUT OF DISK SPACE
OUT OF DIRECTORY SPACE
DISK ERROR

You may also get program error messages:

xx ERROR
PROGRAM CONTAINS n UNMATCHED FOR STATEMENTS
INCLUDE NESTING TOO DEEP NEAR LINE n
WARNING INVALID CHARACTER IGNORED

This last message, the invalid character warning, is one error not serious
enough to stop the compilation process. Every xx ERROR is coded in the
programmer's manual and should be reported to the programmer or
supplier.

CRUN — CBASIC Execution, Compiler Systems, Inc.

Programs written in CBASIC or the later version CBASIC2 are executed
using the CRUN command. This command assumes that a program has
already been compiled (see the previous CBASIC compiler description).
The CRUN command line summary:

CRUN filename < cr >
General form.

CRUN2 filename < cr >
General form for version 2 (CBASIC2).

CRUN204 filename < cr >
General form to run revision of CBASIC2 (revision .04 in this
case).

CRUN filename TRACE line #1, line #2 < cr >
Special form used to turn on the run-time debugging function
from line #1 to line #2.

The CRUN command loads the CRUN run-time module. This set of

computer instructions interprets the program contained in filename.INT.
When the run-time module is loaded into the computer, you will see the
message:

CRUN VERSION 2.04

This message will appear several lines below the CRUN command. It may
take a few seconds for this message to appear; the run-time module is
long and requires a few moments to load.

Once the run-time module is loaded, CRUN looks for the file name you
specified. Note that you did not type the CP/M file extension in your
command. CRUN always assumes that an INT file is to be run. Again,
several seconds will pass before anything else happens, especially if the
program you specified is a long one.

Your program is executed as soon as it has been loaded. Almost all
programs hve some sort of sign-on message or greeting to let you know
execution has begun.

Error Messages

NO INTERMEDIATE FILE

You typed the file name incorrectly, you accidentally typed the
file extension (INT), or you forgot to specify a file name.

A few moments after the error message appears the CP/M
prompt (A >) returns. Verify the file really exists by displaying
the directory (see DIR command) before trying again. If the INT
file (filename.INT) for the program does not exist, check to see
if the source code (filename.BAS) does. If the source code is
there, you will need to compile the program before proceeding
(see the CBASIC compiler command).

IMPROPER INPUT — REENTER

Your entry differs from the expected input. For example, you
might have typed letters where the executing program
expected numbers. Unfortunately, this message is not terribly
precise; it could also mean that the program was expecting
several numbers, each separated by a comma, and you typed
only one number. Consult the manual for the program
involved.

xx ERROR

It is possible for a number of other error messages to be
displayed. All other error messages generated by CBASIC are
presented in this form, where xx represents a two-letter code.
Consult Appendix B in the CBASIC manual for an explanation
of the exact meanings. In almost every case, however, these
error messages indicate a program error.

CP/M error messages
Note that the usual CP/M error messages may also be
generated. These include BDOS ERROR ON x:.

XREF — CBASIC Cross Reference, Compiler Systems, Inc.

The XREF program creates an alphabetized cross reference file of all
variables in a CBASIC program. Programmers need to verify that proper
variables exist in the program and any changes to variables are
consistently made throughout the program. The XREF command is
primarily used by programmers in the program *debugging*, or error
correction stage; it is never exercised by end users. The XREF command
line summary is as follows:

XREF filename < cr >
General form.

XREF filename x: < cr >
General form creates the cross reference file on drive x.

XREF filename 'title' < cr >
General form; puts a title at the top of each page in the cross
reference listing.

XREF filename x: $ABCDE 'title' < cr >
Special form includes commands to the cross reference
program (see the discussion below).

The cross reference list is normally stored in filename.XRF. As with the
compile statement (see the CBASIC compiler command), several special
instructions may be passed to the cross reference program. Here is a brief
summary:

A   Listing also goes to printer.

B   Suppresses listing to a disk file.

C   Suppresses creation of a disk file while sending
        listing to the printer; same as AB.

D   Changes assumed width of printer to 80
        columns instead of 132 columns.

E   Suppresses line numbers; only variable names
        and usage are included.

Note that the "title," if desired, must be the last parameter in the XREF
command line.

C — BDS C, BD Software

C is a high level language designed by Bell Laboratories for use in minicomputer systems. It is a structured programming language. Several implementations of C are available. Supporters of C as a programming language generally call on its speed and structure. The C command line summary is as follows:

CC1 filename -options <cr>
General form for command parser.

CC2 filename <cr>
General form for code generator.

CLINK filename options <cr>
General form for program linker.

CLIB <cr>
General form for library loader.

The BDS C compiler consists of four distinct programs, each of which must be used to create an executable program. These are identified in the command line summary, and explained below.

1. *Parser*. The *parser* is a pseudo-compiler which takes source code and checks it for syntax errors. Assuming no errors, the parser then creates an intermediate code file (i.e., one in which keywords and commands have been condensed to a more useful form for the computer). A number of options can be specified when running the parser. Almost all of these options modify the size of the *symbol table* created.

2. *Code generator*. The code generator takes the intermediate file created by the parser and *crunches* it (creates a smaller, runnable program file). No options are specified.

3. *Linker*. Not all of the information needed to create a runnable program is created by the code generator. In addition, you must use the linker to link your program with predefined functions and definitions (ones that never change, like square roots). Also, the linker creates a COM-type file. The options of the command line must reference all files needed to created the finished product. You can include common subroutines you have written.

4. *CLIB*. CLIB contains a way to see, manipulate or combine predefined functions to be used with your system. BDS C allows you to create individualized routines. The result of CLIB is a program function library.

CIS COBOL — Micro Focus Limited

CIS COBOL is a COBOL compiler that has been adopted to run on a number of microcomputers and minicomputers. The General Services Administration (GSA) has approved CIS COBOL as meeting the standards necessary for government use.

There are a number of unique features in CIS COBOL. First, unlike most COBOL language implementations, CIS COBOL includes a sophisticated forms utility to use with CRT displays. The user may specify indexing of file records. To fully implement these features, a program called CONFIG tells CIS COBOL about the CRT display features, and to use special load parameters when initializing a program.

The forms utility consists of a program (written in COBOL) which writes and stores the ACCEPT and DISPLAY statements for a program. To be specific, the user "edits" a screen to show where information should be presented to the program user and where information may be accepted from the user, and the forms utility writes COBOL statements into a disk file for later inclusion into another program. The forms utility is run by typing one of the following statements:

    RUN -R FORM48.INT < cr >
    RUN -R FORM64.INT < cr >
    RUN -R FORMS.INT < cr >
    FORM48 < cr >
    FORM64 < cr >
    FORMS < cr >

The number of possibilities reflects the assignment of different names on different systems (FORM48, FORM64, or just FORMS), and the program may not have been compiled yet (the first three examples reflect this). The numbers 48 and 64 give the size of your CP/M system. FORM64 adds an extended help facility to FORM48. FORM64 is actually misnamed, as it will run in 54K or larger CP/M system.

In COBOL, you must compile a program before you can run it. The CIS COBOL command line summary for both these functions:

    COBOL filename < cr >
        General form to compile a source code file.

    COBOL filename parms < cr >
        General form to compile a source code file with selected
        parameters.

    RUN filename.INT < cr >
        General form to execute a compiled program.

    RUN loadparm=linkparm filename.INT < cr >
        Special form to run a program which needs to be linked to the
        run-time modules.

As indicated in the second and fourth command lines, several parameters (or directives, as Micro Focus calls them) may be used both when compiling a CIS COBOL program and when executing it. First, here are the compiler parameters:

ANS

COBOL is a standardized language. Every few years the standard is updated, but between updates COBOL creators sometimes introduce extensions that are not supported by the standard. The CIS COBOL ability to interactively accept from and display information to the CRs one such extension. If you specify the ANS parameter, CIS COBOL will allow only statements that meet the ANSI 74 standard. If ANS is not supplied, it is assumed that you want the extensions.

RESEQ

A numbered listing of your program allows you to quickly find a section of code. RESEQ tells the compiler to produce a source listing of your program that includes line numbers (in increments of 10).

NOINT

To check your COBOL program for syntax (i.e., spelling or typing mistakes) use the NOINT parameter. This requests COBOL to compile your program, but not to produce any intermediate file for later execution. You wish to verify that your program is syntactically correct, but do not wish to run it. Verifying that each subtask is correct before proceeding improves the final result.

NOLIST

Specifying NOLIST will cancel creation of a list file during compilation. Ordinarily the list file is produced.

COPYLIST

You may include the listings of included COBOL programs or modules by specifying the COPYLIST parameter. Normally listings of included programs are not in the list file.

NOHEADING

COBOL inserts form feed characters (to properly align 8-1/2 × 11 inch paper) and headings that describe the program being compiled when a list is created. You may cancel the form feeds and headings by using the NOHEADING parameter.

ERRLIST   For program debugging purposes, you may want to produce a listing of those statements that COBOL cannot recognize or understand. To do so, specify the ERRLIST parameter. The resultant list file will contain only those statements with errors, along with the appropriate error messages.

INT filename   To direct the compiled program to a file other than filename.INT, use the INT parameter:

                   COBOL ECHO.COB INT ECHOTEST.INT

                would compile the source program ECHO.COB into a file named ECHOTEST.INT. Normally the compilation would create a file named ECHO.INT to store the compiled program.

LIST filename   Direct the list file to a file other than the one specified. The command line:

                   COBOL SHIP.COB LIST TOPORT.PRN

                compiles the program SHIP.COB into a file named SHIP.COB and places the list file in TOPORT.PRN. The list file would otherwise have been named SHIP.PRN.

FORM nn   Set lines printed per page. To tell COBOL that your printer can list more than 60 lines on a page (normally there are 60 lines with 6 spaces between pages), you use the FORM parameter. The FORM parameter must be followed by an integer number "nn" greater than 5.

NOECHO   As the COBOL compiler encounters errors, error messages are displayed on the console device unless NOECHO is specified.

More than one parameter may be specified by separating each one with at least one space. Some parameters are mutually exclusive. It does not make sense to specify both LIST and NOLIST, for example.

There are also several run-time parameters that can be included in the RUN command line. If no parameters are included, the Indexed Sequential, Relative I/O, and Nucleus modules are included in the run-time module. The parameters used with RUN are:

      +D   Also include the Interactive Debugger in the

runtime module. This option takes the most
memory space.

−I   You do not wish to include the Indexed
Sequential module.

−R   You wish only the Nucleus run-time module to
be included. This option takes the least amount
of memory space. ANSI Standard COBOL
programs need only this option to operate.

The following are the file types used by CIS COBOL during
compilation:

PROGRAM.COB──── compilation ────→PROGRAM.COB (source)
(source)   PROGRAM.INT (compiled)
                                                 PROGRAM.PRN (listing file)

PROGRAM.COB────forms48/64────→DATA.DDS (descriptions)
(source)   DATA.CHK (debugging check)
                                               DATA.Sxx (screen images)

CIS COBOL uses the following files:

    COBOL.COM
    RUN.COM or RUNA.COM
    FORM48.COM, FORM64.COM or FORMS.COM
    CONFIG.COM.

F80 — Microsoft FORTRAN, Microsoft, Inc.

FORTRAN-80 (F80) is Microsoft's version of the ANSI standard
FORTRAN known by number keepers as X3.9-1966. In addition to the
standardized version of FORTRAN, Microsoft provides a number of
subroutines (primarily specialized math functions) that may be integrated
into user programs. The F80 command line summary is as follows:

F80 <cr>
    Loads FORTRAN compiler into memory.

F80 destination,listing=source /parms <cr>
    Normal form for compiling a FORTRAN program.

F80 =source <cr>
    Shorthand compilation execution.

FORTRAN-80 conforms to Microsoft's standardized compilation
scheme. The destination file stores the relocatable code, the listing file
stores the file listings, and the source file contains the original source
code program (i.e. the FORTRAN statements to be compiled).

The optional parameters are:

/O	Print all addresses in octal rather than hexadecimal.
/H	Print all addresses in hexadecimal (the default).
/N	Do not produce a listing file.
/R	Generate a relocatable machine language file even if no name is specified.
/L	Generate a listing file even if no name is specified.
/P	Provides an extra 100 bytes of stack space during compilation (should be used only if stack overflow error is received).
/M	Generate code that can be placed into ROM memory.

Once a relocatable machine code file exists, you should run L80 to create an executable program (see below).

The following files are used by FORTRAN-80:

PROGRAM.FOR ——————— compilation ——————→PROGRAM.FOR (source)
(source)   PROGRAM.REL (relocatable
                                                                                              object)
                                                                         PROGRAM.PRN (listing file)

PROGRAM.REL ——————— linking——————→PROGRAM.REL (relocatable
                                                                                      object)
                                                                 PROGRAM.COM (executable
                                                                                              object)

FORTRAN-80 uses the files F80.COM, FORLIB.REL, and L80.COM.

L80 — Microsoft Linking Loader, Microsoft, Inc.

L80, Microsoft's Linking Loader program, takes compiled code generated by Microsoft BASIC, FORTRAN, COBOL or Pascal compilers, and allows either a trial run or saving the compiled code onto disk as a CP/M command (COM) file. The L80 command line summary is as follows:

L80 < cr >
General form to initiate linker.

L80 filename,filename2 < cr >
General form to execute linker and create executable code

Like most Microsoft utilities, a number of user-defined options may be specified in the command line that loads and executes L80. The file names specified in the command line are the input and output file names, respectively. Specify options by typing a space and a / at the end of the command line, followed by single letter option indicators:

/R	Resets the linker to its initial state.
/E	Exits linker.
/G	Starts the program after loading it into memory.
/N	Saves the program on disk as a .COM file after loading.
/U	Lists the beginning and ending memory locations of program.
/M	Lists the beginning and ending memory locations of the data area.
/S	Searches the file to satisfy any undefined global parameters needed by the linker (see Microsoft manual).
/P: xxxx	Loads program into memory beginning at hexadecimal memory location xxxx.
/D: xxxx	Specifies data area begins at hexadecimal memory location xxxx.

The linker program is not easily summarized. There is a good deal of specialized information that may or may not be necessary to use it successfully. Once you have compiled a BASIC, FORTRAN, COBOL, or Pascal program (which does not use subroutines stored in other files), you use the following sequence of commands:

A > L80 filename/E,filename/N < cr >   note: filenames are same

[210C 301A 48]   message from L80
A > SAVE 48 filename.COM < cr >   note origin of "48"

This session loads the object file into memory, then exits, displaying some important information. The last number contained in the square brackets is the number of decimal pages of memory to SAVE when creating your .COM file. Once you have created a .COM-type file from your compiled program, to load and run your program you only need type:

A > filename < cr >

MBASIC — Microsoft BASIC Interpreter, Microsoft, Inc.

MBASIC loads the high level language Microsoft BASIC and also runs a program, if named. Microsoft BASIC exists in a number of versions. It was one of the first commercially available high level languages. It is still popular since Radio Shack, Apple, and Ohio Scientific all use versions of this BASIC for their computers. The MBASIC command line summary is as follows:

MBASIC < cr >
General form to load interpreter.

MBASIC filename < cr >
General form to load interpreter and run program filename.

MBASIC filename /options < cr >
General form to load interpreter, run program and change the default options (see discussion below).

MBASIC4 < cr >
Specifies version 4.0 of MBASIC.

MBASIC5 < cr >
Specifies version 5.0 of MBASIC.

Microsoft BASIC always signs on with a message identifying itself, the version number, and the amount of free memory available. Unlike some other languages, this BASIC always displays "OK" to indicate it is ready to accept a command.

To run programs automatically upon loading, specify the file name for the program to be run when you type the command line. In addition, several options may be specified. These options may be included only when Microsoft BASIC is loaded from CP/M (i.e., when the command is typed to load Microsoft BASIC). All options are identified with a slash (/) followed by the parameter. The options are:

/S:nnn   where "nnn" is the maximum size of a random disk file record. The default is the standard CP/M record length of 128 bytes.

/F:nnn   where "nnn" is the decimal number of files that can be used by BASIC at one time. The default is 3.

/M:nnn   where "nnn" is the decimal number of the highest memory location you wish MBASIC to use. This is useful in keeping a portion of memory free for subroutines or data storage.

To specify multiple options precede each with a space, and don't forget the slash. For example:

MBASIC COMPLEX /S:256 /F:4 /M:48112 < cr >

PASCAL — Pascal Z, Ithaca Intersystems

Pascal Z is a Pascal compiler optimized for Z80 microprocessors using the CP/M operating environment. Several extensions have been added to the Niklaus Wirth version.

Unlike Pascal/M, Pascal Z creates true machine language code for the Z80 processor. All options are specified within the source code (as opposed to the CP/M command line, thus Pascal Z is extremely convenient for newcomers to computers; there is only one compilation instruction to learn. The Pascal Z command line summary is as follows:

PASCAL filename < cr >
General form to compile program.

ASMEL filename < cr >
General form to assemble program.

LINK destination /parms:source /parms < cr >
General form to create an executable file.

The program PASCAL.COM loads and executes yet another program, PAS2, which actually performs the compilation. A program is compiled into assembly language source code. You must then invoke ASMEL to create a relocatable machine language file. You then use LINK to create an executable COM-type file.

The flexibility of this three-step process is enormous. First, you may combine any Pascal program or program fragment with assembly language code. Second, you may locate the resultant program anywhere within memory. Third, because the result is a true assembly language program, the execution speed is fast. The disadvantages are also great: Pascal Z suits assembly language programmers and software developers; the number of options and steps needed to create the executable program can overwhelm the user, and the extra step of assembling the compiler's output before linking it means that the process of making small changes can be extremely time-consuming.

Here is how Pascal Z uses files:

PROGRAM.PAS——compilation→ PROGRAM.PAS (source)
                           PROGRAM.SRC (assembly
                               language)
                           PROGRAM.LST (listing file)

PROGRAM.SRC——assembly →PROGRAM.SRC (assembly
                               language)
                           PROGRAM.REL (relocatable)

PROGRAM.REL———linking——→PROGRAM.REL (relocatable)
                           PROGRAM.COM (executable)

In addition, Pascal Z uses PAS2, PASCAL.COM, ASMEL.COM, LINK.COM and LIB.REL during compilation and creation of the executable code.

Application Programs

It is impossible to describe every application program compatible with CP/M. Remember, the application program is the level of programming furthest from machine language.

Most application programs are written in a high level language; most business programs available for CP/M systems are written in either CBASIC2 or MBASIC. Only a few application programs are currently available in FORTRAN, COBOL, or Pascal. Application programs written in these other languages will become available as they increase in popularity among microcomputer users.

RUNNING APPLICATION PROGRAMS

Distinguish application programs written in compiler languages from those written in interpreter languages, because this affects the way programs are supplied to users.

A program in its original form, showing instructions as typed in by the programmer, is called a *source program* or *source code*. If you know the program language, you can read the source program and understand the programmer's instructions.

If the programmer used a compiler language, most likely you will receive the program in either *intermediate* or *object code* . The original instructions were submitted to the compiler, which reduced them to a form the computer runs, but you can neither read nor understand. As described earlier in this chapter, intermediate code is a compact code that can be interpreted by a run-time module. Full word instructions which we can easily read are reduced to single-character instructions which result in faster program interpretation and execution.

The object program is in machine language. It can be run directly on the computer without additional interpretation.

Steps needed to execute a particular program depend upon whether the program is supplied in source code, intermediate code, or machine code. Table 5-1 outlines what you need to run a program.

You can change a source code program using an editor. You cannot do this with intermediate or object code, since the program consists of computer-understood instructions, and these are not easily changed. If

TABLE 5-1. Running Application Programs

Type of Language Used	Form of Program Supplied		
	Source Code	Intermediate Code	Machine Code
Interpreter	Load the source code interpreter and the source program	Load the intermediate code interpreter and the intermediate code	Not applicable
Compiler	Compile the program into intermediate code or machine code, then see boxes at right	Load run-time module and intermediate code	Run the program directly, as it is usually a COM file

you must make changes to a program, be sure the source code is available to you.

If the supplied program is in intermediate or object code, you may not need the entire language. In fact, software vendors often supply only the portions of a language needed to execute a program with intermediate or run-time code. CBASIC programs, for instance, if supplied in intermediate code, require only the CRUN module. Most Pascals also have separate compilation and run-time modules.

Many programs must be *installed* before they can be used. When you install a program you specify a number of your system's features to be added to the program (or at least stored in a data file the program checks for system information). Occasionally these installations are quite complex. The programmer installing the program must know a number of specific features of the terminal, printer and disk drives on the system. Unfortunately, there are no standards for the equipment, the information entered or the entry format. If you have problems, call either the program retailer or the software vendor who wrote the program. Improper program installation results in improper operation.

WORD PROCESSORS

One of the most useful application programs youcan purchase is a word processor or text editor. The Digital Research editor (ED.COM, described in Chapter 3) provides basic editing functions. You may need a versatile editor with CP/M for several reasons:

- To create and edit programs.
- To create and edit data files
- To perform emergency maintanence on text files
- To create and edit documents (letters, articles, documentation, etc.)
- To format documents and print them

Some questions immediately come to mind. The first may be; "Why do I need to do all that? I thought the programs I bought would take care of everything I need."

Your computer primarily creates and stores information. A typewriter does the same thing, using paper as the storage media. You would not attempt serious typing without some method of correcting your mistakes, and serious computing also requires a way to correct the information you put on disk. A good editor performs this function for you.

We will briefly describe four word processor/text editor programs which work on the CP/M operating system: Magic Wand, Electric Pencil, SCOPE, and WordStar.

Magic Wand, Small Business Applications

Magic Wand is a no-nonsense, straightforward editor suitable for word processing. Magic Wand does not sacrifice ease of use for a reduced number of features. The Magic Wand command line summary is as follows:

EDIT source destination < cr >
    General form to edit a file.
PRINT filename < cr >
    General form to print a file.

The EDIT module consists of two modes: command and edit. To edit a document, you need to learn only a few commands for cursor movement, character insertion and character deletion. The EDIT module is screen-oriented; you see the changes as they are made. A single-key command takes you from the edit mode to the command mode. In the command mode you may specify a number of other instructions to Magic Wand. Most of these additional instructions manipulate information in disk files or instruct Magic Wand to format and print the information.

The PRINT module prints the document created using Magic Wand. Depending upon the document you wish to print, this session can be automatic, or may request information from you before the printing begins.

Magic Wand can incorporate information from separate data files into a document being printed. This is especially useful for generating form letters or for adding a personalized touch to an otherwise standard document. Magic Wand can incorporate names and addresses into a letter, and can print envelopes as well as letters.

Electric Pencil, Michael Shrayer Software, Inc.

Electric Pencil was one of the first dynamic screen-oriented word processors available for the CP/M operating environment. A number of Electric Pencil versions are available. You need the version designed specifically for the memory-mapped video system in your computer. Electric Pencil will not work with serial terminals. The Electric Pencil command line summary is as follows:

PENCIL < cr >
General form.

Once Electric Pencil has been loaded, it will present a copyright message on an otherwise clear screen. You can then choose either the typing, disk, or print mode. Enter the typing mode by beginning to type. Enter the disk mode by typing Control-K. Enter the print mode by typing Control-P.

Files created by Electric Pencil are not immediately usable as program or data files under CP/M because Electric Pencil inserts carriage returns without line feeds into the text. To use Electric Pencil to create program or data files, you must purchase a program called CONVERT from Michael Shrayer, Inc. A convert program can also be obtained from the CP/M Users' Group.

SCOPE — Screen Oriented Program Editor, Vector Graphic, Inc.

SCOPE is a sophisticated program editor compatible with Vector Graphic computers. It creates source code and data files under CP/M.

Whereas the Digital Research editor was originally designed for a teletypewriter console and has been updated to include some CRT features, SCOPE makes full use of CRT console capabilities. As with most word processing systems, display of the file being edited is dynamic: you can move the cursor anywhere in the file and see it as it does the move. The next insertion or deletion will be at the point where the cursor appears.

In addition to change and insert modes, a number of other useful functions, including global search and replace, and the ability to insert disk files into the current text file, are present.

The SCOPE command line summary is as follows:

SC < cr >
　　General form to begin editing.

SC filename < cr >
　　General form to edit filename.

SC filename options < cr >
　　General form to edit filename with user-defined options (see
　　discussion below).

Three options may be specified when the command to load SCOPE
and edit a file is given. These options are:

A	Read in as much of the text file as possible (depends on the amount of memory you have) for editing.
H	Delete the HELP screen from memory (gives more room for the file being edited).
T	Substitute a TAB character in place of nine consecutive space characters when the file is saved on disk (conserves disk space).

An example of loading SCOPE with options is as follows:

SC VECTOR.GR AT < cr >

This would load SCOPE into memory, then load as much of the file called
VECTOR.GR as possible into memory, and set the TAB mode for file
storage.

WordStar, MicroPro International

WordStar is a text processing program which emulates dedicated word
processing systems. Every now and then a program comes along that is
well suited to computer novices. WordStar is one of those programs. The
WordStar command line summary is as follows:

WS < cr >
　　General form to edit or print.

WS filename.typ < cr >
　　General form to edit a document file.

INSTALL < cr >
　　General form to define the CRT and printer devices you are
　　using (only done once).

Once WordStar is loaded into the computer, you may specify the size
of the *help menu*, a constantly displayed list of command choices.

Note: Just because the program displays excellent on-screen aids is no reason to skip reading the manual.

You must give WordStar information about the operating environment before you use it the first time. Use the INSTALL command. If you have "standard" equipment, the installation process is straightforward. If your equipment is not listed as one of the predefined choices available under INSTALL, then consult your computer dealer or WordStar vendor.

This book was written using WordStar. Two features dictated choice of WordStar: the ability to see the text format on the screen exactly as it would print out, and the ability to perform the number of manipulations necessary for numerous major revisions.

6

MP/M, CP/NET, and
CP/M Derivatives

The immense popularity of CP/M has spawned a number of similar operating systems. Like Cromemco CDOS, some are direct descendants of CP/M , but are not totally compatible. Other lookalikes, TS/A and SDOS for example, retain total CP/M compatibility and claim to improve on CP/M features. Digital Research expanded CP/M capabilities with MP/M and CP/NET.

CP/M sales exceed those of all other microcomputer operating systems except Apple DOS and Radio Shack TRSDOS. CP/M is even available for both the Apple and the Radio Shack TRS-80. The popularity of CP/M has generated a growing library of CP/M-compatible software. Compared to application programs for other operating systems, CP/M-compatible software has developed largely for business applications.

You may have consciously chosen CP/M, you may not have had a choice, or you may simply have bought another operating system because you felt it offered additional useful features. In any case, learn the relationship between your operating system and CP/M to determine if your computer will run CP/M-compatible software.

The degree of compatibility between CP/M and other operating systems varies. Early versions of CDOS could not be used on an 8080-based system since CDOS included some Z80 instructions. CDOS also has several extensions. Other operating systems, like TSA/OS, correct several CP/M "faults," but otherwise retain compatibility. Some, like TPM, are not completely compatible, since they run only on certain computers.

Erroneous assumptions about the compatibility between operating systems and application programs cause problems for everyone. This chapter clarifies compatibility between selected operating systems, and discusses the features of MP/M and CP/NET which increase the appeal of CP/M.

Multi-user and Multitasking Systems

Until now, we have described computer systems which perform one task for one user at a time.

Multitasking computer systems perform a number of chores concurrently. Other names which refer to this computer setup include: multi-user, time-sharing, time-slicing, multiprogramming, and multiterminal. Unfortunately, the microcomputer industry changed some definitions that had previously referred to minicomputer and mainframe computer systems. In this text, multitasking refers to a system performing two or more jobs simultaneously.

How does a multitasking computer system work? In a normal computer system, a sequence of events occurs for each task. For example, when you strike a key on a keyboard, the following (simplified) sequence occurs:

1. You strike a key.
2. The keyboard sends the character to the computer.
3. The I/O device within the computer *captures* the character.
4. The CPU gets the character from the I/O device.
5. The CPU processes the character according to a set of instructions in memory.

While Steps 1 through 3 take place at one keyboard, the CPU could perform Step 5 (processing a character) for a second keyboard. If the CPU is waiting for the character from the first keyboard, it is idle.

Multitasking, in its simplest form, requires the CPU to perform a second job while it *waits* to continue processing for the first job. The computer appears to perform two things simultaneously, since the tasks outlined above are measured in thousandths or millionths of a second.

Were everything as simple as our description, all computer systems would be multitasking devices. We must address one problem to fully describe the concept of multiple jobs on a single computer. Quite simply put, how do you know the two tasks will not interfere with each other? How does the CPU know when to work on which task?

The answer is: computer designers cheat. In a multitasking system as we described, the designers make some assumptions and take one of two conventional approaches:

1. Each user is given a *time slice*. If the slice of CPU time is a particular length, the two users of the system are not aware of the other's presence on the computer. Nor do they notice any appreciable slowing of the system since the computer wastes time in waiting for the user to do something. Multitasking has certain advantages. For *I/O bound* systems where time is spent on input to and output from various devices — for example, a word processing system — the computer waits for keys to be depressed; this is clearly a good candidate for the time slice system.

2. The CPU can also switch jobs each time it must wait for another device. A related method processes one job until another job demands CPU attention. The differences between these two methods are fairly subtle.

   These may or may not be satisfactory methods to divide CPU time. If the CPU rarely waits for I/O in one job, the second job may not be activated for quite some time. On the other hand, if one device constantly demands attention, the other devices will be ignored.

   These methods have been inaccurately described as *polling* systems. Polling is checking to see if a device is ready. A *time slice* system may include polling. It is also possible to implement these schemes without polling.

Microcomputer multitasking systems often combine these methods. Each user has a time slice, but if the CPU must wait during that time slice, or another device demands attention, the CPU will alternate to another job before the time slice ends. This solves any problems resulting from unequal demands on the CPU from either the devices or the operator.

One way jobs demand attention from the CPU involves *interrupts*. When you strike a key, a character needs to be processed; your input must reach the CPU. A special line monitored by the CPU is triggered, and the CPU immediately switches to the routine that will fulfill that process. When this routine is done (the *interrupt task*), the CPU returns to the *interrupted* task.

A method of pseudo-multitasking involving multiple connected computers which share devices is known as *networking*. This concept involves two primary considerations:

1. The computers must be linked by a physical means (like a telephone connection or a simple cable) and a software means. The software means is the *protocol*.

2. The way computers are linked together depends on the interfacing capabilities of each computer in the network. In some instances all computers can use all devices on all other computers, while in others a *hierarchy* operates; one machine acts as a host to several others, or only certain linkages are allowed.

With this introduction to multitasking, we will now consider MP/M and CP/NET.

MP/M

The letters MP/M stand for Multi-Processing Monitor Control Program. MP/M is an operating system which can control more than one console terminal and more than one program at each terminal. Thus several users can each run several programs, all "simultaneously" on one computer.

DIFFERENCES IN USING MP/M AND CP/M

You will notice three general differences between the operation of MP/M and CP/M: the prompt is different, there are new control characters, and there are new commands. Let us examine the differences between using MP/M and CP/M:

1. The prompt. Like CP/M, MP/M displays the drive identifier of the currently logged drive (A, B, C, etc.) followed by a >, but MP/M also includes the currently logged user number (0 to 15, inclusive) before the drive identifier:

   CP/M prompt: A>   Drive A is the default
                   B>   Drive B is the default
                   C>   Drive C is the default

   MP/M prompt: 0A>   User 0 with drive A
                 7A>   User 7 with drive B
                 2C>   User 2 with drive C

   Each user number is associated with a group of files on disk. Enter the USER command to switch to another user area on the disk.

2. Extra control characters. MP/M recognizes several control characters that CP/M does not. These are:

    ^ D   *Detach* console from current job
    ^ Q   Obtain *ownership* of a printer
    ^ Z   End input from console

Control-D lets you *detach* the console from a job. This is useful when a job requires little or no input from the console or when you wish to suspend one job while starting another. You may *reattach* a job by typing ATTACH < cr > in response to the MP/M prompt.

Control-Q lets you *claim* a printer; it ensures no other task will access the printer while you use it. Type another ^ Q when you finish printing to allow other tasks to print.

Control-Z ends the input from the console device. You will rarely need ^ Z. When the console functions like a disk device ^ Z sends an *end-of-file* marker.

3. Additional Commands. MP/M has several new commands:

DIR S	Displays a system file directory
ERAQ	Enables a query mode for erasure of files
CONSOLE	Displays the console number
DSKRESET	Enables user to change disks
GENHEX	Creates a HEX file from a COM file
PRLCOM	Creates a COM file from a PRL file
GENMOD	Creates a PRL file from a special HEX file.
SPOOL	Sends printer output to spooling device
STOPSPLR	Stops spooler output
TOD	Sets or displays time and date
SCHED	Schedules a task to be run automatically
ABORT	Aborts a task, even if detached from console.

Detailed descriptions of these new commands follow in the next section.

MP/M COMMANDS

When you purchase MP/M you receive a number of programs unique to MP/M. All MP/M commands, except for the control characters, are transient commands or programs. We will briefly summarize each MP/M program.

DIR S

Type any valid DIR (directory) command followed by a space and an S to receive a directory of files which includes system files. *System* files would not otherwise appear in the directory display.

ERAQ

The ERAQ command is an extension of the CP/M ERA (erase) command. When you use ERAQ instead of ERA, MP/M asks about each file; the Q stands for *query*. For example:

```
OF>ERAQ *.* <cr>
F: IRAN      OIL?  y
F: SAUDI     OIL?  n
F: ISRAELI   PEO?  n
F: AFGHAN    REB?  n
OF>
```

In our example, we erased IRAN.OIL but not the other three files on the disk. Using the ERAQ command instead of ERA decreases accidental erasures.

CONSOLE

There can be up to 16 independent console devices in MP/M. These terminals are numbered console device number one, console device number two, etc.

The console number is distinct from the user number, and the distinction is important. One fixed console number is assigned to each terminal. The user number, on the other hand, is associated with a group of files on disk.

To see which console you are using, type CONSOLE<cr> and MP/M will reply:

Console = x

where x is your console number.

DSKRESET

Unfortunately, several users may share one or two disk drives. What if one user must change the disk in the drive to access a different disk, or to load another program? Remember, after changing disks in CP/M you must perform a warm start. With MP/M you want to perform that warm start for your job only, not for everyone else's.

DSKRESET selectively changes disks. Type the command with no other parameters to reset all disk drives on the system. Follow the command with a list of valid drive identifiers (A:, B:, etc.), each separated by a comma, to reset only the drives you specify:

DSKRESET E:,N:,D: < cr >   Resets drives E:,N:,and D:

MP/M will not allow you to reset a drive if some task is using files on that drive. When this happens, you see:

Disk reset denied, Drive x: Console y Program zzzzzz

This message informs you which console and program still have open files on that disk. If your console is specified, complete your use of the program (at least finish using the files it is addressing) and then retry DSKRESET. If your console is not listed, you must wait until the other user finishes before you can reset that disk drive, or check for another available drive.

GENHEX

This program is the opposite of LOAD; it reads a COM-type file and creates a HEX-type file to be used either by LOAD or by GENMOD. End users will not need this program.

PRLCOM

Files destined for MP/M with the extension of PRL may be changed to files usable on CP/M-based systems (i.e., COM files) by using PRLCOM. The format of this command is:

PRLCOM PRLTYPE.FIL COMTYPE.COM < cr >

This command line violates the common NEW=OLD convention of most computer commands.

GENMOD

With CP/M, LOAD changes the HEX file created by the assembler to a

COM file to be loaded and executed by typing its name. MP/M locates an individual user program at the beginning of the memory dedicated to that user, but COM files always load beginning at 0100_{16}. GENMOD converts a HEX file into a PRL file which can be loaded at some other address.

GENMOD reads a file consisting of two assembled versions of a program (each assembly with a different beginning location) and creates a file with the extension of PRL. Two assemblies are required at different beginning locations since GENMOD compares the two resulting sets of object code to ascertain where specific addresses appear in the program. Since MP/M does not assume any one beginning location for a program, it identifies portions of the program which use specific locations so they can be changed to reflect the memory area where the program is loaded.

SPOOL

Several users on a system may share a single printer. Instead of sending your information directly to the printer, with MP/M you normally send your output to a disk file, and then use SPOOL to print the file.

SPOOL maintains a *queue* of files to be printed. If User 1 asks for a file to be printed using SPOOL, and User 2 asks for some printed report moments later, SPOOL will finish printing User 1's report first, then print the information for User 2. When you invoke SPOOL, it summarizes the queue and then returns the MP/M prompt to your console. You are free for other jobs; the printer automatically prints your document according to the queue.

To get your files into the SPOOLer queue type:

SPOOL filename.typ,filename.typ,filename.typ, etc. < cr >

You may specify any number of files to add to the queue, each separated by a comma, up to the limitation of the command line length.

STOPSPLR

To stop the SPOOL function type STOPSPLR followed by your console number. If you have any files waiting to be printed, they will all be removed from the queue. This is a drastic action, and may result in a partially printed report; be sure you want to stop the printing of your files.

TOD

MP/M maintains a clock to track both date and time. Do not assume complete accuracy. First, if the computer shuts down for any time period, even a fraction of a second, MP/M restarts the clock. Second, the clock's accuracy depends on how your MP/M system was implemented. If you are using a Digital Microsystems computer, or an Intel MDS-based system, the clock will function exactly as Digital Research intended. Other implementations may or may not function properly.

To set the clock, type:

TOD mm/dd/yy hh:mm:ss < cr >

Type in the month, day, year, hours, minutes, and seconds in exactly that format. Here is a valid entry:

TOD 01/16/80 10:00:00 < cr >

This tells the computer it is the 16th day of January, 1980, and the time is 10 a.m. When you type the above command, MP/M responds:

Strike key to set time
THU 10/16/80 10:00:00

Press any key to begin the clock and return you to MP/M. Now any time you type TOD < cr >, you will see the current date and time, as MP/M maintains it. (You might keep a computer in a different time zone than its physical location if it is in constant communication with another computer or device in a different location.) Typing TOD P < cr > will continuously display the date and time until you press another key.

SCHED

A clock allows automatic scheduling of tasks. The computer could perform a task when no one else uses the system. This is especially useful for long reports that might slow the computer's response time. To do so, type:

SCHED mm/dd/yy hh:mm task < cr >

where task is a valid MP/M command line and the mm/dd/yy hh:mm is the exact date and time you wish the task to begin. You cannot specify execution of tasks in increments shorter than one minute.

ABORT

To cancel a scheduled task (one invoked using SCHED), type:

ABORT task < cr >

If you initially scheduled the task from a different console, you must add the console number, n, from which you scheduled the task:

ABORT task n < cr >

MP/M INTERNAL DETAILS

MP/M is very similar to CP/M. MP/M equipment requirements are:

1. An 8080, 8085, or Z80 CPU,
2. At least 32 Kbytes of memory,
3. At least one disk or diskette drive,
4. A keyboard for input of characters,
5. A printer or CRT for output of characters.

Consider how CP/M loads into memory (see Chapter 1). Load MP/M with a cold start loader just like CP/M. Or, use the special MP/M loader, a CP/M transient program, to load and execute MP/M. CP/M is either replaced by MP/M, or left in memory with MP/M for later use.

The internal structure of MP/M is similar to CP/M. Where CP/M had a Transient Program Area (TPA), Console Command Processor (CCP), Basic Input/Output System (BIOS), and Basic Disk Operating System (BDOS), MP/M has the following parts:

TPA	Transient Program Area
MEMSEG	Between 1 and 8 memory segments, one for each user
BNKBDOS	BaNK-switching memory management system
XDOS	eXtended Disk Operating System
BDOS	CP/M's Basic Disk Operating System
XIOS	eXtended Input/Output System
----	Miscellaneous data areas containing information about each user

See Chapter 7 for further discussion of the MP/M internal structure. Chapter 7 applies to both MP/M and CP/M. MP/M adds to the CP/M structure; it does not significantly alter CP/M. Remember, MP/M has been expanded to include more disk operations and more than one terminal. Where CP/M BIOS describes one user terminal, reader, punch, and printer, MP/M XIOS describes these devices for each user. In other words, the concept has not changed, but the operating system has been expanded to include information about all users. This is one reason why MP/M requires more memory space than CP/M.

MP/M functions slightly differently from CP/M. CP/M always loads a utility program beginning at 0100_{16} and stores it in a COM file.

MP/M retains this feature, but adds the ability to use PRL (Page ReLocatable) type files and place/execute them beginning at any interval of 0100_{16} (0100, 0200, 0300, etc.).

Suppose two users each have 48 Kbytes of memory, and each job requires only 20 Kbytes of memory. If both jobs must start at location 0100_{16} there is a major problem: each user would try to use 20 Kbytes of memory beginning at 0100_{16}, and the top 28 Kybtes would be not used.

Some programs you buy from vendors other than Digital Research come only as COM files. They must be loaded and executed beginning at 0100_{16}. Can two users use that program concurrently?

No. But fortunately there is a solution. Most MP/M computers utilize a feature called *bank selectable memory*. The 8080/8085/Z80 microprocessors can directly address only 64 Kybtes of RAM memory. The key word is *directly*. Imagine you can tell a memory section to ignore all processes until it receives a special coded signal from the CPU. Another memory section pays attention to all processes until it receives that special coded signal, then ignores the proceedings. Your imagined system is a bank selectable memory system.

With MP/M, each user usually gets one bank of memory. If you have two *banks* of 64 Kbytes of RAM memory in your system, the first user has 48K from the first bank, the second user has 48K in the second bank, and 8K is reserved for MP/M. A sample *memory map* is shown in Table 6-1. Notice the *addresses* in the middle column. Both User 1 and User 2 use the same addresses for their programs; they do not interfere with one another because MP/M uses only the currently active memory bank. You do not need to tell the system when to change memory banks; this is done automatically by MP/M.

TABLE 6-1. An MP/M Memory Map

Bank 1 64 Kbytes of RAM memory	Memory Address (Hexadecimal)	Bank 2 64 Kbytes of RAM memory
	————0000————	
Reserved for MP/M	————0100————	Reserved for MP/M
User 1 Program (TPA)		User 2 Program (TPA)
	————C000————	
Not Used		User 3 Program (Optional)
	————E000————	
MP/M		
	————FFFF————	

If your memory space begins at an address other than 0100_{16}, you must use PRL files rather than COM files. Digital Research provides their programs as .PRL files. In addition, the Digital Research MAC assembler can create PRL files from assembly language programs. You can do this with ASM, but with greater difficulty.

CP/NET

CP/NET is the Digital Research networking addition to the CP/M family of operating systems. CP/M is designed for a single user on a single computer system; MP/M is designed for multiple users on a single computer system; CP/NET is designed for multiple users on multiple computer systems.

The concept of computer *networks* differs slightly from multitasking. Multitasking tends to be hierarchical:

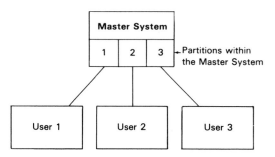

Each user is a separate entity; multitasking allows little or no interaction between users.

CP/NET operates on a different concept:

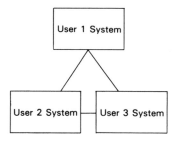

Each of the three users are represented as *systems*, not merely users. The logical *linking* between each user is more direct; there is no *master* system.

CP/NET differs slightly from the concept we illustrated. CP/NET requires at least one *node* in the network to act as a *master*. One user manages the *network*. The master node must have MP/M and disk drives. Other nodes may consist only of an 8080/8085/Z80 CPU and a minimum of 16 Kbytes of memory. While these nodes need no other components, a terminal, more memory, and disk drives will increase a node's functions. Considering these requirements for a CP/NET system, we will modify our diagram as follows:

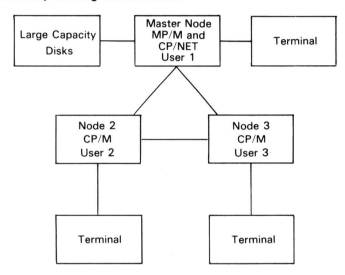

There are two primary advantages to a network system of computers: sharing of resources and speed of execution.

The primary shared resource for a microcomputer network is high capacity disk drives. Hard disk drives are expensive. It may be unreasonable to buy three hard disk drives for three computer systems. Large database applications (storage, maintenance, and use of large bodies of data) may require all users to share one common file or group of files.

Another shared resource is usually a printer. Typewriter-quality printers are both expensive and slow. There may be a typewriter-quality printer at one node, while another may have a faster but less readable dot matrix printer. Each user in this network system may send output to either printer. For rough drafts you might use the faster printer and produce final copies with the typewriter-quality printer.

Each node on a CP/NET system can function independently; each node may be a separate computer. Nodes need connect to the network only to share a resource in the network. A business might use CP/NET to consolidate several different machines into one system.

CP/NET COMMANDS

CP/NET nodes can use all MP/M or CP/M commands and programs. The exceptions are minimal; nodes cannot use commands or programs which require missing devices. For example, if the node has a CPU and memory, but no console or disk drives, it cannot accept input or display output; it must be controlled from another node. Minimal nodes are primarily used for dedicated applications: to monitor another device or monitor a building's thermostat and maintain a constant temperature.

CP/NET includes some new commands. Detailed descriptions of these new commands follow.

LOGIN

This command logs the user into the master node to use its facilities. To access a master node when more than one master node exists in the network, enter an eight-character password and the master node identification code:

LOGIN password id < cr >

Some CP/NET systems are not protected by a password. To access the network resources type only:

LOGIN < cr >

LOGOFF

To remove your node from the network type LOGOFF followed by the master node identification code, if required. Logging off the network allows you to use your system independently once again.

SNDMAIL

The network system conveys messages between nodes. To send a message to another node type:

SNDMAIL (id) "message" < cr >

where "id" is the number of the receiving node and "message" is the message text, enclosed by quotation marks. If your CP/NET system has more than one master node, you may also have to specify the master node to which you are connected.

RCVMAIL

To check your messages type RCVMAIL <cr>. CP/NET displays all messages and their origin that have been received since you last checked for messages.

BROADCST

The master node may send a message to all nodes using only one command, instead of typing individual SNDMAIL messages to each. The format is similar to the SNDMAIL command:

BROADCST "message" <cr>

The BROADCST command may be used by the master node only.

MRCVMAIL

The master node receives its mail by typing MRCVMAIL instead of RCVMAIL.

NETWORK

To enable one node to use the network devices, type the NETWORK command:

NETWORK localname=mastername id <cr>

localname identifies the local device by either the logical or physical name like LST:, A:, etc. mastername identifies the master node device by either a logical or physical device name, and id is the master node number.

To use the master node's second disk drive as your primary local drive type:

NETWORK A:=B: id <cr>

LOCAL

After using the NETWORK command, some devices on your system are replaced by the master node's devices. To reassign the devices to your local configuration, type:

LOCAL localname <cr>

This returns the device localname to its normal configuration. LOCAL A: <cr> returns the designation of device A: to your node's normal definition: a local disk drive.

DSKRESET

The DSKRESET command operates exactly like the MP/M DSKRESET command.

SPOOL

All users may use the master node spooler to print in an organized fashion. Check the SPOOL command in the section on MP/M commands.

ENDLIST

The ENDLIST command sends a Control-Z to the list device to terminate list output to the network.

Operating Systems Similar to CP/M

Many software creators have tried to improve CP/M control over the computing process. Most of these attempts have been based upon CP/M version 1.4.

A number of other manufacturers provide CP/M-compatible operating systems. Some, like ADDS (Applied Digital Data Systems), have written their own operating system to function like CP/M. Others have simply licensed CP/M from Digital Research and added a few features that reflect specific abilities of their equipment.

Figure 6-1 summarizes how the major operating systems that are similar to CP/M were developed. Several other operating systems might fit into this outline. Subtle changes in an operating system (CP/M 1.41 versus 1.42, for instance) are not reflected in this illustration; only major changes are shown.

CROMEMCO CDOS

Cromemco was one of the first microcomputer manufacturers. Its first products were not microcomputers, but components used with IMSAI and Altair microcomputers. Rapid growth and careful attention to the order of new product development allowed Cromemco to introduce a complete system.

Cromemco's first disk-based system was the Z-2 computer. This

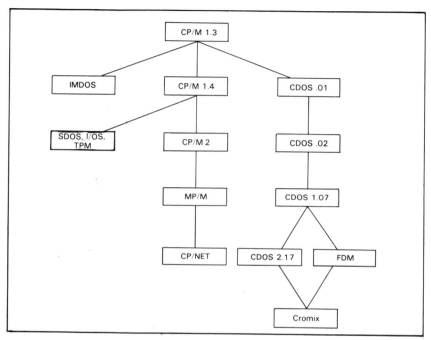

FIGURE 6-1. The Evolution of CP/M-like Operating Systems

system was housed in a rugged industrial-grade cabinet and included two
built-in diskette drives. Later, Cromemco designed System 3, a computer
for the business environment. Both computer systems were introduced
with an operating system named Cromemco Disk Operating System
(CDOS).

Originally, CDOS was little more than a rewrite of CP/M; it took
advantage of the enhanced abilities of the Z80 microprocessor. CDOS,
however, continuously evolved, with more subtle refinements than CP/M.
Cromemco has been able to update CDOS because they have full control
over the design of the computer systems that utilize it. CDOS functions
only with the Cromemco disk controller and a Z80 CPU. Digital Research
has no control over the microcomputers that utilize CP/M, necessitating
fewer changes.

CDOS Compatibility with CP/M

Cromemco includes this notice regarding CDOS compatibility with CP/M
with each copy:

> The Cromemco Disk Operating System (CDOS) is an original
> product designed and written in Z80 machine code by

Cromemco, Inc. for its own line of microcomputers. However, due to the large number of programs currently available to run under the CP/M operating system, CDOS was designed to be upwards CP/M-compatible. Cromemco is licensed by Digital Research, the originator of CP/M, for use of the CP/M data structures and user interface. This means that most programs written for CP/M (versions up to and including 1.33) will run without modification under CDOS. This also means that programs written for CDOS will not generally run under CP/M.*

CDOS evolved from the first commercially available version of CP/M, version 1.3; it does not include features Digital Research added in later versions. This is only a minor inconvenience if you use CDOS and try to run programs written for CP/M version 1.4; the differences between CP/M 1.3 and 1.4 are not as extreme as those between 1.4 and 2.0.

A program written using features of CP/M 2.0 or later will most likely not run on a CDOS-equipped computer. However, most programs written for CP/M 2.0 do not necessarily use the added features. A program developed to run with EBASIC works equally well with CP/M version 1.4 or 2.0, and retains compatibility with CDOS. Versions of Microsoft BASIC and CBASIC2 probably will not work correctly on your CDOS-equipped computer. Some versions of each of these BASICs may appear to execute correctly using some versions of CDOS, but may not be maintaining the disk files exactly as CP/M requires.

Do not believe that a program written for CP/M will run correctly on your CDOS system just because you can load and execute it. To guarantee everything works correctly, you may:

1. Test the programs thoroughly, or
2. Buy a CP/M operating system for your Cromemco machine.

The preferred choice is the second one. Remember Cromemco's advice on CDOS-CP/M compatibility: the CDOS file structure is the same, but some of the system functions are not. Use a CP/M operating system on your Cromemco machine to execute a CP/M program. This is more reliable and economical than modifying CP/M programs to fit CDOS.

CDOS Commands and Utilities

CDOS commands look like CP/M commands:

BYE	Returns to the Cromemco System Monitor
DIR	Displays a diskette file directory
ERA	Erases a file or files from a diskette

---

* From *Cromemco Users Bulletin*, Issue #1, December 1978.

REN	Renames a file
SAVE	Saves a portion of memory in a diskette file
TYPE	Displays an ASCII file on the console device

Cromemco includes these utility programs:

BATCH	Submits a list of commands for execution
DUMP	Displays hexadecimal representations of a disk file's contents
EDIT	A simple character-oriented editor
INIT	Initializes (formats and prepares) a diskette
WRTSYS	Copies CDOS from one disk to another
XFER	Transfers files from disk to disk; transfers to and from devices, like CP/M's PIP utility
STAT	Displays statistics on the diskettes

These are the minimum commands and utilities supplied. New versions of CDOS (i.e., 1.07 and 2.17) include other utilities and enhance other commands and utilities. Early versions of the STAT program, for example, display the amount of disk space left, the number of directory entries, the names of any *null* files, and an error message for diskette problems. The latest versions of CDOS include a STAT program which displays all of the above plus specific information on disk status, usage, and device assignments. To detail the differences between each version of CDOS and explain how all of the commands work requires another book.

Some versions of CDOS include several other utility programs:

CDOSGEN	Creates a different sized operating system like MOVCPM
DEBUG	Tests assembly language programs; a debugging tool like DDT
LINK	A linker program which takes compiled program code from Cromemco FORTRAN, COBOL, or assembler and creates an executable file (i.e., a COM file)
SCREEN	A sophisticated editor (works only with Cromemco terminals) used for program development and/or minimal word processing tasks
MEMTEST	Tests Cromemco RAM memory and reports errors; provides easy location and repair of defective components; used primarily to assure that the system is running correctly.

CDOS Relatives

Cromemco has spawned two derivatives of CDOS. The first is not so much a unique operating system as it is an extension of CDOS. This relative is a multi-user system based on Cromemco Multi-User BASIC. Cromemco has also developed an operating system similar to some popular minicomputer operating systems, called Cromix.

The Multi-User BASIC system allows seven users to independently and simultaneously run BASIC programs. Alternatively, one user can run up to seven independent programs simultaneously. Almost complete compatibility exists between Multi-User BASIC and CDOS-developed programs and disk files.

Cromix operates in a completely different user environment. First, a single-user Cromix system requires twice as much memory (64 Kbytes for the operating system plus 64 Kbytes for the user) as does CDOS (16 Kbytes for the operating system plus 48 Kbytes for the user). Cromix allows:

- File names up to 24 characters long
- Files which are directories of other files. This is known as a *tree-structured directory* ; if you were to sketch a complex file system, your structure would look like an upside-down tree
- Twelve commands, as opposed to six for CDOS
- Over 35 utility programs
- *Privilege* levels, i.e., protection of files from unauthorized users
- Multiple tasks and multiple users
- Date and time support

Cromix is not directly compatible with CDOS; Cromix maintains information on the disk in a different fashion (a 24-character file name would not fit into a CP/M directory). Cromemco provides utility programs to convert CDOS files to Cromix files and vice versa. Thus, programs developed with CDOS can still be used. Consider Cromix and CP/M as totally different operating systems with no compatibility. To run a CP/M-compatible program with Cromix requires a multi-step conversion process, with no guarantee of success. Converting Cromix files and programs back to CP/M-compatible ones is theoretically possible, but so fraught with complications that a non-programmer should not attempt it.

For a Cromemco user, Cromix and Multi-User BASIC are worth considering, as each has specific abilities that transcend the abilities of both CDOS and CP/M. For a CP/M user, neither offers any improvements that can easily be transferred to the CP/M environment.

SDOS

SDOS is the SD Systems version of CP/M. A number of changes are readily apparent:

1. The system prompt is changed from A > to [A].
2. Several additional commands are provided:
   GET loads a HEX file into memory.
   MON returns to the computer system monitor.
   SET assigns output to either console or printer.
   ATTRIB changes file attributes.
3. Several additional utility programs are included:
   B1-SIDED assumes one-sided diskettes.
   B2-SIDED assumes double-sided diskettes.
   DCOPY copies a diskette.
   DSKDIAG performs simple disk diagnostics (tests).
   DSKDUMP displays and modifies any part of a diskette.
   ERASE conditionally erases files (i.e., it asks you
      about each file).
   FORMAT formats a diskette (initializes it).
   LINK concatenates files.
   ZASM is a Z80 assembler.
4. Some additional BDOS functions are provided.

For the most part, SDOS is an improved CP/M version 1.4. The current version is not compatible with programs which utilize CP/M 2.2 BDOS or MP/M.

I/OS

TSA/OS also attempts to improve upon CP/M version 1.4.

TPM

TPM is a Z80 version of CP/M. It will not run on 8080-based computers, nor will it run on 8085-based computers. Primarily TPM increases speed with the more powerful Z80 instruction set.

CP/M FOR HEATH, ZENITH, POLYMORPHIC, AND
RADIO SHACK COMPUTERS

Two versions of CP/M are sold specifically for Heathkit and TRS-80

Model I and III computers. While the CP/M operates exactly the same, its memory location has been moved to reflect design differences in Heathkit and Tandy computer systems. This relocation of CP/M requires modification of many programs. Make sure a program version is suitable for your machine if you use any of the following computers with CP/M:

- Poly 88
- Polymorphic 8813
- Radio Shack TRS-80 Model I
- Radio Shack TRS-80 Model III
- Heathkit H8
- Heathkit H89
- Zenith Z89

7
Technical Aspects of CP/M

This chapter is not for everyone. An occasional end user may benefit from reading this description of the internal structure of CP/M; it does explain a few idiosyncracies of CP/M. Other readers will find this material extremely boring, since it covers the more technical aspects of CP/M. In previous chapters we presented information you must know to use CP/M. This chapter presents information the assembly language programmer must know to program effectively in the CP/M environment.

If you bogged down reading about assembly language in Chapter 4, then skip this chapter. If you are extremely curious or find computers fascinating, by all means read on.

The Structure of CP/M

When you *cold start* CP/M in your computer, CP/M itself is loaded at the topmost free memory block, which is generally 7168 bytes (7 Kbytes) long. Also, two jump instructions are placed at the bottom of your memory area. The first is placed at memory location 0000_{16} and is called the *Warm Start Vector*. The second is located at 0005_{16} and is called the *FDOS Entry Vector*. You may use all memory between 0100_{16} and the bottom of CP/M as identified by the address in the FDOS Entry Vector. After booting, your computer memory contains the following:

Memory Location (Hexadecimal)	Memory Contents (Hexadecimal)	Function
0000	C3	Warm Start Vector
0001	03	
0002	xx	
0003	00	IOBYTE (usually)
0004	00	Currently Logged Disk Drive
0005	C3	FDOS Entry Vector
0006	06	
0007	yy	
0008-005B		Interrupt, scratch, and reserved areas
005C-007C		Default File Control Block
007D-007F		Default Random Record Position (CP/M 2.0)
0080-00FF		Default Disk Buffer
0100-(yy0D-1)		Transient Program Area (TPA) where programs are loaded and executed
yy00-zzFF		CP/M Operating System (consists of several sections: CCP, BDOS, and BIOS)

Note: xx, yy, and zz are used as substitutes here for actual hexadecimal memory addresses, which vary depending upon the size of your CP/M system.

Another way to depict the memory structure of CP/M follows:

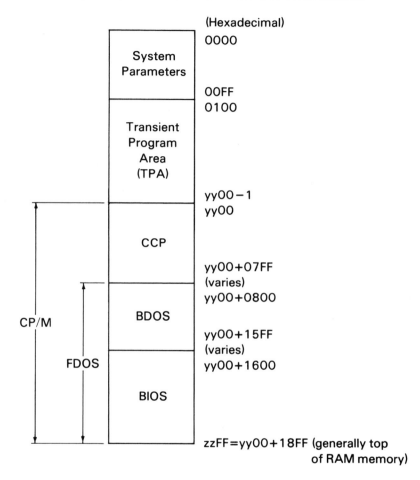

This simplified representation of the CP/M structure is not drawn to scale; the Transient Program Area (TPA) is by far the largest section of memory (about 58 Kbytes of memory in a 64K CP/M system). The CP/M area consists of three primary divisions: CCP, BDOS and BIOS.

CCP — THE CONSOLE COMMAND PROCESSOR

The CCP module interprets the CP/M commands you type. This portion of CP/M is generally only relevant when you see an A > (or the prompt for another drive) on your terminal. The CCP recognizes six or seven

CP/M commands; it also recognizes several *special* characters, the sub-commands (see Chapter 2).

When the CCP does not recognize your command, it checks the disk directory for a COM-type file whose name matches the first eight characters (or up to the first space in the command line). The "matched" program is loaded into memory and execution is passed to that program. Digital Research calls this a *transient command*.

BDOS — THE BASIC DISK OPERATING SYSTEM

All disk drive activity passes through this section of CP/M. BDOS is not accessible through direct commands at the console. Instead, the CCP or Transient program places the number of the desired function in Register C (a storage area in the CPU) and then executes a CALL to location 0005_{16}.

Among others, BDOS contains the following disk functions:

- Disk system reset
- Drive selection
- File creation
- File opening
- File closing
- Directory search
- File delete
- File rename
- Random or sequential read from file
- Random or sequential write to file
- Interrogate available disks
- Interrogate selected disk
- Set DMA address
- Set/reset file indicators

In addition, some BDOS routines perform logical console, reader, punch, and list input and output functions.

If a function requires several parameters, they are usually passed to it using register pair DE. Some functions return information to the calling program upon completion. Information "returns" through the internal registers of the CPU. The Digital Research manuals *CP/M Interface Guide* and *CP/M 2.0 Interface Guide* provided with CP/M outline the exact functions included with your CP/M. An example of BDOS functions appears later in this chapter.

BIOS — THE BASIC INPUT/OUTPUT SYSTEM

A great deal of confusion about CP/M originates with BIOS. Many people purchase CP/M and discover that the BIOS section (and possibly the BDOS section as well) is not configured properly for their particular machine. Configuring CP/M is fairly straightforward for software developers and computer dealers but can be frustrating for the computer novice. Like the BDOS, the BIOS provides several routines that may be called by other software. The BIOS is provided by the dealer or software vendor, not by Digital Reseach. The BIOS functions you need include:

- Read a character from the console device
- Write a character to the console device
- Read a character from the reader device
- Write a character to the punch device
- Write a character to the list (printer) device
- Get or set I/O status
- Write a string to the console device
- Read a string from the console device
- Interrogate the console for ready status

We can now begin to understand what CP/M does when it is first loaded into memory, and how it functions during operation.

The Cold Start Process

When you first *boot* the system, the disk controller moves the *cold start loader* into memory. The loader is then executed. It loads CP/M into memory and moves it to its proper location at the top of your RAM memory, as you specified when you used MOVCPM to create your CP/M image.

Once CP/M loads into memory, execution passes to the first routine in the BIOS section of CP/M: the *Cold Start* or *Cold Boot* routine. The Cold Start routine initializes (puts beginning information into) all memory locations used by your devices when operating with CP/M, and displays a sign-on message to verify CP/M has been loaded.

On completion, the Cold Start routine returns control to the CCP (Console Command Processor). The CCP sets up a few initial memory locations it must track, displays the system prompt A >, and waits for your command. The CCP collects characters in the command buffer until you press the carriage return; then it processes them.

Programs that have been translated into COM-type files function like the CCP: they capture characters, then use selected portions of BDOS (depending upon the characters received) to perform the requested task. This is not always true, however. Some programmers take shortcuts or otherwise modify the standard CCP and BDOS processes. Microsoft BASIC and some word processing software detect errors and take over control so that CP/M cannot issue a BDOS ERR ON x: message. Other programs do not use BDOS to provide console input and output but use BIOS routines at their assumed locations. This rules out the use of XSUB and possibly SUBMIT.

How to Use the BDOS Functions in Assembly Language Programs

BDOS can perform 37 functions (assuming CP/M version 2.0 or newer). Table 7-1 summarizes these functions.

To use any BDOS function, a program simply loads the function number into Register C, loads other registers as required, and calls BDOS. BDOS performs the function and returns control to the calling program.

We will demonstrate this by displaying a string on the console. Table 7-1 lists 9 as the function number for "Print String." The DE register pair must contain the address of the string, and the string must be terminated by a $ in order to function properly. To display a string:

1. The program places the string somewhere in memory, terminated with a $.
2. The program places 09 in Register C.
3. The program places the address of the string in register pair DE.
4. The program calls BDOS.
5. BDOS displays the string on the screen and returns execution to the program.

One way to perform these steps in assembly language follows:

```
BDOS        EQU        0005H          ; the location of BDOS
STRING      EQU        09H            ; the Print String function number
LABEL:  DB  'DOCTOR, MY PROBLEM IS $' ; the string itself
MVI         C,STRING                  ; put Print String function # in C
LXI         D,LABEL                   ; put address of string in DE
CALL        BDOS                      ; do it!
```

Most experienced programmers use equates (EQU directives) to

TABLE 7-1. BDOS Functions for CP/M 2.0

Function Number (Decimal)	Function Name	Input Parameters	Output Parameters
0	System Reset	None	None
1	Console Input	None	A=ASCII character
2	Console Output	E=ASCII character	None
3	Reader Input	None	A=ASCII character
4	Punch Output	E=ASCII character	None
5	List Output	E=ASCII character	None
6	Direct Console I/O	E=FF$_{16}$	A=ASCII character or A=00
6	Direct Console I/O	E=ASCII character	None
7	Get I/O Byte	None	A=IOBYTE
8	Set I/O Byte	E=IOBYTE	None
9	Print String	DE=String Address	None
10	Read Console Buffer	DE=Buffer Address	(Data in buffer)
11	Get Console Status	None	A=00 or A=FF$_{16}$
12	Return Version Number	None	HL=BA=Version Number
13	Reset Disk System	None	(Several)
14	Select Disk	E=Disk Number	None
15	Open File	DE=FCB Address	A=Directory Code
16	Close File	DE=FCB Address	A=Directory Code
17	Search for First	DE=FCB Address	A=Directory Code
18	Search for Next	None	A=Directory Code
19	Delete File	DE=FCB Address	A=Directory Code
20	Read Sequential	DE=FCB Address	A=Error Code
21	Write Sequential	DE=FCB Address	A=Error Code
22	Make File	DE=FCB Address	A=Directory Code
23	Rename File	DE=FCB Address	A=Directory Code
24	Return Login Vector	None	HL=BA=Disk Login Bits
25	Return Current Disk	None	HL=Current Disk Number
26	Set DMA Address	DE=DMA Address	None
27	Get Addr (Alloc)	None	HL=Allocation Vector Address
28	Write Protect Disk	None	None
29	Get R/O Vector	None	HL=Disk R/O Bits
30	Set File Attributes	DE=FCB Address	A=Directory Code
31	Get Disk Parm. Block Addr.	None	HL=DPB Address
32	Set/Get User Code	E=FF$_{16}$	A=Current User Number
32	Set/Get User Code	E=User Code	None
33	Read Random	DE=FCB Address	A=Error Code
34	Write Random	DE=FCB Address	A=Error Code
35	Compute File Size	DE=FCB Address	(Random Record Field)
36	Set Random Record	DE=FCB Address	(Random Record Field)

Source material used with permission of copyright owner, Digital Research, Inc., Pacific Grove, CA. Modified by author.

assign values to the functions they are going to use and to the location of
BDOS. This practice makes the program easier to understand. A novice
might perform the same assembly language program like this:

```
ORG       0100H
DB        'DOCTOR, MY PROBLEM IS $'
MVI       C,9
LXI       D,0100h
CALL      5
```

While this is functionally accurate, it is unnecessarily vague.

The BIOS

BIOS stands for Basic Input Output System. Digital Research provides a
sample BIOS with CP/M, but someone must tailor the BIOS to the
particular equipment it is run on. Sometimes a distributor or dealer
performs this service for a prepackaged and complete computer system.
Sometimes, however, the end user is left to configure CP/M: to tell CP/M
how to manipulate the various devices attached to the system.

If you do NOT know assembly language, or if you do NOT have a
working computer system, or if you are a newcomer to microcomputers,
then *do NOT try to write a BIOS section for CP/M!!!*

The BIOS section performs crucial functions for CP/M. It tells CP/M
how to access the various devices, and most important, how to move the
head of the disk drive from place to place. Any problems in the BIOS
section of CP/M are your responsibility. They can cause CP/M to function
improperly or not at all.

BIOS begins with a series of *jump instructions* arranged in a particular
order. An example of the first instructions in your BIOS routine follows
(we use extra-long *labels* for clarity):

```
ORG       BIOSBEGIN          ; the beginning of BIOS
JMP       COLDSTART          ; COLD START routine
JMP       WARMSTART          ; WARM START routine
JMP       CONSOLESTATUS      ; GET CONSOLE STATUS routine
JMP       CONSOLEINPUT       ; CONSOLE INPUT routine
JMP       CONSOLEOUTPUT      ; CONSOLE OUTPUT routine
JMP       LISTOUT            ; PRINTER OUTPUT routine
JMP       PUNCH              ; PUNCH OUTPUT routine
JMP       READER             ; READER INPUT routine
JMP       HOME               ; HOME HEAD OF DISK routine
JMP       SELDISK            ; SELECT DISK routine
JMP       SETTRACK           ; SET TRACK routine
JMP       SETSECTOR          ; SET SECTOR routine
JMP       SETDMA             ; SET DMA ADDRESS routine
```

```
JMP        READ               ; READ DISK SECTOR routine
JMP        WRITE              ; WRITE DISK SECTOR routine

;VERSIONS 2.0 AND LATER ALSO NEED:

JMP        LISTSTATUS         ; GET PRINTER STATUS routine
JMP        SECTRANSLATE       ; SECTOR TRANSLATION routine
```

Each of these instructions jumps to a routine included in your BIOS. An example of a BIOS routine for output to a printer (which the BIOS finds with JMP LISTOUT) follows:

LIST OUTPUT ROUTINE

This routine provides output to the CP/M LST: device
through a Vector Graphic Bitstreamer II I/O board
at Port 2. The following is assumed:

-Bitstreamer is initialized in Cold Start Routine
-Character to be printed is in Register C
-Bitstreamer is addressed at Port 2
-The printer is plugged into the third serial port
  on the Bitstreamer board
-LISTST has been EQUed to status port
-LISTDATA has been EQUed to data port

```
LISTOUT:
IN         LISTST             ;get the current printer status
ANI        1                  ;check to see if printer ready
JNZ        LISTOUT            ;if not ready, keep trying

    printer is ready, now send character:

MOV        A,C                ;get character into accumulator
OUT        LISTDATA           ;send it
RET
```

Each routine within the BIOS concludes with a *RET* (return from subroutine) instruction. Our sample routine consists of only six instructions; the comments explain the operation of the routine.

HOW TO MODIFY BIOS

Most CP/M suppliers provide a sample BIOS with the original diskette. Digital Research provides both a *skeletal* BIOS (just the bones and a number of comments; the routines do not include specific instructions) and a completed one for the system they use. Many microcomputer manufacturers remove these two sample BIOSs and include their own CP/M. Some "hide" the BIOS from the end user and supply only the routines that may need changing (the printer, punch, and reader routines). To create a new or modified BIOS perform the following steps.

1. On a freshly initialized/formatted diskette, copy the sample BIOS, an editor program, ASM.COM, DDT.COM, and any SYSGEN/MOVCPM utilities. Use SYSGEN to copy an unmodified CP/M system onto the diskette.

2. Print a copy of the sample BIOS (if you can; you may be changing the BIOS to include routines for a printer). Study the copy carefully. Become familiar with its structure, the individual routines required, and the comments included in the sample.

3. Invoke your editor and edit the sample BIOS. Begin by inserting a comment to indicate the date, your name, the reason you are changing the BIOS, and any other identification to trace problems later.

4. Minor additions or changes should not prove too difficult, assuming you understand assembly language and the device you wish to manipulate. An example of a simple modification follows. Examine a portion of a sample BIOS before modification:

```
SIGNON:         DB              14h,0Dh,0Ah
                DB              'CP/M version 2.2',0Dh,0Ah,'$'
                LXI             H,SIGNON
MOVEIT:         MOV             A,M
                CPI             '$'
                RZ
                MOV             C,A
                CALL            CONOUT
                INX             H
                JMP             MOVEIT
```

This routine displays the CP/M sign-on message and initializes the terminal screen with the 14h that starts the message. But the terminal requires a 04h to be initialized (cleared), and this change is to be identified by a special sign-on message:

```
SIGNON:         DB              04h,0Dh,0Ah
                DB              'Thom Hogan's Vectrola 1.1',0Dh,0Ah
                DB              '----------------------------',0Dh,0Ah
                DB              0Dh,0Ah
                DB              'CP/M 2.2 — 10/17/80 last update',0Dh,0Ah
                DB              'no printer installed',0Dh,0Ah,0Ah,0Ah
                DB              '$'
```

The first version of the BIOS signs on:

```
[clear screen]
CP/M version 2.2
A>
```

The new version displays:

```
[clear screen]
Thom Hogan's Vectrola 1.1
----------------------------

CP/M 2.2 — 10/17/80 last update
no printer installed

A>
```

In this example we have not changed anything important. Notice the DB '$' line remains so CP/M will know the end of the message. Basically there are three types of changes to make to the BIOS:

- Inserting new material
- Deleting old material
- Changing existing material

When you insert information into BIOS, previously entered information remains unchanged. You can easily backtrack your steps and restore the BIOS to its original form. We suggest you identify where you have inserted new material to locate it later. A line of hyphens (i.e., ---------) can separate individual routines. Equals signs can delineate instructions added later (i.e., ==================). A section of the BIOS might look like this:

```
------------------------------------------------------------------------------
MODEM ROUTINES — substitute for PUNCH/READER

MODEM           EQU         TRUE        ;yes, I have a modem today
DCH             EQU         FALSE       ;no, I don't have a DCHayes
                                        yet

MODEMCTL        EQU         03h         ;modem control port
MODEMSBIT       EQU         80h         ;modem send control bit
MODEMRBIT       EQU         40h         ;modem receive control bit
MODEMDATA       EQU         02h         ;modem data port


==================================================
10/17/80 Oh my gosh! I got a D.C.Hayes board
         for my birthday. Here are the EQUs I think I
         need to substitute for my modem ones above:
IF                          DCH
MODEMCTL        EQU         82h         ;D.C. Hayes control port
MODEMSBIT       EQU         2           ;modem send control bit
MODEMRBIT       EQU         1           ;modem receive control bit
MODEMDATA       EQU         80h         ;modem data port
MODEMCTL2       EQU         81h         ;second control port needed
  ENDIF

==================================================
LXI                         H,0
DAD                         SP
SHLD                        STACK
etc.
```

The routines for the D.C. Hayes and Associates Micromodem 100 are not yet implemented, but you can see how to identify the inserted section.

When you delete a section from an existing BIOS, do not erase it; make it a comment instead. Insert semi-colons in front of each line you wish to make inoperative. Add a note to explain the deletion.

```
RCVSOH        MVI      B,1           ;TIMEOUT = 1 SEC
              CALL     RECV          ;GET SECTOR
              JC       RCVSTOT       ;GOT TIMEOUT
              MOV      D,A           ;D=BLOCK NUMBER
              MVI      B,1           ;TIMEOUT = 1 SEC
              CALL     RECV          ;GET CMA'D SECT #
NEXT JUMP CANCELLED 10/1/80 TO DISABLE TIMEOUT
              JC       RCVSTOT       ;GOT TIMEOUT
              CMA                    ;CALCULATE COMPLEMENT
              CMP                    ;GOOD SECTOR #?
              JZ       RCVDATA       ;YES, GET DATA*
```

By making the *deleted* statement a comment, you can easily restore the file to its original form; just remove the semicolon.

Changing an area of the BIOS is more difficult; it is not as easy to document changes. To trace changes, make the original line a comment, and insert the new line below it. Unfortunately, with many changes the results are difficult to read. Be sure you always have a copy of the original BIOS; name it BIOS.OLD or BIOS1.1 to indicate it is not a current version. Each time you edit the BIOS, save a copy of the previous version, and date all versions.

5. Before leaving the editor, return to the beginning of the BIOS file and examine the ORG (origin) directive and any labels named BIOS, BIAS, or OFFSET. Instructions to the assembler on where to start assembling the BIOS differ among programmers. Usually the BIOS is either origined absolutely (by a statement like ORG 0E000h) or is calculated using a method suggested by Digital Research:

```
BIAS          EQU      2900          ;for 16K CP/M version 1.4
PATCH         EQU      1500h+BIAS
              ORG      PATCH
```

You check the CP/M capacity of the BIOS. If it matches the CP/M size you are using, go to the next step. If it does not match, or if you cannot tell, do not proceed (size means 48K CP/M, 56K CP/M, etc.). Unfortunately, there is no absolute rule about the relationship of the BIOS section with the base location of CP/M. Knowing the starting location of CP/M does not necessarily mean you can calculate the beginning location of the BIOS section. Digital Research has tried to standardize this, but several distributors and computer manufacturers continue to change the pattern. An easy way to locate the BIOS follows:

```
A>DDT<cr>
DDT Vers 2.2
L0,2<cr>
JMP 9603
- ^C
A>
```

---

* Routine from MODEM527.ASM by Ward Christiansen — a public domain program available from CP/M Users' Group.

We asked DDT to display the instruction stored at locations 0000_{16} through 0002_{16}. There the jump to the warm start routine of the BIOS is stored. Almost every BIOS begins with the 15 (or 17) jump instructions, and the warm start jump is the second one. In the above example, the beginning of the BIOS would be 9600_{16} (the cold start jump takes three memory locations).

Some BIOS modules can begin with something other than the jump table. Look at the BIOS listing that came with the machine. If any instructions appear before the jump table, then you have a unique BIOS, and you must determine where the BIOS module starts.

Change the origin directive at the start of the BIOS to match the size of your CP/M.

6. Assemble the new BIOS. If the BIOS assembles without any error messages, proceed to the next step. Always correct your errors before proceeding.

7. Load and execute DDT (type DDT < cr >). Use DDT to load the file BIOS.HEX (the HEX-type file containing your assembled BIOS). For some versions of CP/M, the creator suggests you use an offset value, as their BIOS consists of relocatable instructions only and can be assembled beginning at any address. Assuming you performed Step 5, however, to get the BIOS to *overlay* your current BIOS, type:

```
-IBIOS.HEX < cr >
-R < cr >
-
```

If you receive the DDT prompt (-) back, then at least you have not failed catastrophically. If the DDT prompt does not return, then you have major problems: either the BIOS was loaded at the wrong address or it does not work properly. If it does not work, return to Step 3.

Assuming the DDT prompt returned, try out the changes you made (i.e., if you added a printer driver, try typing a ^ P to send information to the printer). If the changes do not work, or the system stops responding, reboot the computer, load DDT and the BIOS, and use the DDT single-step and trace functions to discover where the problem occurs.

8. When everything works properly, make the new BIOS a permanent addition to your CP/M. Re-edit the BIOS.ASM file to reflect the BIOS location in the MOVCPM module. Reassemble the BIOS. Load and execute DDT and use it to load MOVCPM.COM, then BIOS.HEX. Note the NEXT number DDT displays when MOVCPM.COM is loaded. Use ^ C to get out of DDT and return to CP/M. Now SAVE the number of pages of memory indicated by the NEXT display you noted earlier. Call the new MOVCPM NEWMOVE.COM. Here is a sample session:

```
A > DDT < cr >
DDT Vers 2.2
```

```
—IMOVCPM.COM<cr>
—R<cr>
  NEXT  PC
  3000  0100
—IBIOS.HEX<cr>
—R<cr>
NEXT  PC
3000  0100
—∧C
A>SAVE 48 NEWMOVE.COM<cr>
A>
```

    9. Now use NEWMOVE just as you would MOVCPM to create your new CP/M system.

THE IOBYTE

The concept of the IOBYTE predates CP/M by many years. Gary Kildall used it in some sample implementations of CP/M, and he documents its use in several of the Digital Research manuals. Other software creators writing BIOS modules have elaborated upon the IOBYTE concept, but have not changed its basic function.

    The IOBYTE is a reserved byte of memory that indicates the current assignment of physical devices to logical devices. In CP/M, you have four logical devices:

      CON: Console device
      LST: List device
      RDR: Reader device
      PUN: Punch device

When you have two different printers, terminals, or paper tape readers, the IOBYTE indicates which device is to be used.

    The IOBYTE is normally located at address 0003_{16}. The byte is treated as four separate two-bit indicators:

Bit 7	Bit 6	Bit 5	Bit 4	Bit 3	Bit 2	Bit 1	Bit 0
LIST		PUNCH		READER		CONSOLE	

Table 7-2 shows how CP/M interprets the two bits for each device. The device names should look familiar. They are the physical devices that PIP and STAT address. An IOBYTE value of 00100100 (24_{16}) means the physical devices are currently assigned to logical functions as follows:

The TTY: device is performing the CONSOLE function.

TABLE 7-2. Interpreting the IOBYTE

Logical Device or Function	Physical Device			
	00	01	10	11
Console (CON:)	TTY:	CRT:	BAT:	UC1:
Reader (PTR:)	TTY:	RDR:	UR1:	UR2
Punch (PTP:)	TTY:	PUN:	UP1:	UP2:
List (LST:)	TTY:	CRT:	LPT:	UL1:

The PTR: device is performing the READER function.

The UP1: device is performing the PUNCH function.

The TTY: device is performing the LIST function.

A BIOS routine you or your computer vendor wrote examines IOBYTE to see where to send or receive information. The CONSOLE STATUS, CONSOLE INPUT, CONSOLE OUTPUT, READER, PUNCH, and LIST jumps in the BIOS jump table all point to a special routine to see which device to use. This routine proceeds as follows:

1. Get the IOBYTE.

2. Determine which device to use.

3. Go to the routine for that device.

For further information in the internal structure of CP/M consult the annotated bibliography in Appendix F. A number of excellent articles about specific portions of CP/M have appeared in trade publications.

8

Putting it All Together:
The Systems Approach

Although CP/M is a versatile, yet simple, operating system, it has not always been well understood. The public has often criticized the documentation and mistaken hardware problems for software problems.

Selling business systems to the general public includes a responsibility for thorough training and product reliability. The microcomputer industry has often been deficient in this regard. Educating the general computing public in the use of CP/M has been left to computer manufacturers, distributors, and dealers.

To simply complain about the industry's neglect of the end user avoids the main problem: how does the end user learn to use CP/M? While this book provides one answer, it cannot possibly solve the entire problem.

The following pages present a series of recommendations to CP/M end users. These offer a *system* solution to problems you may encounter. *System* includes the entire universe of people, equipment, paper, information, and resources involved in the use of a computer. Buying a computer, some software, and this book is not enough. You must integrate each component of the system into your current needs and procedures.

System Recommendations

Misleading advertising and consumer naïveté cause many end users to buy a computer system according to price. If two computer sellers promote the XY system, the customer buys from the firm with the best price. This is dangerous. While it is possible to solve a business' computer needs inexpensively, salespeople often make promises they can never keep.

Most end users purchase CP/M because the application program they need requires it. CP/M, however, places some additional requirements upon the computer system in which it operates.

To operate CP/M effectively, you need at least:

- Two disk drives
- 500 Kbytes of disk storage space
- 48 Kbytes of main computer memory
- A 24 × 80 character video terminal, and
- A printer

We will examine each of these components individually.

TWO DISK DRIVES

You need two disk drives for several reasons. As we discussed in Chapter 1, diskettes are fragile; they are easily bent, are useless when dirty, and they can be tampered with, lost, or stolen. In short, they are not a permanent storage medium. Thus you need to copy a diskette for *backup* purposes; copying is far easier with two disk drives.

While you can operate a computer system with only one drive, if that drive malfunctions, you have no system. With two drives you can continue to operate, although in a limited fashion, if one drive breaks down.

It is inconvenient to operate with only one drive. If your computer system is difficult to use, as it would be if you had to transfer diskettes in and out of a single drive, you might stop using it. Almost every serious business application program compatible with CP/M requires two disk drives.

500 KBYTES OF DISK STORAGE SPACE

Five hundred thousand characters of information seems like a lot of information. For example, this book is about 450,000 characters. In general, most computer users tend to underestimate the volume of information they use and generate.

Serious accounting programs (like the Structured Systems Group Integrated Accounting package or the Peachtree Integrated Accounting package) use 700,000 characters of disk space just for the programs, although this is split among several diskettes. The volume of information a business keeps for tax and auditing purposes is staggering. For example, tracing the meter readings and payments of 1000 utility district customers for one year takes up about 300 Kbytes.

Consider a typical retail business which averages 100 transactions a day. With only 100 characters of information per transaction, one year of transactions will occupy almost four million characters of information.

It is unrealistic to try to store all the information you need on a single diskette. Instead, apportion the information into *logical* blocks and save each block on an individual diskette. The reason for this suggestion is simple. Suppose your annual business transactions require four million characters of information and you want to see the transactions for the second week of August. On many systems the program must first wade through January to July before it finds the August data, taking a considerable amount of time just to identify the data. A more useful and convenient method assigns each month's information to a single diskette. Only rarely do accounting systems address all data at the same time.

There is another advantage to floppy disk systems with capacities ranging from 500 Kbytes to 1 Mbyte when you use accounting software. Many accounting systems *close* all transactions every month and carry forward only the balances. Usually you cannot look at the details of each transaction in a *closed* month. If you make an extra copy of your data (by making a duplicate diskette), you can recover the individual transactions whenever necessary. While exact figures are impossible to project due to the variables involved, a month's worth of information could fit comfortably on a single diskette with a capacity of 256 to 500 Kbytes. With any less storage space, the entire month's information will not fit. With a greater disk storage capacity you may be tempted to continue filling that diskette rather than maintaining logically distinct groupings of data on a diskette (i.e., you may start trying to fit three month's data on a diskette, but end up with only two months and a week's worth, which is not a very logical breaking point).

For general accounting purposes, 500 Kbytes to 1 Mbyte of disk storage space tends to be convenient. Maintaining the inventory of an electronics parts distributor, though, would require more.

48 KBYTES OF MAIN MEMORY

The program which created this book (WordStar) occupies 44 Kbytes of computer memory. This leaves 4000 characters of information you can scan at one time (without accessing the disk drive). Many programs now require between 32 and 48 Kbytes of memory to operate, and some require 64 Kbytes.

Program size is not the only consideration in determining the proper amount of memory, however. Most accounting or database programs must first sort the information stored on the diskette in order to process it. A good sort routine uses all of the computer's memory; the more memory available for the sort routine at one time, the faster it will operate. To give you an idea of the amount of memory versus the efficiency of the sort, consider the following figures:

An inefficient sort running in 16 Kbytes of free memory sorting 706 items by two *fields*.	3 hours, 10 minutes
An efficient sort running in 48 Kbytes of free memory sorting 525 items by five *fields*.	1 minute, 25 seconds

There are other variables involved, but giving the inefficient sort more memory resulted in a sort time of slightly over two hours. This example typifies real business packages sold by computer stores.

Buy a minimum of 48 Kbytes of memory. Buy 64 Kbytes if you can afford it. The 64 Kbyte memory is very common.

A 24 × 80 CHARACTER TERMINAL

The terminal should have a video screen which can display 24 lines of 80 characters each. This recommendation entails several considerations. One of the most practical uses of a computer system is *word processing:* writing letters and storing and retrieving information. Terminal screen size determines how much of the document or *record* you create or edit can be viewed at one time. Terminals which show 16 lines of 64 characters each show a maximum of 1024 characters at a time. A 24-line by 80-character terminal can show you almost twice as many (1920).

The number of characters on the screen at one time can enhance or impair readability: the program may leave extra space between blocks of information, making it more readable, or it may pack it close together, making the display confusing. Some of the more sophisticated word processing programs use two or more lines of the screen display to show you the status of a document being edited. WordStar, for example, provides the following information on your current location.

```
        B:SECTION7.CPM  PAGE 4 LINE 52 COL 44    INSERT ON
        L!----!--------------------------------------------------------R
```

The example shows you are editing the file SECTION7.CPM on drive
B:, page four, line 52, and the cursor is in column 44. INSERT ON means
you are inserting information into some previously prepared text. The
following line shows the left (L) and right (R) margins and tab stops (!).
This is valuable information, but if it occupies two lines of a 16-line
screen, there is little room left for the document.

Unfortunately, many software creators have assumed the *least
common denominator* (the 16 × 64 terminal) for their programs; users
of 24 × 80-character terminals waste some terminal capabilities.

A PRINTER

Recall we described diskettes as fragile and temporal records which you
must copy to insure against accidental loss of the information stored. We
will take this argument one step further.

First the scare tactic. The Internal Revenue Service (IRS) does not
always consider computer documents (i.e., disk files) as auditable
material. In many cases, the use of a computer for accounting or
information storage has not kept the IRS from demanding *printed* copies
of the information. If the agency allowed computer audits in all cases, it
would have to acquire knowledge of a variety of computers and
computer software to insure the integrity of the information. While
standards exist for auditing a company's books, the accounting
profession has been negligent in adopting and enforcing standards for
computerized record keeping. It is unlikely you will find standards
adopted outside of very large corporations.

Now for the practical approach. End users are often hesitant to
commit valuable information to a medium they cannot *read*. The first of
the copyright cases concerning computer software made specific note of
the inability of anyone to read the information contained within the
computer, on diskette, or in Read-Only Memory (ROM). This implies the
same information printed on paper has a different status. Perhaps the
current generation of children, growing up with both television and
computers, will solve the *official acceptance* problems with information
stored as magnetic impulses. Until then, we are limited by a society which
places special emphasis on the printed word. The smart computer user
creates printed documents to supplement magnetic information storage.

Another reason to keep printed records is the lack of standards among
computers. At last count, there were over 25 different formats of

diskette storage (all using CP/M), making reliance on magnetic media for all *readers* unrealistic. Where computers are not yet accessible, the print medium will continue to dominate.

In summation, use a printer to:

1. Save information for audit purposes
2. Create human-readable information
3. Make the information portable

Making paper copies of your data also provides an additional backup measure.

Procedure Recommendations

Now for some specific recommendations for using CP/M wisely and efficiently.

1. Understand what you want the computer to do (see the section on system design at the end of this chapter). Read all manuals, even if you do not understand them all at this point. If you are confused or not sure of your skills at using the computer, request help from an expert on microcomputers such as your computer dealer.

2. Figure out how many diskettes you need, both originals and backup diskettes, and format them for use with CP/M.

3. Create *use* copies of all program diskettes. Never use the original diskette. The original copy of the programs (and this includes the original CP/M diskette) should be put in a safe place such as a safe, safe-deposit box, or lockable file cabinet. Label all diskettes as they are created or modified. Date the label, indicating the dates you created and modified the diskette.

4. Use the SYSGEN program to copy CP/M onto every diskette you will use with your system. Copy the same CP/M on all diskettes; do not put a 48K CP/M on one diskette and a 56K CP/M on another. You never know when you may have to reboot (warm start) CP/M because of a disk error or an accidental interruption of the computer. If all your diskettes have the same CP/M you will always know how to recover from the error.

5. Establish a rational backup procedure and stick to it. The following is recommended for business applications: Do not

trust the computer to remember everything; do not eliminate the current system you use to keep information. Keep any information the computer prints out; file it as you would any other information. Regard the computer as you would any another employee. If you think it important enough to pay for health insurance for employees, get some for the computer, too; a service contract should guarantee the maximum length of time you will be without a computer.

If you are using the computer to replace a current accounting or information processing system, do not sell or throw away the old system. If the computer provides word processing (typing letters, etc.), do not sell all your typewriters. Likewise, do not lay off every employee who knew the old system. Occasionally your computer will have problems, and you need to be prepared for them.

Computers are productivity boosters, not surrogate employees. Use the computer to augment your operation and increase its efficiency, not to replace people. Making your business or personal data handling more efficient may decrease your need for an individual's participation, but that should not be your intention, nor should you overlook the political ramifications of such an action.

6. Cut out the *computerese*. Why force someone to use a command like PIP when it really means COPY? Use the REN command in CP/M to create program names that are meaningful to you. Here are some suggestions:

Change		to	
	PIP	to	COPY
	CRUN204	to	RUN
	ED	to	EDIT
	CBAS2	to	COMPILE
	ASM	to	ASSEMBLE
	MOVCPM	to	MOVE-CPM
	WS	to	WORDSTAR

A number of other programs can be changed so you and the others using the system can immediately recognize each disk file and you are not intimidated by acronymns. In addition, ask your computer dealer to change (or show you how to change) the following:

Change BDOS ERROR ON x: to DISK ERROR ON x:

Other small changes can eliminate some of the rampant computer jargon that confuses end users. For instance, the following might be useful changes to CP/M:

a. On any diskette which includes an automatic execution instruction whenever CP/M is started (or restarted), CP/M could issue this message:

AUTOMATIC EXECUTION OF program name
OCCURRING

Since some programs take a long time to load, and provide no indication of what is happening, panic sometimes sets in. "What's happening?" is a frequent exclamation at this point and is usually accompanied by a strong desire to press the RESET button to start over. A message might relieve some of the frustration.

b. Programs without adequate error handling techniques can be improved by notifying the user of the error and by providing an option to retry rather than to abort the program and return to CP/M. Rewrite error messages so the user cannot ignore them. Error messages which require the user to consult a manual for further interpretation can be rewritten to provide something more informative.

c. Train everyone using the computer. This book will fulfill a portion of this need. Also, choose a computer dealer who will not desert you but will provide after-sale training and education.

The foregoing should improve the day-to-day operation of a computer system.

The microcomputer industry is a young and competitive one. Share your problems with others. There are a number of publications which pride themselves on being advocates of the end user. These include *InfoWorld, Kilobaud Microcomputing, Creative Computing*, and *Interface Age*. Let others know of your problems and frustrations. Do not continue to buy products from a firm which "burned" you the first time.

The Systems Approach

This issue is not directly related to CP/M, but may affect your ability to use it: many computer users should not be using computers. Often our society believes it can solve any problem with new and better technology. This just is not true. To make sure you do not fall into the *technology trap*: Stop.

Analyze your current use of the computer. See if you can answer the following questions.

1. Did you buy the computer because someone promised it would solve specific problems?
2. Or because you were fascinated by technology?
3. Can you do the work the computer does just as efficiently by hand?
4. Is the computer used less than an hour a day?
5. Can you afford to hire another employee, or can you afford to devote more of your time to the computer?

If you answered yes to any of these questions, you have not developed a systems approach to your computer.

Consider this example to clarify the systems approach: You work for a company, Postal Service, that sells tennis equipment by mail. You wish to computerize order processing, inventory, and periodic reports of mail and phone orders to your chief executive, Clayton Court. You can buy a computer and software to perform the order processing, inventory and report tasks, but is that all you need? Definitely not.

Postal Service receives orders through the mail and occasionally by phone. Your complete *system* must detail how the computer receives mail and phone information. In addition, you receive the invoices, merchandise, packing slips, and pricing updates from wholesale companies. The computer must receive this information, too. And how about order cancellations, queries about order status, lost merchandise, and damaged goods?

Postal Service employs ten people. Do all ten use the computer? Does everyone in the firm have access to all the information stored in the computer?

The computer is a small part of the system. Talk with the people who sold you your computer and software. If more than one firm is involved, bring them together for the discussion. If you bought the system mail-order to save money, consider it a lesson learned and find someone locally to provide the necessary support for both the software and hardware.

Discuss your system with everyone. Make sure that everyone knows you are looking for a complete integration of the computer into your business environment. Deal only with people who accept a systems approach to problems. Remember, a computer dealer who knows everything about *wait states*, *NAND gates*, and *vectored interrupts* but nothing about cash flow, inventory valuation, and charge procedures, will be of no use to you.

Your discussion will inform you which computer equipment and software you need as well as how the computer will fit into your operating environment. You may find it helpful to create a systems flowchart to learn how your business really works.

Once you are positive the computer and software will work for your system instead of against it, proceed with the acquisition. See demonstrations of the equipment and software functioning as it will in your environment. A computer store will use a computer for some portion of their own operation. If not, they are not interested in end users, they are *hardware freaks*, and they are more interested in computers as toys or gimmicks.

Train personnel and ready the business for the computer *before* the computer arrives, not afterward. Where will you place it? Can Joe Nicotine smoke his ten packs a day around it? Does everyone have to learn typing? A hundred more questions need to be considered before the equipment arrives and you try to use it.

What about your old system? If you currently prepare all the order and inventory records by hand, do you stop writing? There are several approaches to introducing a new computer system. You may start using the new system:

Cold turkey : One day you stop using the old system and start using the new one.

Phased in : You separate each task into its component parts and convert one at a time. When one part works fine on the new system, you convert the next part. It is a series of small *cold turkeys*.

Parallel : Use your old system and the new system at the same time. You can compare the two side by side to ensure the new system performs the job correctly and completely. You can easily show employees the differences between the systems.

Now look at your projected use of the computer. Is it part of a system? Do the rest of the pieces work with the computer, or is the computer an *island* ?

To reiterate the lessons of this section:

1. A computer is a tool.

2. A computer is not a complete solution to any problem.

3. You control the computer; do not let the computer control you.

Buying a computer is not a necessity. Evaluate how a computer relates to all your business needs.

A

CP/M Command
Summary

This appendix summarizes the command line format and the function of each CP/M built-in and transient command. The commands are listed in alphabetical order.

In the space below, fill in the command line format for your disk copy and disk format (initialize) programs. See Chapter 5 for more information.

ASM Command Lines

ASM filename < cr >

> Assemble the file filename.ASM; use the currently logged disk for all files.

ASM filename.opt < cr >

> Assemble the file filename.ASM on drive o: (A:,B:,...,P:). Write HEX file on drive p: (A:,B:,...,P:), or skip if p: is Z:.
>> Write PRN file on drive t: (A:,B:,...,P:), send to console if p: is X:, or skip if p: is Z:.

DDT Command Lines

DDT < cr >

> Loads DDT and waits for DDT commands.

DDT x:filename.typ < cr >

> Loads DDT into memory and also loads filename.typ from drive x into memory for examination modification, or execution.

DDT COMMAND SUMMARY

Assss < cr >

> Enter assembly language statements beginning at hexadecimal address ssss.

D < cr >

> Display the contents of the next 192 bytes of memory.

Dssss,ffff < cr >

> Display the contents of memory starting at hexadecimal address ssss and finishing at hexadecimal address ffff.

Fssss,ffff,cc $<$ **cr** $>$

> Fill memory with the 8-bit hexadecimal constant cc starting at hexadecimal address ssss and finishing with hexadecimal address ffff.

G $<$ **cr** $>$

> Begin execution at the address contained in the program counter.

Gssss $<$ **cr** $>$

> Begin execution at hexadecimal address ssss.

Gssss,bbbb $<$ **cr** $>$

> Set a breakpoint at hexadecimal address bbbb, then begin execution at hexadecimal address ssss.

Gssss,bbbb,cccc $<$ **cr** $>$

> Set breakpoints at hexadecimal addresses bbbb and cccc, then begin execution at hexadecimal address ssss.

G,bbbb $<$ **cr** $>$

> Set a breakpoint at hexadecimal address bbbb, then begin execution at the address contained in the program counter.

G,bbbb,cccc $<$ **cr** $>$

> Set breakpoints at hexadecimal addresses bbbb and cccc, then begin execution at the address contained in the program counter.

Ifilename.typ $<$ **cr** $>$

> Set up the default file control block using the name filename.typ.

L $<$ **cr** $>$

> List the next eleven lines of assembly language program disassembled from memory.

Lssss $<$ **cr** $>$

> List eleven lines of assembly language program disassembled from memory starting at hexadecimal address ssss.

Lssss,ffff <cr>

List the assembly language program disassembled from memory starting at hexadecimal address ssss and finishing at hexadecimal address ffff.

Mssss,ffff,dddd <cr>

Move the contents of the memory block starting at hexadecimal address ssss and ending at hexadecimal address ffff to the block of memory starting at hexadecimal address dddd.

R <cr>

Read a file from disk into memory (use I command first).

Rnnnn <cr>

Read a file from disk into memory beginning at the hexadecimal address nnnn higher than normal (use I command first).

Sssss <cr>

Display the contents of memory at hexadecimal address ssss and optionally change the contents.

Tnnnn <cr>

Trace the execution of (hexadecimal) nnnn program instructions.

Unnnn <cr>

Execute (hexadecimal) nnnn program instructions, then stop and display the CPU registers' contents.

X <cr>

Display the CPU registers' contents.

Xr <cr>

Display the contents of CPU register or flag r and optionally change it.

DIR Command Lines

DIR x: <cr>

Displays directory of all files on drive x:. x: is optional; if omitted, the currently logged drive is used.

DIR x:filename.typ < cr >

> Displays directory of all files on drive x: whose names match the ambiguous or unambiguous filename.typ. x: is optional; if omitted, the currently logged drive is used.

DUMP Command Line

DUMP x:filename.typ < cr >

> Displays the hexadecimal representations of each byte stored in the file filename.typ on drive x:. If filename.typ is ambiguous, displays the first file which matches the ambiguous file name.

ED Command Line

ED x:filename.typ < cr >

> Invokes the editor, which then searches for filename.typ on drive x: and creates a temporary file x:filename.$$$ to store the edited text. filename.typ is unambiguous. x: is optional; if omitted, the currently logged drive is assumed.

ED COMMAND SUMMARY

> Note: Non-alphabetic commands follow the Z command.

nA

> Append lines. Moves "n" lines from original file to edit buffer: 0A moves lines until edit buffer is at least half full.

+/−B

> Begin/Bottom. Moves CP:
> +B moves CP to beginning of edit buffer
> −B moves CP to end of edit buffer

+/−nC

Move by characters. Move CP by "n" character positions:
+ moves forward
− moves backward

+/−nD

Delete characters. Deletes "n" characters before or after the CP in the
edit buffer:
+ deletes before the CP
− deletes after the CP

E

End. Ends edit, closes files, and returns to CP/M; normal end.

nFstring ^ Z

Find string. Find the "n"th occurrence of string, beginning the search
after the CP.

H

Move to head of edited file. Ends edit, renames files, then edits former
temporary file.

I < cr >

Enter insert mode. Text from keyboard goes into edit buffer after the CP;
exit with Control-Z.

Istring ^ Z

Insert string. Inserts string in edit buffer after the CP.

Istring < cr >

Insert line. Inserts string and CRLF in the edit buffer after the CP.

nJfindstring ^ Zinsertstring ^ Zendstring ^ Z

Juxtaposition. Beginning after the CP, finds findstring, inserts insertstring
after it, then deletes all following characters up to but not including
endstring; repeats until performed "n" times.

+/−nK

> Kill lines. Deletes "n" lines:
> > + deletes after the CP
> > − deletes before the CP

+/−nL

> Move by lines. Moves the CP to the beginning of the line it is in, then
> moves the CP "n" lines forward or backward:
> > + moves forward
> > − moves backward

nMcommandstring ^ Z

> Macro command. Repeats execution of the ED commands in
> commandstring "n" times.
> "n"=0, "n"=1, or "n" absent repeats execution until error occurs.

nNstring ^ Z

> Find string with autoscan. Finds the "n"th occurrence of string,
> automatically appending from original file and writing to temporary file
> as necessary.

O

> Return to original file. Empties edit buffer, empties temporary file, returns
> to beginning of original file, ignores previous ED commands.

+/−nP

> Move CP and print pages. Moves the CP forward or backward one page
> then displays the page following the CP. nP displays "n" pages,
> pausing after each.

Q

> Quit edit. Erases temporary file and block move file, if any, and returns to
> CP/M; original file is not changed.

R < cr >

> Read block move file. Copies the entire block move file X$$$$$$$.LIB
> from disk and inserts it in the edit buffer after the CP.

Rfilename <cr>

> Read library file. Copies the entire file filename with extension LIB from the disk and inserts it in the edit buffer after the CP.

nSfindstring ^Zreplacestring ^Z

> Substitute string. Starting at the CP, repeats "n" times: finds findstring and replaces it with replacestring.

+/−nT

> Type lines. Displays "n" lines:
> + displays the "n" lines after the CP
> − displays the "n" lines before the CP
> If the CP is not at the beginning of a line:
> 0T displays from the beginning of the line to the CP
> T displays from the CP to the end of the line
> 0TT displays the entire line without moving the CP

+/−U

> Upper case translation. After +U command, alphabetic input to the edit buffer is translated from lower case to upper case; after −U, no translation occurs.

0V

> Edit buffer free space/size. Displays the decimal number of free (empty) bytes in the edit buffer and the total size of the edit buffer.

+/−V

> Verify line numbers. After +V, a line number is displayed with each line displayed; ED's prompt is then preceded by the number of the line containing the CP. After −V, line numbers are not displayed, and ED's prompt is *.

nW

> Write lines. Writes first "n" lines from the edit buffer to the temporary file; deletes these lines from the edit buffer.

nX

> Block transfer (Xfer). Copies the ''n'' lines following the CP from the edit buffer to the temporary block move file X$$$$$$$.LIB; adds to previous contents of that file.

nZ

> Sleep. Delays execution of the command which follows it. Larger ''n'' gives longer delay, smaller n gives shorter delay.

n:

> Move CP to line number ''n.'' Moves the CP to the beginning of line number ''n'' (see +/−V)

:m

> Continue through line number ''m.'' A command prefix which gives the ending point for the command which follows it. The beginning point is the location of the CP (see +/−V).

+/−n

> Move and display one line. Abbreviated form of +/−nLT.

ERA Command Lines

ERA x:filename.typ < cr >

> Erase the file filename.typ on the disk in drive x. filename and/or typ can be ambiguous. x: is optional; if omitted, the currently logged drive is used.

ERA x:*.* < cr >

> Erase all files on the disk in drive x:. x: is optional; if omitted, the currently logged drive is used.

Line Editing Commands

Control-C

Restarts CP/M if it is the first character in command line. Called *warm start*.

Control-E

Moves to beginning of next line. Used for typing long commands.

Control-H or Backspace

Deletes one character and erases it from the screen (CP/M version 2.0 and newer).

Control-J or Line Feed

Same as carriage return (CP/M version 2.0 and newer).

Control-M

Same as carriage return (< cr >).

Control-P

Turns on the *list device* (usually your printer). Type it again to turn off the list device.

Control-R

Repeats current command line (useful with version 1.4); it verifies the line is corrected after you delete several characters (CP/M version 1.4 and newer).

Control-S

Temporarily stops display of data on the console. Press any key to continue.

Control-U or Control-X

> Cancels current command line (Control-X in CP/M version 1.4 and newer).

Rubout (RUB) or Delete (DEL)

> Deletes one character and echoes (repeats) it.

LOAD Command Line

LOAD x:filename < cr >

> Reads the file filename.HEX on drive x: and creates the executable program file filename.COM on drive x:.

MOVCPM Command Line

MOVCPM < cr >

> Prepare a new copy of CP/M which uses all of memory; give control to the new CP/M, but do not save it on disk.

MOVCPM nn < cr >

> Prepare a new copy of CP/M which uses "nn" Kbytes of memory; give control to the new CP/M, but do not save it on disk.

MOVCPM * * < cr >

> Prepare a new copy of CP/M, which uses all of memory, to be saved with SYSGEN or SAVE.

MOVCPM nn * < cr >

> Prepare a new copy of CP/M, which uses "nn" Kbytes of memory, to be saved with SYSGEN or SAVE.
>
> "nn" is an integer decimal number. "nn" can be 16 through 64 for CP/M 1.3 or 1.4. "nn" can be 20 through 64 for CP/M 2.0 and newer.

PIP Command Lines

PIP < cr >

> Loads PIP into memory. PIP prompts for commands, executes them, then prompts again.

PIP pipcommandline < cr >

> Loads PIP into memory. PIP executes the command pipcommandline, then exits to CP/M.

PIP COMMAND SUMMARY

x:new.typ=y:old.top[p] < cr >

> Copies the file old.top on drive y: to the file new.typ on drive x:, using parameters p.

x:new.typ=y:old1.top[p],z:old2.tip[q] < cr >

> Creates a file new.typ on drive x: which consists of the contents of file old1.top on drive y: using parameters p followed by the contents of file old2.tip on drive z: using parameters q.

x:filename.typ=dev:[p] < cr >

> Copies data from device dev: to the file filename.typ on drive x:.

dev:=x:filename.typ[p] < cr >

> Copies data from filename.typ on drive x: to device dev:.

dst:=src:[p] < cr >

> Copies data to device dst: from device src:

PIP PARAMETER SUMMARY

B	Specifies *block mode* transfer.
Dn	Deletes all characters after the "n"th column.

E	Echoes the copying to the console as it is being performed.
F	Removes form feed characters during transfer.
Gn	Directs PIP to copy a file from user area n.
H	Checks for proper Intel Hex File format.
I	Ignores any :00 records in Intel Hex File transfers.
L	Translates upper-case letters to lower-case.
N	Adds a line number to each line transferred.
O	Object file transfer (ignores end-of-file markers).
Pn	Issues page feed after every "n"th line.
Qs ^ Z	Specifies quit of copying after the string "s" is encountered.
R	Directs PIP to copy from a system file.
Ss ^ Z	Specifies start of copying after the string "s" is encountered.
Tn	Sets tab stops to every "n"th column.
U	Translates lower-case letters to upper-case.
V	Verifies copy by comparison after copy finished.
W	Directs PIP to copy onto a R/O file.
Z	Zeros the "parity" bit on ASCII characters.

PIP DESTINATION DEVICES

CON:	PUN:	LST:	Logical devices
TTY:	PTP:	LPT:	
CRT:	UP1:	UL1:	Physical devices
UC1:	UP2:		
	OUT:	PRN:	Special PIP devices

PIP SOURCE DEVICES

CON:	RDR:		Logical devices
TTY:	PTR:		
CRT:	UR1:		Physical devices
UC1:	UR2:		
NUL:	EOF:	INP:	Special PIP devices

REN Command Line

REN newname.typ=oldname.typ < cr >

> Finds the file oldname.typ and renames it newname.typ.

SAVE Command Line

SAVE nnn x:filename.typ < cr >

> Save a portion of the Transient Program Area of memory in the file filename.typ on drive x: where nnn is a decimal number representing the number of pages of memory. x: is the optional drive specifier.

STAT Command Lines

STAT < cr >

> Displays attributes and amount of free space for all diskette drives accessed since last warm or cold start.

STAT x: < cr >

> Displays amount of free space on diskette in drive x:

STAT x:filename.typ < cr >

> Displays size and attributes of file(s) filename.typ on drive x:. filename.typ may be ambiguous. x is optional; if omitted, currently logged drive is assumed.

STAT x:filename.typ $atr < cr > **(CP/M and newer)**

> Assigns the attribute atr to the file(s) filename.typ on drive x:. filename.typ may be ambiguous. x: is optional; if omitted, currently logged drive is assumed.

STAT DEV: < cr >

> Reports which physical devices are currently assigned to the four logical devices.

STAT VAL: < cr >

>Reports the possible device assignments and partial STAT command line summary.

STAT log:=phy: < cr >

>Assigns the physical device phy: to the logical device log: (may be more than one assignment on the line; each should be set off by a comma).

STAT USR: < cr > (CP/M 2.0 and newer)

>Reports the current user number as well as all user numbers for which there are files on currently logged disks.

STAT x:DSK: < cr > (CP/M 2.0 and newer)

>Reports the characteristics of disk drive x:.

STAT x:=R/O < cr > (CP/M 1.4 and newer)

>Assigns a temporary write-protect status to drive x:.

SUBMIT Command Lines

SUBMIT filename < cr >

>Creates a file $$$.SUB which contains the commands listed in filename.SUB; CP/M then executes commands from this file rather than the keyboard.

SUBMIT filename parameters < cr >

>Creates a file $$$.SUB which contains commands from the file filename.SUB; certain parts of the command lines in filename.SUB are replaced by "parameters" during creation of $$$.SUB. CP/M then gets commands from this file rather than the keyboard.

SYSGEN Command Line

SYSGEN <cr>

Loads the SYSGEN program to transfer CP/M from one diskette to another.

TYPE Command Line

TYPE x:filename.typ <cr>

Displays the contents of file filename.typ from drive x: on the console.

USER Command Line

USER n <cr>

Sets the User Number to "n", where "n" is an integer decimal number from 0 to 15, inclusive.

x: Command Line

x: <cr>

Changes the currently logged disk drive to drive x:. x can be A through P.

B

ASCII Character Codes

The American Standard Code for Information Interchange (ASCII) consists of a set of 96 displayable characters and 32 non-displayed characters. Most CP/M systems use at least a subset of the ASCII character set. When CP/M stores characters on a diskette as text, the ASCII definitions are used.

Several of the CP/M utility programs use the ASCII character code. Text created using ED is stored as ASCII characters on diskette. DDT, when displaying a ''dump'' of the contents of memory, displays both the hexadecimal and ASCII representation of memory's contents.

ASCII does not use an entire byte of information (i.e., eight bits) to represent a character. ASCII is a seven-bit code, and the eighth bit is often used for *parity*. Parity is an error checking method that assures that the character received is the one transmitted. Many microcomputers and microcomputer devices ignore the *parity bit*, while others require one of two forms of parity:

Even Parity : The number of binary *1's* in a byte is always an even number. If there is an odd number of 1's in the character, the parity bit will be a 1; if there is an even number of 1's in the character, the parity bit is made a 0.

Odd Parity: The total number of 1 bits in the character, including the parity bit, is always odd.

Alternative ways of *coding* the information stored by the computer include the 8-bit EBCDIC (Extended Binary Coded Decimal Interchange Code), used by IBM, and a number of *packed binary* schemes, primarily used to represent numerical information.

TABLE B-1. ASCII Character Codes

b7 →					0	0	0	0	1	1	1	1
b6 →					0	0	1	1	0	0	1	1
b5 →					0	1	0	1	0	1	0	1
b4	b3	b2	b1	Column / Row	0	1	2	3	4	5	6	7
0	0	0	0	0	NUL	DLE	SP	0	@	P	`	p
0	0	0	1	1	SOH	DC1	!	1	A	Q	a	q
0	0	1	0	2	STX	DC2	"	2	B	R	b	r
0	0	1	1	3	ETX	DC3	#	3	C	S	c	s
0	1	0	0	4	EOT	DC4	$	4	D	T	d	t
0	1	0	1	5	ENQ	NAK	%	5	E	U	e	u
0	1	1	0	6	ACK	SYN	&	6	F	V	f	v
0	1	1	1	7	BEL	ETB	'	7	G	W	g	w
1	0	0	0	8	BS	CAN	(	8	H	X	h	x
1	0	0	1	9	HT	EM	)	9	I	Y	i	y
1	0	1	0	10	LF	SUB	*	:	J	Z	j	z
1	0	1	1	11	VT	ESC	+	;	K	[	k	{
1	1	0	0	12	FF	FS	,	<	L	\	l	|
1	1	0	1	13	CR	GS	-	=	M	]	m	}
1	1	1	0	14	SO	RS	.	>	N	Λ	n	~
1	1	1	1	15	SI	US	/	?	O	—	o	DEL

NUL	Null		DC1	Device control 1
SOH	Start of heading		DC2	Device control 2
STX	Start of text		DC3	Device control 3
ETX	End of text		DC4	Device control 4
EOT	End of transmission		NAK	Negative acknowledge
ENQ	Enquiry		SYN	Synchronous idle
ACK	Acknowledge		ETB	End of transmission block
BEL	Bell, or alarm		CAN	Cancel
BS	Backspace		EM	End of medium
HT	Horizontal tabulation		SUB	Substitute
LF	Line feed		ESC	Escape
VT	Vertical tabulation		FS	File separator
FF	Form feed		GS	Group separator
CR	Carriage return		RS	Record separator
SO	Shift out		US	Unit separator
SI	Shift in		SP	Space
DLE	Data link escape		DEL	Delete

TABLE B-2. ASCII Character Codes in Ascending Order

Hexadecimal	Binary	ASCII	Hexadecimal	Binary	ASCII
00	000 0000	NUL	40	100 0000	
01	000 0001	SOH	41	100 0001	A
02	000 0010	STX	42	100 0010	B
03	000 0011	ETX	43	100 0011	C
04	000 0100	EOT	44	100 0100	D
05	000 0101	ENQ	45	100 0101	E
06	000 0110	ACK	46	100 0110	F
07	000 0111	BEL	47	100 0111	G
08	000 1000	BS	48	100 1000	H
09	000 1001	HT	49	100 1001	I
0A	000 1010	LF	4A	100 1010	J
0B	000 1011	VT	4B	100 1011	K
0C	000 1100	FF	4C	100 1100	L
0D	000 1101	CR	4D	100 1101	M
0E	000 1110	SO	4E	100 1110	N
0F	000 1111	SI	4F	100 1111	O
10	001 0000	DLE	50	101 0000	P
11	001 0001	DC1	51	101 0001	Q
12	001 0010	DC2	52	101 0010	R
13	001 0011	DC3	53	101 0011	S
14	001 0100	DC4	54	101 0100	T
15	001 0101	NAK	55	101 0101	U
16	001 0110	SYN	56	101 0110	V
17	001 0111	ETB	57	101 0111	W
18	001 1000	CAN	58	101 1000	X
19	001 1001	EM	59	101 1001	Y
1A	001 1010	SUB	5A	101 1010	Z
1B	001 1011	ESC	5B	101 1011	[
1C	001 1100	FS	5C	101 1100	\
1D	001 1101	GS	5D	101 1101	]
1E	001 1110	RS	5E	101 1110	ʌ
1F	001 1111	US	5F	101 1111	—
20	010 0000	SP	60	110 0000	`
21	010 0001	!	61	110 0001	a
22	010 0010	''	62	110 0010	b
23	010 0011	#	63	110 0011	c
24	010 0100	$	64	110 0100	d
25	010 0101	%	65	110 0101	e
26	010 0110	&	66	110 0110	f
27	010 0111	'	67	110 0111	g
28	010 1000	(	68	110 1000	h
29	010 1001	)	69	110 1001	i
2A	010 1010	*	6A	110 1010	j
2B	010 1011	+	6B	110 1011	k
2C	010 1100	,	6C	110 1100	l
2D	010 1101	—	6D	110 1101	m
2E	010 1110	.	6E	110 1110	n
2F	010 1111	/	6F	110 1111	o
30	011 0000	0	70	111 0000	p
31	011 0001	1	71	111 0001	q
32	011 0010	2	72	111 0010	r
33	011 0011	3	73	111 0011	s
34	011 0100	4	74	111 0100	t
35	011 0101	5	75	111 0101	u
36	011 0110	6	76	111 0110	v
37	011 0111	7	77	111 0111	w
38	011 1000	8	78	111 1000	x
39	011 1001	9	79	111 1001	y
3A	011 1010	:	7A	111 1010	z
3B	011 1011	;	7B	111 1011	{
3C	011 1100	<	7C	111 1100		
3D	011 1101	=	7D	111 1101	}
3E	011 1110	>	7E	111 1110	~
3F	011 1111	?	7F	111 1111	DEL

C

Comparison of CP/M Versions 1.3, 1.4, and 2.0

Line Editing Commands

Command	Version 1.3	Version 1.4	Version 2.0
Control-C	Yes	Yes	Yes
Control-E	No	Yes	Yes
Control-H or Backspace	No	No	Yes
Control-J or Line Feed	No	No	Yes
Control-M or Carriage Return	Yes	Yes	Yes
Control-P	Yes	Yes	Yes
Control-R	No	Yes	Improved
Control-S	Yes	Yes	Yes
Control-U	Yes	Yes	Improved
Control-X	No	Same as Control-U	Backspace and erase
Delete or Rubout	Yes	Yes	Yes

New or Changed Commands

Command	Version 1.3	Version 1.4	Version 2.0
DIR	Yes	Yes	New: Displays 4 file names per line. Displays only DIR file names. Displays file names for current user only.
ED	Yes	New: +/−V 0V nX 0X nnnn: :mmmm Singly only: E,H,Q,O Tabs always echo as spaces.	New: +V is default. Cannot alter R/O file. Cannot access SYS file.
ERA	Yes	New: Asks ALL? after ERA *.*	New: Erases files of current user only.
PIP	Yes	New: Option parameters. Physical device names. Ambiguous file names.	New parameters: Gn R W
SAVE	Yes	Yes	New: Does not alter user memory (TPA).

New or Changed Commands (Continued)

Command	Version 1.3	Version 1.4	Version 2.0
STAT	Yes Displays free disk space only.	New: Displays size of each file. log:=phy: x:=R/O Detects switched disks. Displays free space on all active disks.	New: VAL: menu DSK: x:DSK: USR: $S File attributes: R/W, R/O DIR, SYS
SUBMIT	Yes	Yes	New: XSUB
USER	No	No	Yes

Disk Differences

Item	Version 1.3	Version 1.4	Version 2.0
Maximum number of drives	2	4	16
Maximum storage per drive	1 Mbyte	1 Mbyte	16 Mbyte
Maximum number of files	64	64	Expandable
Access method	Sequential	Sequential	Sequential or random
Location of disk charac- teristics	BDOS	Disk parameter block	BIOS

New or Changed BDOS Functions

Function	Version 1.3	Version 1.4	Version 2.0
6-Direct Console I/O	No	No	Yes
10-Read Console buffer	Yes	Yes	Improved line editing
12-(see right)	Lift Disk Head	Lift Disk Head	Return Version Number
15-Open File	Yes	Yes	Improved
17-Search for First	Yes	Yes	Improved
18-Search for Next	Yes	Yes	Improved
19-Delete File	Yes	Yes	Improved
22-Make File	Yes	Yes	Improved
23-Rename File	Yes	Yes	Improved
24-Return Login Vector	Yes	Yes	Improved
28 through 36	No	No	Yes

D

CP/M Prompts

x >	CP/M waiting for command; drive x is currently logged drive.
nx >	MP/M waiting for command; drive x is currrently logged drive; current user number is n.
*	PIP waiting for command.
*	ED waiting for command.
nnnn:*	ED waiting for command; character pointer is at line number nnnn.
*	Also used by Microsoft BASIC, EDIT, FORTRAN, COBOL, and Pascal when waiting for a command.
-	DDT waiting for command.

In the space below, write in the prompts of other programs you use.

Diskette Selection

Within each category below, diskettes may be single-density or double-density. Be sure to choose the proper density for your system. Double-density systems can usually be operated in single-density mode, so you may be using both varieties if you have such a system.

SYSTEMS WHICH USE 8-INCH
SOFT-SECTORED DISKETTES

Altos
Cromemco FDC controller
Cromemco System 3
Delta
Digital Microsystems
Discus
Dynabyte DB8/4
iCOM 3712, 3812
IMS 8000
IMSAI FDC2
IMSAI VDP-80
Intecolor (ISC) 8063, 8360, 8963
Intel MDS

Micromation
Morrow Discus
Mostek
Ohio Scientific C3
Pertec PCC 2000
Radio Shack TRS-80 Model II
Radio Shack TRS-80 Model I/Micromation
Radio Shack TRS-80 Model I/Omikron (8-inch)
Radio Shack TRS-80 Model I/Shuffleboard (8-inch)
Research Machines (8-inch)
SD Systems (8-inch)
Spacebyte
Tarbell
TEI (8-inch)
Thinkertoys
TRS-80. *See* Radio Shack
Vector Graphic System 2800

SYSTEMS WHICH USE 8-INCH
HARD-SECTORED DISKETTES

MITS 3200, 3202
Processor Technology Helios II

SYSTEMS WHICH USE 5.25-INCH
SOFT-SECTORED DISKETTES

Apple/SoftCard
AVL Eagle
BASF System 7100
Cromemco Z2D
Digi-Log Microterm II
Durango F-85
Gnat
iCOM 2411 Micro Floppy
IMS 5000
IMSAI VDP-40, -42, -44
Intertec SuperBrain
Kontron PSI-80
MSD (5.25-inch)

Polymorphic 8813
Quay 500, 520
Radio Shack TRS-80 Model I (5.25-inch)
Radio Shack TRS-80 Model I/FEC Freedom
Radio Shack TRS-80 Model I/Omikron (5.25-inch)
RAIR
Research Machines (5.25-inch)
Sanco 7000 (5.25-inch)
SD Systems (5.25-inch)
SuperBrain. *See* Intertec
TEI (5.25-inch)

SYSTEMS WHICH USE 5.25-INCH
HARD-SECTORED 10-SECTOR DISKETTES

Heath H8 and H17, H27
Heath H89
Horizon
Meca (5.25-inch)
North Star Horizon
Vista V80 (5.25-inch)
Vista V200 (5.25-inch)
Zenith Z89

SYSTEMS WHICH USE 5.25-INCH
HARD-SECTORED 16-SECTOR DISKETTES

Blackhawk (40 TPI)
CDS Versatile 3B (40 TPI)
CDS Versatile 4 (100 TPI)
COMPAL-80 (100 TPI)
Dynabyte (Some models)
Exidy Sorcerer (100 TPI)
Micropolis Mod I (40 TPI)
Micropolis Mod II (100 TPI)
Nylac (40 TPI, 100 TPI)
REX (40 TPI)
Sorcerer. *See* Exidy
Vector Graphic (100 TPI)
Vector MZ (100 TPI)
Versatile. *See* CDS

Annotated Bibliography

CP/M GENERAL

Fernandez, Judi, and Ashley, Ruth. *Using CP/M.* New York: John Wiley Sons, 1980.

A self-teaching book; it uses a question/answer format while conveying technical information. A quick primer of CP/M commands and syntax.

Ballinger, Charles. "HDOS or CP/M?" *Interface Age*, September 1980, pp. 88-91.

Compares two disk operating systems available for Heath computers.

Brigham, Bruce, ed. *CP/M Summary Guide.* Glastonbury, Conn.: Rainbow Associates, 1980.

The book reprints and summarizes the commands available with CP/M, DESPOOL, MAC, TEX, CBASIC, and BASIC-80 from Microsoft. A useful computer-side reference.

Epstein, Jake, and Terry, Chris. "Introduction to CP/M; The CP/M Connection." *S100 Microsystems*, September/October 1980, pp. 10-32.

Continuation of a series of CP/M articles.

Fritzon, Richard. "The New CP/M: Is It Worth It?" *Kilobaud Microcomputing*, July 1980, p. 66.

Quickly summarizes the differences between versions 1.4 and 2.0 of CP/M.

Miller, Alan. "Diagnostics Package for CP/M." *Interface Age,* October 1980, p. 104.

Reviews the Supersoft CP/M Diagnostics package; these programs test memory, CPU, disk, printer and console.

North, Steve. "The CP/M Disk Operating System." *Creative Computing,* November/December 1978, pp. 52-53.

A short summary of the CP/M operating system and the programs that accompany it.

Stewart, John. "CP/M Primer; a Most Sophisticated Operating System." *Kilobaud Microcomputing,* April 1978, pp. 30-34.

An early detailed description of the CP/M operating system.

"Upgraded CP/M Floppy Disc Operating System." *Dr. Dobbs,* November 1976, p. 51.

A detailed summary of the features of CP/M revision 1.4. Includes descriptions of the accompanying 1.4 manuals.

Warren, Jim. "First Word on a Floppy-Disc Operating System." *Dr. Dobbs,* April, 1976, p. 5.

Provides first available information on CP/M.

Warren, Jim. "The Time for Floppys is Just About Now!" *Dr. Dobbs,* August, 1976, p. 5.

Reviews the available floppy disk systems of the time, and summarizes CP/M features.

Zaks, Rodnay. *The CP/M Handbook With MP/M.* Berkeley: Sybex, 1980.

Discusses CP/M and MP/M commands, programs, and facilities.

CP/M-COMPATIBLE SOFTWARE

Collins, Rosann; Hines, Theodore; and Rowan, George. "Manipulating Pencil Files; Convert Them to BASIC." *Creative Computing,* August 1979, pp. 98-99.

Illustrates how to use files created with Electric Pencil using Processor Technology BASIC; applicable to many different CP/M-compatible BASICs.

Craig, John. "A New Kind of Pencil!" *Creative Computing,* February 1979, pp. 30-33.

Thoroughly reviews the Electric Pencil word processor.

Didday, Rich. "Universal Data Entry System; In a Car Pooling
Application." *Creative Computing*, May 1980, pp. 102-10.
Reviews UDE from the Software Store and demonstrates the program.

Eubanks, Gordon. "Notes on CP/M's BASIC-E." *Dr. Dobbs*, October
1977, p. 35.
Letter to the editor describing the versions of BASIC-E, its public
domain status, and how to obtain revised versions. (Note: Gordon
Eubanks developed BASIC-E for a Master's thesis project; it is the
ancestor of CBASIC and CBASIC2).

Fitzgerald, Jim. "Off-the-Shelf Word-Processing System." *Kilobaud
Microcomputing*, September 1980, pp. 92-94.
Describes a CP/M system using Electric Pencil.

Foster, Charlie. "Pascal with a Z80." *Interface Age*, November 1980,
pp. 60-62.
Reviews Pascal/Z from Ithaca Intersystems, emphasizes its
differences from UCSD Pascal.

Hallen, Rod. "Super Word Processors." *Kilobaud Microcomputing*, June
1980, pp. 214-17.
Summarizes the features of ED, EDIT, Electric Pencil, WordStar, and
The Magic Wand; makes no conclusions or recommendations.
Provides a brief bibliography of acticles on word processing.

Hallen, Rod. "Tarbell Disk BASIC." *Kilobaud*, May 1980, pp. 168-70.
Summarizes the features of Tarbell Disk BASIC; emphasizes the
features of Tarbell BASIC distinct from other interpreters.

Hallen, Rod. "The Battle of The Word Processors." *Creative Computing*,
November 1979, pp. 48-53.
Reviews ED, TEX, EDIT, and Electric Pencil.

Hamilton, R.W. "WPDaisy Word Processing System." *Creative
Computing*, May 1979, pp. 36-41.
Reviews a little-known, but powerful, word processing system.

Hart, Glenn. "A New BASIC From Tarbell." *Creative Computing*, January
1980, pp. 20-23.
Reviews a slightly different BASIC available for CP/M systems.

Hart, Glenn. "Magic Wand Word Processor." *Creative Computing*,
August 1980, pp. 38-45.
Reviews the features of the Magic Wand word processing system.

Heintz, Carl. "Analyst: Another Data-base Manager." *Interface Age*, December 1980, pp. 42-44.
Reviews the Analyst data base management system from Structured Systems.

Heintz, Carl. "Maxiledger." *Interface Age*, September 1980, pp. 42-44.
Reviews the Maxiledger general ledger accounting system available from Compumax Associates.

Heintz, Carl. "A Peach of a General Ledger Program." *Interface Age*, October 1980, pp. 46-48.
Reviews the Peachtree General Ledger system.

Heintz, Carl. "Pearl — A Novel Programming Gem." *Interface Age*, November 1980, p. 47.
A program which "writes" programs; Pearl writes custom application packages from user input. Explains the power inherent in such a concept.

Heyman, Victor. "IDSWORD — The Comprehensive Processing System for Home and Business." *Creative Computing,* May 1979, pp. 43-44.
Reviews another little-known word processing system compatible with CP/M systems.

Hogg, Douglas. "How Good is Microsoft's FORTRAN-80?" *Creative Computing*, January 1979, pp. 62-67.
Reviews Microsoft's FORTRAN-80 and examines the FORTRAN implementation on a microcomputer.

Johnson, Bob. "Business Software Review." *Interface Age*, August 1979, pp. 38-39.
Reviews the Graham Dorian Apartment Management and Payroll software packages.

Kendall, Wallace. "Prettyprinting With Microsoft BASIC." *Kilobaud Microcomputing*, May 1979, p. 80.
Presents a simple way to format program listings using Microsoft BASIC.

Knecht, Ken. "CBASIC Review." *80 Microcomputing*, April 1980, pp. 130-32.
Compares CBASIC features with Microsoft BASIC; introduces FMG's CP/M operating system for the TRS-80.

Lindsay, John. "New Version of BASIC." *Kilobaud*, May 1980, pp. 72-74.

Summarizes the features of Microsoft BASIC version 5. Discusses the differences between versions.

Lutz, Dick. "Sharpening Your Pencil." *Creative Computing*, March 1980, pp. 30-35.

Reviews a program designed to add to the features of Electric Pencil.

Magruder, Bob. "The New WPDaisy: Word-Processing Software." *onComputing*, Fall 1980, pp. 68-74.

Extensively reviews WPDaisy.

McClure, James. "CBASIC — A Review." *Creative Computing*, September 1979, pp. 48-51.

Reviews a frequently used high level language. Provides timing comparisons for a series of standardized benchmarks, indicating CBASIC's relatively slow speed on many tests.

McClure, James. "Microsoft vs. MicroFocus COBOL." *Creative Computing*, March 1980, pp. 20-29.

Compares the features of the two primary implementations of COBOL available to CP/M users.

McClure, James. "A Personal Finance System." *Kilobaud Microcomputing*, June 1979, pp. 74-78; July 1979, pp. 50-56; August 1979, pp. 66-75.

An extensive CBASIC2 program for managing personal finances.

Miller, Alan. "BASCOM: Microsoft's BASIC Compiler for the 8080/Z80." *Interface Age*, July 80, pp. 124-26.

Discusses the difference between compilers and interpreters, emphasizing the features of Microsoft's compiler BASIC. Presents sample programs.

Miller, Alan. "CBASIC: A Business-Oriented Language for CP/M." *Interface Age,* August 1979, pp. 116-19.

Summarizes and reviews the CBASIC high level language for CP/M.

Miller, Alan. "CP/M for the TRS-80 Model II: Lifeboat and FMG Corp. Versions." *Interface Age,* November 1980, pp. 94-98.

A detailed comparison of two different implementations of CP/M for the Model II.

Miller, Alan. "The Electric Pencil for CP/M." *Interface Age*, August 1978, pp. 148-49.

A review of a popular word processing package.

Miller, Alan. "Pascal for CP/M: Digital Marketing's PascalM." *Interface Age*, September 1980, pp. 96-103.

Reviews Pascal/M and discusses the difference between Pascal and other high level languages.

North, Steve. "Creative Computing Reviews Five Software Packages — Tiny C, Microsoft BASIC 5.0, Research Machines Z80 Algol, Structural Analysis SP80 Macros, Digital Research CP/M 2.0 and MP/M." *Creative Computing*, March 1980, pp. 40-44.

Summarizes the features of the titled packages.

Pournelle, Jerry. "Omikron TRS-80 Boards, NEWDOS+, and Sundry Other Matters." *Byte*, July 1980, pp. 198-208.

A rambling look at Pournelle's experiences with microcomputers in writing; a popular science fiction writer (*Mote in God's Eye, Lucifer's Hammer*, and others), Pournelle offers a personal and fascinating account.

Press, Larry. "A Review of Four Text-Formatting Programs." *onComputing*, Fall 1980, pp. 48-54.

Reviews S-80, TEX, TPS, and Textwriter.

Press, Larry. "Word Processors: A Look at Four Popular Programs." *onComputing*, Summer 1980, pp. 38-52.

A detailed review of Auto Scribe, Electric Pencil, Magic Wand, and WordStar.

Sanger, Joseph. "The Electronic Librarian." *Kilobaud Microcomputing*, November 1979, pp. 44-62.

A BASIC-E program for maintaining an information database.

Sjowall, Tor. "CP/M to UCSD Pascal File Conversion." *Dr. Dobbs*, October 1980, pp. 16-19.

Pascal source code for converting CP/M files to the UCSD Pascal format.

VanHorn, Eric. "SuperSort by MicroPro International." *Creative Computing*, July 1979, pp. 34-37.

Reviews the features of SuperSort.

CP/M AND ASSEMBLY LANGUAGE PROGRAMMING

Barbier, Ken. "CP/M For Single-Drive Systems." *Kilobaud Microcomputing*, September 1980, pp. 94-98.

Explains the problems with using a single-drive CP/M system; includes an assembly language single-drive file copy program source listing.

Barker, Lee. "Help With OSI's CP/M." *Dr. Dobbs*, May 1980, pp. 36-37.

A modification of the BIOS for OSI computers using CP/M to eradicate problems encountered.

Biese, Leo, and Iannuccillo, Emilio. "MASTHEAD: Why Not Title Your Printouts?" *Interface Age*, August 1980, pp. 122-27.

A method of printing large titles on program listings, with source code in both assembly language and Microsoft BASIC.

Cecil, Alex. "ACT:An 8080 Macroprocessor." *Dr. Dobbs,* March 1978, pp. 20-45.

A "TRAC"- like text interpreter, ACT is written in PL/M. Computer programming students will be interested in the source code.

Christensen, Ward. "An 8080 Disassembler." *Dr. Dobbs*, February 1977, pp. 30-43.

A complete assembly language source listing for an 8080-based disassembler. Documentation explains disassembly to assembly language programmers.

Cotton, Gene. "How to Solve Your Damaged Disk Dilemma." *Interface Age*, September 1980, pp. 80-86, 130-31.

An assembly language program to save bad spots on a diskette as a file named [unused].bad. Contains a fairly detailed explanation of how CP/M maintains information on the diskette.

Epstein, Jake. "An Introduction to CP/M." *S-100 Microsystems*, January/February 1980, pp. 6-10; March/April 1980, pp. 28-33; May/June 1980, pp. 12-17.

An excellent introduction to CP/M for computer programmers; details specific technical information.

Foster, Charlie, and Meador, Richard. "8080 Dynatrace." *S-100 Microsystems*, July/August 1980, pp. 22-31.

A dynamic screen-oriented assembly language debugging system: Source code is in 8080 assembly language. Article assumes expertise required to modify the output routines.

Frantz, James. "Turn-Key CP/M Systems." *Creative Computing*, December 1979, p. 104-07.

Step-by-step directions to make CP/M automatically execute a program after a cold start.

Friedman, David. "Las Vegas Super Slot: A CP/M Game Machine Program Using Flashwriter I Graphics." *Dr. Dobbs*, November/ December 1980, pp. 10-22.

A game program in assembly language for CP/M systems using the Vector Graphic Flashwriter I board.

Gagne, Jim. "Vice Versa — Pencil to CP/M and Reverse." *Dr. Dobbs*, March 1979, pp. 26-29.

How to reformat Electric Pencil files to CP/M format and vice versa. Assembly language source code provided.

Haanstra, Bruce. "Optional Printing with CP/M and Microsoft BASIC." *Interface Age*, November 1980, pp. 84-86.

Illustrates how to circumvent Microsoft BASIC's interception of the ^ P character used to turn the printer on and off in CP/M.

Hallen, Rod. "Battle of the Assemblers." *Creative Computing*, December 1979, pp. 42-45.

Compares ASM, supplied with CP/M with ASMB, an assembler available from Technical Systems Consultants. Briefly describes an assembler called "SASSY."

Hoffer, W.C. "Data and Time for the CP/M Operating System." *Interface Age*, August 1978, pp. 152-56.

Assembly language routines enable a CompuTime board to perform automatic time and dating of program listings.

Kildall, Gary. "Simple Technique for Static Relocation." *Dr. Dobbs*, February 1978, pp. 10-13.

The author of CP/M describes CP/M relocation technique.

Miller, Alan. "CP/M Part 2 — A Macro Assembler & Other Goodies." *Interface Age*, December 1978, pp. 130-35.

Reviews the MAC assembler available from Digital Research, the SID symbolic instruction debugger also from Digital Research, and a sample CBIOS for a North Star CP/M system.

Miller, Alan. "An Interrupt-Driven Keyboard Buffer." *Interface Age*, October 1980, pp. 106-07, 137-41.

A different approach for implementing a keypress detection routine for North Star BIOS in CP/M.

Miller, Alan. "Structured Assembly-Language Programming for the 8080." *Interface Age*, November 1979, pp. 153-155.
Reviews SP80, a structured assembly language set of macro routines available for CP/M systems. Compares the Digital Research MAC assembler with SP80.

Miller, Alan. "ZSID Z80 Debugger for CP/M." *Interface Age*, August 1980, pp. 88-90.
Reviews the ZSID symbolic debugger for assembly language programs available from Digital Research; also mentions the DESPOOL program, from Digital Research.

Parsons, Ronald. "UCSD Pascal to CP/M File Transfer Program." *Dr. Dobbs,* August 1979, pp. 12-16.
Assembly language program transfers from UCSD Pascal format to CP/M file structure.

Pugh, Tim. "Intelligent Terminal Implementation on S100 Bus." *Dr. Dobbs,* June/July 1978, pp. 4-16.
A well-commented assembly language program that allows communication between any CP/M system using a IDS-88 modem board and any other computer system.

Terry, Chris. "The CP/M Connection." *S-100 Microsystems*, July/August 1980, pp. 32-35.
Discusses the CP/M relocation method and how to interface CBIOS and make other modifications to a relocated system.

Van Buer, Darrel. "A Table-Driven Assembler on CP/M." *Dr. Dobbs*, February 1980, pp. 18-25.
A PL/M source code for a macro assembler.

Willoughby, Steve. "Hardcopy Device Driver Programs for CP/M." *Dr. Dobbs,* September 1980, pp. 34-37.
Assembly language routines to be included in CP/M CBIOS section for Diablo 1650 or Teletype printers.

ASSEMBLY LANGUAGE PROGRAMMING

8080/8085 Assembly Language Programming Manual. Santa Clara, Calif.: Intel Corp., 1980.

Leventhal, Lance, *8080A/8085 Assembly Language Programming.* Berkeley: Osborne/McGraw-Hill, 1978.

Leventhal, Lance A., *Z80 Assembly Language Programming.* Berkeley: Osborne/McGraw-Hill, 1979.

Myers, Glenford, *Reliable Software Through Composite Design.* Van Nostrand Reinhold, 1975.

Zaks, Rodnay. *Programming the Z80.* Berkeley: Sybex, 1979.

CP/M Address Book

Sources of CP/M Compatible
Languages, Programs, and Computers

Word Processing Programs

Magic Wand	Small Business Applications, Inc.
Microsoft Edit	Microsoft, Inc.
Electric Pencil	Michael Shrayer Software, Inc.
SCOPE	Vector Graphic, Inc.
WordStar	MicroPro International

Languages

C	Whitesmiths, Ltd.
CBASIC	Compiler Systems, Inc.

CBASIC2
    CRUN (CBASIC run-time module)
    XREF (CBASIC debugging module)	

CIS COBOL	MicroFocus, Inc.

Microsoft BASIC	Microsoft, Inc.
BASCOM (Compiler)	
MBASIC (Interpreter)	
L-80 (Linking Loader)	
FORTRAN-80	Microsoft, Inc.
(Microsoft FORTRAN)	
Pascal Z	Ithaca Intersystems, Inc.
FORTH	Forth, Inc.
PL/I-80	Digital Research, Inc.

Data Management Systems

SELECTOR-IV	Micro.AP, Inc.
Pearl	Computer Pathways Unlimited
HDMS	Micro Data Base Systems

CP/M Derivative Operating Systems

CDOS	Cromemco, Inc.
SDOS	SD Systems
TPM	Computer Design Labs
I/OS	TSA Software

Alphabetical Listing of Companies Mentioned in this Book

Altos Computer Systems
2360 Bering Drive
San Jose, CA   95131
(408) 946-6700

American National Standards Institute (ANSI)
1430 Broadway
New York, NY   10018
(212) 354-3300

Apple Computer
10260 Bandley Drive
Cupertino, CA   95014
(800) 538-9696 (except California)
(800) 662-9238 (from California)

Applied Digital Data Systems (ADDS)
100 Marcus Boulevard
Hauppauge, NY   11787
(516) 231-5400

BD Software (BDS)
See Lifeboat Associates

Bell Laboratories — C Language
Patent License Organization
Western Electric Company
P.O. Box 25000
Greensboro, NC   27420
(919) 697-6530

Byte Publications, Inc.
70 Main Street
Peterborough, NH   03458
(603) 924-9281

Compiler Systems, Inc.
P.O. Box 145
Sierra Madre, CA   91024
(213) 355-4211

Computer Design Labs
342 Columbus Avenue
Trenton, NJ   08629
(609) 599-2146

Computer Pathways Unlimited
2151 Davcor Street S.E.
Salem, OR   97302
(503) 363-8929

CP/M Users Group
1651 Third Avenue
New York, NY   10028
No telephone

Comemco, Inc.
280 Bernard Avenue
Mountain View, CA   94043
(415) 964-7400

Digital Microsystems
1840 Embarcadero
Oakland, CA   94606
(415) 582-3686

Digital Research
P.O. Box 579
801 Lighthouse Avenue
Pacific Grove, CA   93950
(408) 649-3896

DynaByte, Inc.
115 Independence Drive
Menlo Park, CA   94025
(415) 329-8021

Exidy
1234 Elko Drive
Sunnyvale, CA   94086
(408) 734-9410

FORTH, Inc.
2309 Pacific Coast Highway
Hermosa Beach, CA   90254
(213) 372-8493

Heath Data Systems
Hilltop Road
St. Joseph, MI   49085
(616) 982-3200

Industrial Micro Systems
628 N. Eckhoff Street
Orange, CA   92668
(714) 978-6966

Intel Corporation
3065 Bowers Avenue
Santa Clara, CA   95051
(408) 987-8080

Ithaca Intersystems, Inc.
1650 Hanshaw Road
P.O. Box 91
Ithaca, NY   14850
(607) 257-0190

Lifeboat Associates
1651 Third Avenue
New York, NY   10028
(212) 860-0300

Lifelines Publishing Corp.
1651 Third Avenue
New York, NY   10028
(212) 722-1700

Michael Shrayer Software, Inc.
1198 Los Robles Drive
Palm Springs, CA   92262
(714) 323-1400

Micro Data Base Systems
P.O. Box 248
Lafayette, IN   47902
(317) 448-1616

MICRO.AP, Inc.
9807 Davona Drive
San Ramon, CA   94583
(415) 828-6697

Micro Focus Inc.
1620 Civic Center Drive
Santa Clara, CA   95050
(408) 984-6961

Micromation, Inc.
1620 Montgomery Street
San Francisco, CA   94111
(415) 398-0289

MicroPro International Corp.
1299 4th Street
San Rafael, CA   94901
(415) 457-8990

Microsoft, Inc.
10800 NE Eighth
Suite 819
Bellevue, WA   98004
(206) 455-8080

MITS
See Pertec Computer Corp.

MMS
Miller Microcomputer Services
61 Lake Shore Road
Natick, MA   01760
(617) 653-6136

Morrow Designs
5221 Central Avenue
Richmond, CA   94804
(415) 524-2101

Ohio Scientific
1333 South Chillicothe Road
Aurora, OH   44202
(216) 831-5600
(800) 321-6850

Onyx Systems, Inc.
10375 Bandley Drive
Cupertino, CA   95014
(408) 257-8022

Pertec Computer Corp.
20630 Nordhoff Street
Chatsworth, CA   91311
(213) 998-1800

Radio Shack
1300 One Tandy Center
Fort Worth, TX   76102
(817) 390-3700

SD Systems
P.O. Box 28810
Dallas, TX   75228
(214) 271-4667

Small Business Applications, Inc.
3220 Louisiana
Suite 205
Houston, TX   77006
(713) 528-5158

Tarbell Electronics
950 Dovlen Place
Suite B
Carson, CA   90746
(213) 538-4251

Texas Instruments, Inc.
P.O. Box 1444
Houston, TX   77001
(800) 257-7850 (except NJ)
(800) 322-8650 (from NJ)

Thinkertoys
See Morrow Designs

TSA Software
5 North Salem Road
Ridgefield, CT   06877
(203) 438-3954

Vector Graphic, Inc.
31364 Via Colinas
Westlake Village, CA   91362
(213) 991-2302

Whitesmiths, Ltd.
P.O. Box 1132
Ansonia Station, NY   10023
(212) 799-1200

Zenith
See Heath Data Systems

Index

About the Author

Thom Hogan is the editor of *InfoWorld,* a weekly publication for microcomputer users which features the latest in microcomputing news as well as standardized equipment and software evaluations.

His training includes degrees from Washington University and Indiana University, with M.B.A. and Ph.D. coursework in new technology economics and management. Before coming to *InfoWorld,* Mr. Hogan was manager of Data Domain, one of the Midwest's leading computer retailers.

Mr. Hogan frequently consults for the leading microcomputer manufacturers, and is actively engaged in writing software for current state-of-the-art machines, including those based on 16-bit technology. He has recently written books on FORTH and Microsoft BASIC, and future writing projects include a novel and two general audience works on the sociology of new technology.

Other OSBORNE/McGraw-Hill Publications

An Introduction to Microcomputers: Volume 0 — The Beginner's Book
An Introduction to Microcomputers: Volume 1 — Basic Concepts, second edition
An Introduction to Microcomputers: Volume 2 — Some Real Microprocessors
An Introduction to Microcomputers: Volume 3 — Some Real Support Devices
Osborne 4 & 8-Bit Microprocessor Handbook
Osborne 16-Bit Microprocessor Handbook
8089 I/O Processor Handbook
CRT Controller Handbook
68000 Microprocessor Handbook
8080A/8085 Assembly Language Programming
6800 Assembly Language Programming
Z80 Asembly Language Programming
6502 Assembly Language Programming
Z8000 Assembly Language Programming
6809 Assembly Language Programming
Running Wild — The Next Industrial Revolution
The 8086 Book
PET and the IEEE 488 Bus (GPIB)
PET/CBM Personal Computer Guide, 2nd Edition
Business System Buyer's Guide
Apple II® User's Guide
Microprocessors for Measurement & Control
Some Common BASIC Programs
Some Common BASIC Programs — PET/CBM Edition
Practical BASIC Programs
Payroll with Cost Accounting
Accounts Payable and Accounts Receivable
General Ledger
8080 Programming for Logic Design
6800 Programming for Logic Design
Z80 Programming for Logic Design

OSBORNE CP/M® USER GUIDE

While CP/M® is by far the most popular operating system, its literature has been largely aimed at professional programmers. For end users who want to know the basics of CP/M, this User Guide bridges the gap between technical manuals and your working knowledge of microcomputers.

Beginning with the basic, practical information you need to get started, this book details all the CP/M commands and describes compatible support programs. Use of application packages, high level languages (BASIC, Pascal, FORTRAN, Forth and COBOL), and utility programs are all covered. It includes many tables and lists which serve as operating references once you've become familiar with CP/M.

For more advanced users, the relationship between CP/M and other operating systems, such as Cromemco CDOS, is carefully examined. There is also discussion on how to modify CP/M or use CP/M for program development.

Author Thom Hogan offers a wealth of tips and suggestions about using CP/M based on his years of experience working with it.

ISBN 0-931988-44-6